THE SCOTTISH LIBRARY
General Editor: Alexander Scott

SCOTTISH PROSE

1550-1700

Edited and with an Introduction

by

RONALD D. S. JACK

CALDER & BOYARS · LONDON

First published in Great Britain in 1971
by Calder and Boyars Ltd
18 Brewer Street London W1

© Ronald D. S. Jack 1971

ISBN 0 7145 0798 9 Cloth edition
ISBN 0 7145 0799 7 Paper edition

This volume has been produced with the assistance of the Scottish Arts Council and the publishers wish to acknowledge with thanks the substantial help given not only by the Council itself but by its Literature Committee without which this volume and others in the series could not be viably published.

Printed in Great Britain by
Northumberland Press Limited
Gateshead

CONTENTS

(The titles refer to works from which selections have been made.
The date in brackets indicates the date of the manuscript or printed
edition, on which the text has been based. In the case of Diaries,
the dates refer to the years in which the respective entries were
made.)

INTRODUCTION

IF ONE were to rely on Critical Histories of Scottish Literature for one's information on the prose writings of this period, one might be forgiven for thinking it wisest to cast a discreet veil over them, and pass on without further wasting one's time. Kurt Wittig in *The Scottish Tradition in Literature* may be taken as typical in paying a quick reverence to the topic, highlighting only the work of Pitscottie and Knox. Even T. F. Henderson, whose *Scottish Vernacular Literature* gives a slightly more detailed survey, does not consider a fully comprehensive account necessary. Are these reactions fair ones? In the later sixteenth and in the seventeenth centuries, a vast amount of prose, varying in quality and theme, was being produced by Scotsmen. Undoubtedly some of it is of a low literary standard, but such are the riches that remain, that my problem in this Anthology has been what to leave out rather than what to put in.

There are probably three major reasons for past critical condescension. The early Scottish prose writers tended to rely even more on classical writings for their stylistic approach than did their English counterparts. They thus produced complex periodic structures foreign to our ear and somewhat at odds with the Scottish or English vernacular. In its extreme form, this produces the convoluted sentences favoured by George Buchanan, all sounding as if they were translations from an original draft in Latin. This we might have expected, at a time when Scotsmen were still profoundly under the influence of humanism, and any form of the vernacular was a second choice for prose or poetry. Later, when the grip of humanism lessened and James VI in his *Reulis and Cautelis* of 1585, urged that Scottish poetry should imitate the

example of the various European vernacular movements, the artificiality of the classical period was replaced by the mannerised
style favoured by the European rhetoricians, on whose treatises,
James's essay was based. Slowly one type of rhetoric gave way to
another, but the basic artificiality remained. Thus those who come
to this Anthology with twentieth century expectations of an
economical, self-effacing prose style, are liable to be disappointed.
Here, prose is, like the poetry of the same period, a secondary
branch of rhetoric, a medium which does not merely transmit but
also recreates its message.

If one group of people is estranged by the artificiality and erudi-
tion of this prose, there is a further group who reject it on other
grounds. Those critics who like to stress the Scottishness of literature written by Scotsmen, and tend to arrive at their literary
judgments in part on a nationalistic criterion, either ignore or condescend to early Scottish prose. To begin with, there is little doubt
that beside the energetic and inspired writings of Bacon, Browne,
Hooker and others, few Scottish prose writings achieve the same
level of brilliance. Equally, the strong influence of Calvinism, which
obtrudes itself from the beginning of our period, was to a large
degree anglicising. The writings of Wyclif led to those of Knox,
and although the latter was heavily criticised by his contemporaries
for using predominantly English rather than Scots, such was the
power of his prose, that a strong anglicising line in Scottish prose
writing had begun even before the movement south of the Scottish court in 1603. This latter movement then acted as a catalyst,
and many Scottish writers, including James VI himself, began to
revise their works, erasing Scotticisms. Not surprisingly too, when
the prose movement of the sixteenth and seventeenth centuries reached its full flowering, most Scots preferred to follow
either the copiousness of Sir Thomas Browne or the epigrammatic
prose of Bacon, using the ever-expanding English language, rather
than return to the complex Latin periods of earlier Scottish writers,
or to their own vernacular, which if anything was narrowing in
scope and which was anyway fast becoming strange to those Scots
based in London.

If a critic then wishes to indulge in a form of literary patriotism, he will retreat to literary realms where an overall comparison with English writings proves more favourable. In so doing, he will ignore many isolated pieces of excellent Scottish prose. Failing this, he may accept only prose writings in the Scottish vernacular, thus accepting the Histories of Pitscottie and Leslie, but probably rejecting that of Knox. In short he will halve his range of choice at least; while giving an inaccurate reflection of the peculiarly divided state of the Scottish nation and the supra-national quality of much prose during the Renaissance. This is the major reason for excellent Scottish prose writers like Sir Thomas Urquhart and Sir George MacKenzie still awaiting their 'Triumph of Fame'. Ignored by English anthologists on grounds of nationality and by Scots anthologists on grounds of medium, they fall into oblivion between two neat and distorting categorisations. My lengthy selections from both of these writers are an attempt to redress this balance.

Finally, Scottish prose of the sixteenth and seventeenth centuries is underestimated, because it exists for the modern reader either in the *Scottish Text Society* editions, which are for the most part good, but not readily available, or in the inadequate nineteenth century collections of the Maitland and Bannatyne Clubs. Indeed one of the major results of my research in this period, is to discover the very real need for modern, realistically-priced texts for the student and general reader. It is hoped that the present volume will pave the way for further, more detailed studies of particular writers.

Faced with the many choices open both to selector and to editor, I have made the following decisions. As this book is intended mainly for literary students, my search has been confined to literary prose. With regret, I have omitted all record material, consoling myself with the thought, that this is already available in *A Source Book of Scottish History*, ed. Croft-Dickinson, Donaldson, Milne, Vol. 2 (Edinburgh and London, 1963). Then, within the field as defined, I have preferred to isolate a number of writers to be represented in depth. This implies the neglect of a few major figures, but it does ensure against too thin a spread of the material. A further controlling feature is the desire to represent the great variety of Renaissance prose, and to strike an acceptable balance between Scots, Anglo-Scots and English; between copious Ciceronian prose, epigrammatic Senecan prose and the various more eccentric experiments such as Urquhart's imitation of Rabelais or the parodies contained in the *Pretended Conference*. Along with this variety of medium, there is variety of topic and of genre. Examples will be found of historical writings, of theological pamphleteering, of sermons, of political treatises and satires. On a strictly literary level, there is James VI's first essay in literary criticism, along with the first developments of the Scottish essay and the first hesitant movements of Scottish prose romance and Scottish novel. The cult of translation and adaptation is stressed, through the works of Fowler and Urquhart, while more personal prose is preserved in the extracts from letters and diaries of the period.

From an editorial point of view, I have at all times returned to the best manuscript or early printed text and used this as copy. The following concessions have been made to modern conventions. As 'u', 'v', and 'w' were written almost indifferently, I have at all times introduced the modern equivalent. Likewise, when 'i' is used for 'j' or vice versa, I have normalised. The 'ff' form has been normalised to either 'f' or 'v', and where 'y' stands for 'th', the latter form has been employed. All contractions have been expanded, except in the selections from Diaries. Capitals have only been retained, where a modern text would have employed them, or where a special emphasis seemed to be intended. Punctuation presented a more complex problem. As some of the manuscripts possessed little or no punctuation, while in others the punctuation was minimal, I have modernised the punctuation in all my selections. This modernisation however allows for the longer periodic structure, favoured by many of the writers, and in some cases for the rhetorical flow of the speaking voice. Thus, while the aim of the punctuation is to facilitate reading, there is also an attempt to remain true to the spirit of the original and the intentions of the author, where these are discernible. Conditions of space prevent notes but a short introduction precedes each passage. A glossary is provided at the end of the book.

HISTORIES, PAMPHLETS, SERMONS

The period from 1550 till 1700 takes us from the middle of Mary's reign into that of William II and Mary III. It covers one of the most troubled and vivid eras in Scottish history. As these prose writers compose, the young Queen Mary returns to Scotland after the death of her French husband, Francis II. The Hamiltons see their hopes of a marriage alliance dashed by the eventual insanity of Arran. Rizzio is murdered and then Darnley. Mary marries Bothwell, is imprisoned and eventually dies that tragic death, so often celebrated in song and story. After the inevitable regency struggles, her son James VI begins his personal rule in the mid 1580s. Despite constantly having to reconcile the interests of the extremists in both politics and religion, James does, while in Edinburgh, find time to create a group of poets and musicians, called the Castalian band. He also encourages foreign writers, including Constable and Du Bartas to visit Edinburgh. But in 1603, yet another major change occurs. The Union of the Crowns draws James south to London, taking most of his glittering court with him and leaving the Scottish capital a cultural wilderness again. As Helena Shire puts it in the introduction to *Music of Scotland* (*1500-1700*):

> A rich and varied world of Scottish music, sacred and secular, centred in the court of King James VI; but when the monarch moved south in 1603 to inherit the crown of England, that warm hearth was extinguished for ever.

Yet this is only one aspect of the historical background. Equally important is the fact that the sixteenth century also sees the growth in power of the religious reformers. After Wishart's visit to Scotland in 1544-5, Knox begins mercilessly to attack the priesthood, the mass and other central elements in Catholic worship. The primacy of scripture is advocated and faith raised above deeds as the criterion for true Christianity. Wishart is martyred, Cardinal Beaton murdered in expiation and Knox himself serves his period as a slave on the French galleys. As James VI soon discovers, any attempt at enforcing a prayer book on the Scottish people or attempting to increase the system of episcopal government in the church meets with resolute opposition. When his son, Charles, approaches the same problem with more determination and less subtlety, the result is the drawing up of the National Covenant in 1638. This not only opposes popery (as had the Negative Confession of 1581), but resuscitates the old idea of the Scots as a chosen race, analogous to the Israelites of old.

Any of our prosewriters pondering on this last topic, might be forgiven for wondering when this chosen race was at last to come through its trials, for fast on the heels of these earlier dissensions comes the Civil war. The Scots in turn side with the Parliamentarians and then with Charles. In each case they find themselves disillusioned. The Presbyterian link implied by the Solemn League and Covenant means one thing to the Presbyterian English and another to the covenanting Scots. Their political sympathies lie with the King, but his religious views imply that they must oppose him until God opens his eyes to the truth. Thus, the Scottish covenanter-poet, Sir William Mure writes in his *Caledons Complaint*:

> *By Law, not force, wee move, not tumult make,*
> *Wee justice plead, sedition doe forsake:*
> *None with rebellion our attempts will brand*
> *But who themselves to crush religion band,*
> *By act, or by intent.*

Bewildered and shocked at the eventual death of Charles, they promise aid to his son, but the Army of the Scottish Estate was defeated, and the Scots prepare for commonwealth rule, administered by eight commissioners elected by the English parliament.

A reaction sets in during the reigns of Charles II and James II. The Act Rescissory of March 1661 quietly restores the tolerantly episcopalian régime of James VI, which earlier had so bloodily been overthrown. Then by the Test Act, James VII ensures that all holders of public office must forswear the Covenants and accept royal supremacy, while in 1690 the Scots replaced episcopacy by a restored Presbyterian system. Thus in one sense the wheel comes full circle, and in more docile mood than previously Scotland awaits the next momentous development of 1707.

It is usually argued, that this crowded historical era, encompassing the chaotic reign of Mary, the Union of the Crowns, the growth of the reformation, the civil war, the commonwealth and the reaction, had an adverse effect on literature. This may be true as a generalisation, but some reservations will be advanced in the course of this introduction. The first of these is, that prose works dealing directly with the political and religious disputes of Scotland in past and present, began to appear. Many of these possess much intrinsic literary worth. It is therefore misleading to suggest that literature suffered, because the literary men were drawn into commenting on social or religious injustices. Literary men will produce literature whatever the theme.

Of the many Histories written during this period, I have chosen extracts from two of the earliest: *The Historie and Cronikles of Scotland* by Robert Lindsay of Pitscottie and *The Historie of Scotland* by John Leslie, Bishop of Ross. Of these, the first was probably completed in the late 1570s, while the latter was handed to Mary, Queen of Scots as a gift in 1570. To this closeness in time, they add the further link of being written in forceful Middle Scots and of covering roughly the same historical period, from the reign of James II to that of Mary. Moreover, the opening date is determined by a shared dependence on the earlier *Historie and Croniklis of Scotland* by Hector Boece, translated from the Latin by John Bellenden. Leslie confesses that he is adding to Boece's historical treatise, which reached only the reign of James I, while Lindsay opens his History with the comment, "Heir beginnis the historie and cronickillis of Scotland quhilk was left onwrettin be the last translature to wit maister hector boes and maister John Bellentyne quha endit thair cronickill at the slauchter of king James the first." Lindsay remained closer to the Boece-Bellenden approach. Thus when his History is likened to that of Herodotus, in its love of anecdotes and its passion for alternative versions of key incidents, the general parallel may be valid, but the particular application should be to Boece-Bellenden. There too one will find the saga-like approach and the use of alternative versions. Likewise, when parallels with Livy spring to mind, it is well to remember that in 1533 Bellenden had also finished his translation of Livy's *History of Rome*, and that Boece likewise had been influenced by the Latin author.

Despite these basic similarities, the two Histories do diverge markedly. In part this is due to the very different nature of their authors. Lindsay, although he knew Latin, was not a scholar of the same stature as Leslie. His aim as proclaimed in his prologue is to focus on "the fyve kingis of the Stewartis". His recorded sources, other than Boece-Bellenden, are all Scottish—Patrick Lindsay, William Scot of Balwearie, Andrew Wood, John Major and David Lindsay. Apart from already betraying his particular interest in the Lindsay family, soon to reveal itself over and over again in the History, he shows little concern for the classical or English works then popular.

In direct contrast, Leslie begins by citing Cato and admitting a debt to Cicero, Livy and Quintus Curtius. Foremost among the long list of English historians he cites are Polydore Virgil, Bede, Hall and Cooper. These authors suggest a more selfconscious and didactic approach to history than that indicated by Pitscottie. Our suspicions are borne out when Leslie categorises the various types of History as Divine, Natural and Human. His falls into the last class and is held to be more valuable than philosophy itself, in teaching us to follow the good life. While Pitscottie aims at chronicling the lives of Kings, Leslie moves closer to the vices of rebellion and the responsibilities of the subject, as argued by Hall and Polydore Virgil "the subjectis are admonischit to obey thair prince and magistrate; for that rebellioun hes always brocht gryt harme to the comone weill". While Lindsay promises a lengthy historical discourse, Leslie sees his as only an "abbreviatione or summarye of the principell dedis in these dayes", looking forward to the day when a more learned writer will "set fourth the samyn at grytar lenth." Later he was to attempt this himself, using Latin as his medium.

The weaknesses and strengths implied by these prologues are largely borne out by the Histories themselves. Pitscottie's is fuller and more interesting, as almost all critics have confirmed. Leslie on the other hand is not aiming at these effects, and his work does have a more satisfying overall pattern. Pitscottie begins with a somewhat stilted rendering of Boece Chapter XVIII. The reign of James II is too far in the past for detailed vision, and one detects a thinness of content along with many historical errors. At the other extreme are those periods personally known to the author, where his lack of artistic selectivity tempts him into overcrowding his record. Thus one page of the STS edition in the reign of James VI contains information on the relationship of ministers to the regent, a law forbidding export of food, Scottish soldiers killed in Livonia, the regent going to St. Andrews, the birth of a monstrous child, and a man repenting by crucifying himself. The finest portions of this History are contained in the Books on James IV and V. These constitute the not too distant past for Pitscottie, where he has neither to overplay his imagination nor test his unsure sense of relevance. It is no coincidence that the moment of highest comedy (the Scottish Bishop's benediction), the moment of highest tragedy (the death of James V) and the most expertly extended period of drama (Flodden) all are contained in this central portion of the work.

Working more selfconsciously and excluding material more rigorously, Leslie does not present us with a History characterised by different types of artistic vision. In every reign he makes comment on three different levels—foreign policy, domestic events, and incidents likely to boost Catholic prestige. These are interspersed with lists of men, who have either died recently or achieved fame. In the reign of James II for example, he concentrates on the foreign policy towards France and the marriage of Lady Margaret to the Dauphin. On the domestic scene, he describes those civil broils, which culminated when James II personally took over the reigns of government. Meanwhile the Papal Legate's attempt to strengthen obedience to Rome, is but one of the Catholic triumphs highlighted. These three studies are punctuated by lists of nobles, including one enumerating those slain in the battle between Crawford and Huntly. Taken in isolation, passages from Leslie's *History*, may seem loose and unconnected, for the true patterning of leitmotivs only becomes apparent, once the work is regarded as a whole.

This formal unity, however, implies a wider variety of styles than that suggested by Pitscottie's approach. The device of listing and the simple, economical style used for the "abbreviatione" of a series of events, exists beside a heavier, more periodic style, than is at any time used by Pitscottie and may fairly be connected with the rhetorical narrative of Livy. Between these is the controlled, balanced style connected in the classical mind with Isocrates: "At the samyn tyme, be the advyse of the estatis of parliament, thair wes send ane esquier and ane herald in France, Spanye and uther realmes, to se and consider quhair ane honorabill princes mycht be had for mariadge of the King, to the effect that efter thair returning and report made, ambassadouris mycht be send to treat thairapoun". But Pitscottie, in the original portions of his narrative retains more or less the same style throughout. It is a looser, simple narrative style, reminiscent of Herodotus rather than Livy or Isocrates. Although largely dependent on repetition for its effect, and although replete with co-ordinate clauses rather than complex periods, its very simplicity of structure is often used to telling effect, as in the account of James V's death: "He turnit him bak and luikit and beheld all his lordis about him and gaif ane lyttill smyle and lauchter, syne kissit his hand and offerit the samyn to all his lordis round about him and thairefter held upe his handis to god and yeildit the spreit." This sort of style, however, seldom creates an effect on its own, and it is perhaps worthy of note, that it seems halting and repetitive where the tale is itself halting and unexciting, energetic and vivid, where the tale is enthralling.

It is not a misleading generalisation that Leslie's *History* is advanced through overall narrative unity and a variety of styles while Pitscottie's presents a changing artistic vision, but seldom departs from the simple narrative mode. Leslie concentrates on the kingship only as it effects the changing political scene, Pitscottie strongly suggests that the nature of the King determines the nature of the government; Leslie presents a pro-Catholic viewpoint, while Pitscottie is an early voice of the Reformation; in Pitscottie one sees both the influence of classicism and of the mediaeval homily, while Leslie shows a wider knowledge of classical writings, and

English Histories. Finally, Pitscottie intended his History as a finished, extended account of the Stewart line, while Leslie's had the nature of an abbreviated draft handed to a particular monarch, with the specific intention of advising her, that unscrupulous men sought to usurp her control of the government. When considering these roughly contemporaneous histories, covering many of the same incidents, these oppositions in style, tone, form, theme and intention might profitably be kept in mind.

Pitscottie was the first Scot to write a prose history in the vernacular. Although Wyntoun had earlier composed his poetic chronicle in verse, Latin was still the favourite medium and the example of Latin writers influences these early vernacular works. Vernacular histories became comparatively popular however, after the early examples had paved the way. Mention should be made of David Moysie's *Memoirs of the Affairs of Scotland*. A writer and notary public during the early part of James VI's reign, Moysie's account covers in detail the years between 1577 and 1603. Despite excessive repetition of phrases like "At this tyme" and "Efter this ... remanit", Moysie has a pleasing, clearcut style, and skilfully highlights points of crisis, like the 1591 invasion of Holyrood by Bothwell and his party. Moysie's legal training contributes to the exactness of his style, but even more legalistic in medium is the *Diurnal of Occurents*. Although theoretically it covers the period from 1514-75, detailed comment only begins at 1559 and there are many vivid and memorable passages. Of later works, James Kirkton's *History of the Restoration* (1678) especially will repay study. His style is forceful, if excessively influenced by the repetitions and climaxes of the pulpit: "They mockt religious worship, they beat the poor people, the men they bind and wound, they dragg to church and prison, and both with equall violence." At the same time, Kirkton occasionally shows a depth of historical analysis, hitherto unparalleled in Scottish prose. His analysis of the problems raised by Oates' discovery of the Popish plot is particularly thorough in its assessment of motivations and would not disgrace a historian of the modern school.

Before making the slight change of bias, which takes us from general histories to religious histories, I should stress that Scottish writers in the Renaissance decided to compose their histories for a vast variety of reasons. First, like the English writer, Julius Brende, when presenting his translation of Quintus Curtius' *History*, they might feel it to be an act of patriotism: "that we Englishmen might be found as forward in that behalf as other nations, which have brought all worthy histories into their natural language". This should be connected with the growing idea of Scotland as the chosen race, as originally fostered in the Arbroath Declaration and expanded upon in the various Covenants. Also, in the troubled reigns of successive Scottish monarchs, the historian felt, that a reconsideration of the past, might help to solve the problems of the present. Thirdly, the growing dissatisfaction with Latin, led some writers to compose vernacular histories, so that the nation's glories might be made known to a wider circle of people. These motivations arose particularly from the given social context of the late sixteenth century, while after the Union, Scottish historians felt in addition, that works of this sort might to a degree resurrect the lost sense of nationalism. So, writing of Histories flourished, and in an age where the medium was still as important as the message, and every Historian thought in terms of rhetoric and devices of persuasion, these Histories survived as literature, boosting the potential of Middle Scots as a vehicle for prose.

Knox's *History of the Reformation* represents another group of Histories, those dealing with religious developments, rather than wider political problems. In it he scorns details, "such as appertain to an Universal History of the time", and dismisses important economic and social troubles as "trifling questions". It thus presents a contrast to both Leslie's and Pitscottie's, in the concentration of its theme and in the partisan committedness of the author's tone. Knox in the Prologue makes no attempt to present his *History* as an objective account of events. It is part of a conflict: "I see the battle shall be great, for Sathan rageth even to the uttermost; and I am come (I praise my God), even in the bruit of the battle". The enemy is Catholicism: "It is not unknown, Christian Reader, that the same cloud of ignorance that long hath darkened many realms under this accursed kingdom of that Roman Antichrist hath also over-covered this poor realm."

Despite these obvious differences, there is one way in which Knox's *History* does resemble Pitscottie's, for in it too the tone and narrative methods alter as the book progresses. In its simplest terms, the first book of *The History of the Reformation* is descriptive and persuasive, subtly leading the readers into the polemical and heated justification of the Protestant cause in Book 2. Book 3, although still replete with persuasive rhetoric, does make extensive use of historical documents and indeed includes the text of the *Book of Discipline*. This is the approach later to be favoured by Calderwood. In the context of the *History of the Reformation* it provides factual material to back up the reformer's points, but at the same time frees us from the intoxicating power of his own rhetorical presence. The fourth book, by way of contrast, is almost dramatic in form, with a heavy reliance on reported speech, as Knox, Queen Mary and Lethington argue out religious problems, in a fashion always designed to give victory to the protestant side.

These variations of technique along with the presence of a dominating narrator and the ordering of events, to point a specific religious message, imply that Knox's *History* will have many of the charms of the novel. Moreover, the writer is throughout entirely in control of his medium, alternating between passages in eloquent English and others in forceful vernacular Scots. As a rhetorician he is also influenced by the classical periodic structure, but the hypotaxis is controlled by a basic binary rhythm, perhaps suggested by the writings of Calvin: "Our faces are this day confounded, our enemies triumph, our hearts have quaked for fear, and yet they remain oppressed with sorrow and shame. But what shall we think to be the very cause that God hath thus dejected us? If I shall say, our sins and former unthankfulness to God, I speak the truth."

It is, I think no coincidence, that after Knox, Scottish prose tends to become more controlled, more precise than it had been previously. Nor can Knox's great influence be attributed solely to his influential position, for as Carlyle sees, "It must be a little mind that cannot see that he was a poet—one of the wild Saxon kind, full of deep religious melody that sounds like Cathedral music." This poetry does reside mainly in the rhythm, in the rhetoric, in the slow building up of atmosphere or in the sudden incongruous simile, which breaks the continued tonal effect. Not in the associations of imagery (for these Calvin had condemned) but in the rhetorical skill of passages like the one celebrating Queen Mary's first arrival in Scotland, does Knox's poetry reside: "The very face of heaven, at the time of her arrival, did manifestly speak what comfort was brought into this country with her, to wit, sorrow, dolour, darkness, and all impiety. For, in the memory of man, that day of the year was never seen a more dolorous face of the heaven than was at her arrival, which two days after did so continue; for besides the surface wet, and corruption of the air, the mist was so thick and so dark that scarce might any man espy another the length of two pairs of boots". Calderwood's *History of the Kirk in Scotland* is more comprehensive, more accurate, more objective, but as literature, it does not bear comparison with Knox's.

Knox was of course to the forefront in another branch of Scottish prose writing, that of pamphleteering. Here he employs an even wider diversity of rhetorical skills, as his prose style becomes even more exclusively geared to persuasion than narration. *The First Blast against the Monstruous Regiment of Women* is perhaps the finest example of Knox in this mode, although here too one can justifiably see the influence of Calvin. Like Calvin in his polemical works, Knox first of all establishes a complete certainty of tone, presuming that his reader's agreement is *a priori* guaranteed. Like Calvin he uses authorities to back up his point, but by providing them with the same rhetorical style as himself, they soon become mere aspects of his own voice. Thus even the voice of God becomes that of Knox, an energetic second in the Reformer's corner. More subtly, if the authority does not fully support the point in question, both Knox and Calvin are not above inserting a qualifying phrase, such as—"by which he wold plainlie conclude", and then quietly moving the viewpoint into a position more obviously in harmony with their own.

All this builds up the power of the debater's own voice. Francis Higman in *The Style of John Calvin in his French Polemical*

Treatises notes related devices aimed at discrediting one's opponent, almost all of which are employed also by Knox. Each of the reformers tends to use an elevated diction, when putting his ideas forward, but resorts to indigenous words, when stating the opposing case. More obviously, by appealing to commonsense and then mercilessly over-simplifying contrary arguments, they make it difficult for their readers to take their adversaries seriously. All the repulsive images are also associated with the voice of the opponent, so that in the *First Blast*, woman's authority becomes a "wall without foundation", her empire an "idol"; the result of her power, "monsters".

In some ways, Knox surpasses Calvin however, notably in a superior use of dialogue and in a more sophisticated "question and answer" technique. He also looks behind and beyond the point he has reached, with the same sublime certainty of tone, almost suggesting that for him, like God, past and present fuse as one: "As before I have proved the contrarie ... so shal I shortlie do the same by other testimonies". These and many other devices will be found in the extended extract from the *First Blast*, expressed with the power and control of the expert rhetorician. Seldom, if ever, has a Scotsman so successfully realised in practice, that theory of prose, which sees it as a branch of the rhetorical art of persuasion.

The two other examples of pamphleteering presented in this anthology contrast markedly with Knox's. George Buchanan was the finest Latin scholar of his century, but possibly for this very reason, his vernacular prose remains only as a solemn warning that Scots cannot be expected to stretch successfully into lengthy Latin periods. In Buchanan one sees those very dangers of excessive Latinising and lack of rhetorical control, which Knox successfully combated. There are successful passages, but one retains also memories of syntactic chaos. Of these the following is by no means the worst example: "This not obtenit, he obtenit aganis all the said regentis freindis will, to be send to ward in the castell of Edinburgh quhair he wrocht aganis the nature of the Chamaeleon, for he changeit the greitar part of thame of the castell to his colour, sa weill, that the consperacy of the regentis deid lang afoir consavit wes than brocht to effect." Of his two vernacular tracts, *The*

Chamaeleon is more impressive than the *Admonitioun to the Lordis*, partially because of the governing metaphor suggested by the title, and partially because in it, Buchanan maintains his powerful if slightly pedantic satire more forcefully. But the excessive stylistic complexity is common to each, obstructing meaning as often as it underlines it.

The third example of pamphleteering, William Fowler's *Answer to the Calumnious Letter and Erroneous Propositions of an Apostat named M. Io. Hammiltoun*, represents in some ways a mean between the other two. Writing later than Buchanan and with some experience of life in England, he uses more English word forms, without approaching the rigorous anglicisation of Knox. Equally his sentence structures are neither as rambling as Buchanan's nor as controlled as Knox's. Nonetheless, his is a vigorous and adventurous style, probably influenced by the English prose writings of Hoby (who also influenced his *Tarantula* and *Prince*). The base is still the classical period, although this is embellished by features from other traditions. For example, alliteration plays a major part in all Fowler's prose works. A favoured device in the writings of all Scottish poets from Barbour onwards, it is used extensively by Fowler in phrases like " thair libidinous lust and lycherous lyves" or "fostering thair foolishe foly with thair furious fantesies". Alliteration is often introduced at climactic moments in the argument, especially at the end of one of Fowler's long lists of condemnation, reminiscent of the medieval homilists. If the growth of alliterative intensity in one such list, coincides with the classical ideal of balanced comment, the result can be most impressive: "In end, as voyd and emptie vessels rings maist and rattels loudest: even so thou of gritter ostentatioun then of doctrine, of arrogancie then of knawledge, of rasher railing then of solid reason, bosteously after thy blasphemeis thus wayis concludes...." The "nervous Scottish prose" of Buchanan, of Lindsay and of Leslie has now a more confident note, and is drawing its strength from more than one tradition.

It is instructive to compare Fowler's style in this pamphlet with his later translation of the *Prince*, where maturity has produced a more careful, but the need for imitation, a less adventurous style.

Equally one might profitably compare his style with that of other pamphleteers regrettably unrepresented in this anthology. With Knox's most renowned opponent for example, Ninian Winzet, whose syntactic control over very lengthy sentences again argues for increasing confidence in the composition of vernacular prose. Often Winzet adds to a simple statement, in turn a double, then a triple and even a quadruple rhythm: "And give ye have thair maid sacrifice to fals godis—that is, alswa (as ancient fatheris godlie exponis it) hes embraceit fals and erroneous doctryne for the treuth—hes worchippit and adorit erroures, hereseis, and lies for the eternall veritie of Godis Word, and that ye mycht haif youre awin consaitis wicketlie fulfyllit—consider give ye *prurientes auribus* hes not electit preistis and precheaures, and heipit up masteris to your selfis, not descending of the tribe of Levi—that is, not succeeding to the Apostles and thair successouris efter the ordinance appoyntit to be the Word of God." Here the very gradual growth of the complexity, the use of parenthesis as a braking agent, and the introduction of pauses prevent the sort of chaos so often found in Buchanan. Winzet is a good prose writer, although like Knox he is unduly scornful of imagery. To read first Knox's scourgings of Mary and then Winzet's references to her as a "maist noble humane and gentil Soverane" or to compare their reactions to Cardinal Beaton's murder, is perhaps one of the best ways to discover James VI's coveted *"media via"*.

Still in the field of pamphleteering and controversial writings generally, but moving into the later part of the period, one should not ignore the temperate style and tone of Samuel Rutherford's *Plea for Paul's Presbyterie in Scotland* (1642) or the lesser known *Some Remarks on a Scandalous Paper*, written by Alexander Munro in 1695. A reply to the Synods and presbyteries of the Kirk of Scotland, the latter is characterised by a wry humour and a not inconsiderable satiric ingenuity. Having accredited the Reformation with one great discovery—Sin, Munro remarks, "However, I may be allowed to observe, that of late, we were wont to hear the abounding of Sin attributed to the dull, dry, insipid and moral lectures of the Episcopal Curates, as if their dead Sermons had been the only cause of the prevailing power of wickedness." Munro relies on more subtle techniques than Knox or Fowler. Using the *persona* of a puzzled onlooker desperately trying to make sense of the new Presbyterian discoveries, he proves himself a worthy opponent for these earlier religious propagandists. His work also shows that the Scottish Prose writers of the late seventeenth century were moving much closer to the simpler, modern style.

The sermon tradition itself had an influence on these writers. Fowler's long catalogues, his alliteration and love of word pairs, are all devices favoured by Hugh Latimer, perhaps the most influential of all sixteenth century English preachers. In Scotland as in England, sermons still relied on metre, on heavy alliteration and on anecdotes, for their effect. But alongside this, the followers of Wyclif considered many of these devices unfitting for serious religious worship. There was a conflict between the seriousness and loftiness, thought to be apposite for praise of God, and the colloquial speech, necessary to hold the interest of one's congregation. Many of the presbyterian preachers tried to use both extremes in their sermons, thus laying themselves open to the merciless parodying of the *Presbyterian Eloquence*. Elsewhere, variety is the keynote. The impressive rhetoric of Knox still dominates, while in the *Pretended Conference*, we have a malicious description of his mannerisms and "stur and kroking voce". From the pulpit of St. Giles, there is also Robert Bruce's strange mixture of Biblical and patristic theology, expressing itself in a neatly balanced prose, relying on word pairs and an effective overlapping argument: "There is nothing in this world, or out of this world more to be wished by everyone of you than to be conjoined with Jesus Christ, and once for all made one with Him, the God of glory. This heavenly and celestial conjunction is procured and brought about by two special means. It is brought about by means of the Word and preaching of the Gospel, and it is brought about by means of the Sacraments and their ministration." Bruce makes few concessions to his audience, but he does lead them through the argument by defining the words of his text and numbering the heads and sub-heads of the discourse. In England, Lancelot Andrewes favoured the same minute and rigorously logical division. In Scotland the most extreme, yet effective exponent of the "numerological" sermon is Andrew Gray, with his numbered thematic divisions, his simple, staccato style, his short sentences, and his fervent use of repetition and exclamation: "For I take Heaven to be my Witness; I take the Father the first person of the Blessed Trinity; I take Jesus Christ the second; I take the Holy Ghost the third; I take Angels; I take all the glorified Saints about the Throne; I take the stones of this house; I take your selves; I take your selves to witness."

For the vast majority of these preachers, English was the medium for praising God, and Scots, if used at all, was employed for the colloquial anecdotes, or for vigorous castigating of the sins of the congregation. The power of the image also began to grow in the seventeenth century, despite Calvin's mistrust of its usefulness. The Ciceronian periods of Hugh Binning are often punctuated with extended conceits of God as fire, as sun or the city of refuge. The covenanting preachers were, however, the main developers of the associative values of imagery. Alexander Henderson likens the rulers to giants with one foot on the neck of the Church and the other on the neck of the state, but he is by no means an extreme example. Edward Calamy uses the image more frequently and more daringly: "England hath broken Covenant with God, and now God is breaking England in pieces, even as a potter breaks a vessel in pieces ... A Covenant is a bond to ty us to God; and now God hath made an iron whip of that Covenant, which we have broken asunder, to whip us withal." For these conceits, use of colloquialism and sudden juxtaposition of ideas associated with the English metaphysical movement, the Scottish sermon is a more profitable hunting ground than Scottish verse.

John Row's *Red-Shankes Sermon* has been chosen for extended treatment, because it does represent many of the powerful forces in sermon preaching of the late sixteenth and seventeenth centuries. Its theme is the Church of Scotland and the Covenant, certainly the most frequently preached theme of the period, for the idea of a federal theology, had gained a firm hold on the Scottish imagination. There is the neat and ordered development of the argument into heads. There is the use of English predominantly for the argument, but Scots for the anecdote of Balaam and the

Ass, which reminds one at once of the Mediaeval Miracle plays and the Mediaeval preachings of such as John Mirc. There is the controlled sentence length, the use of climactic rhetorical devices and the increasing importance of the image, all characteristic of mid-seventeenth century preaching. For these reasons, as for the skilful development of theme and overall power of appeal, the *Red-Shankes Sermon* must rank as one of the finest examples of the very varied and talented preaching tradition in Scotland.

TRANSLATION, ROMANCE, ESSAY

If a short outline of sixteenth and seventeenth century history provides a useful background to our study of historical and religious writings in the period, so before embarking on the more purely literary writings of the time, one ought to have a general idea of the wider perspective. To begin with, literature was still dominated by poetry. Prose, as we have seen, was still in its embryonic stages. Drama never gained the immense popularity it enjoyed in Elizabethan England. Indeed, within our period only Sir David Lindsay's *Satire of the Thrie Estaitis*, the anonymous comedy *Philotus*, and the turgid Senecan dramas of Sir William Alexander, are of note. Doubtless, other works were written and performed, but drama did remain a secondary genre.

Poetically the period is not nearly so poor as earlier critics supposed. In the 1550s there is still the figure of Sir David Lindsay who had exposed the follies of courtly and public life in satires like the *Papyngo* and taken the mediaeval romance form into the early renaissance with *Squyer Meldrum*. In the 1560s, the combined influences of the rhétoriqueurs in France and the increased interest in courtly music fostered by the Scottish Chapel Royal, produce some of the most polished of Scottish courtly lyrics, with the poet-musician Alexander Scott leading the way. He is followed in the 1570s by Alexander Montgomerie, who expertly plays the voices of humanist, musician and rhetorician against each other. At the same time he introduces a more popular note into his verse, without transgressing courtly form.

Yet, although prose romances, especially Sidney's *Arcadia* were popular, no Scottish writer had successfully followed this example. In part this was because Scottish writers, unlike English, lacked a critical manifesto, setting out clear guidelines for literary practitioners. In part it was because, despite isolated writers of talent, the troubled times prevented any co-ordinated interest in art. These, anyway, were the conclusions James VI reached. The latter problem he solved by setting up his Castalian band of writers and musicians, headed by himself as Maecenas and by Montgomerie as "maister poete". This group included the English Hudson brothers, John Stewart of Baldynneis and William Fowler. Although, on leaving for England, the Castalians split up, the concept of the literary group remained, with William Alexander and Robert Ayton dominating, and writers like Alexander Craig travelling south to join it.

More pertinently, James solved the first problem by producing in 1585 his own critical treatise, those *Reulis and Cautelis* from which we have already had occasion to cite. As James's views were largely based on the practice of earlier Scottish writers, and as his position at court carried their influence into the future, this work provides a good mirror of Scottish literary tastes over a period of many decades. To begin with, the treatise is at once national and international. It supports the use of the Scottish vernacular. Nor is Scots to be confounded with English, for "we differ from thame in sindrie reulis of Poesie". Yet his very argument for a Scottish linguistic and poetic autonomy, is advanced with the same "tree and branch" metaphor employed by Du Bellay in *La Deffence et Illustration de la Langue Françoyse*. Elsewhere one hears the influence of Ronsard, Puttenham, Gascoigne and even of Trissino. This looks forward to a period, when Scots poets, inspired primarily by the influence of the *pléiade* sought to express their nationalism through imitation and invention, by producing work based on the writings of Petrarch, Ariosto, Saint Gelais, Desportes, Spenser, Daniel and many others. In prose, this movement was to produce Fowler's translation of *Il Principe* and Urquhart's rendering of Rabelais among others.

The idea of art as a branch of rhetoric is also strengthened in the *Reulis*. James is mainly concerned with devising rules for rhyme, rhythm and stanza formation. In a discussion on decorum he extends Puttenham's definition of levels of style by introducing a system of graded levels of diction, while extending the principle to include modes of argument. These ideas on art as mannerised, teachable, and working within a framework of set rhetorical devices and grades of diction begin to fade only in the latter half of the seventeenth century.

Before this however, a second critical essay had appeared, Sir William Alexander's *Anacrisis*, composed about 1634. There the internationalism remains, with Alexander expressing his admiration of Virgil and Ovid, Statius and Lucan, Tasso and Du Bartas. Sidney's *Arcadia* is adjudged, "the most excellent work that, in my judgment, hath been written in any Language", although the reasons advanced are more moral ("affording many exquisite types of perfection") than literary. Apart from the increasing interest in pastoral poetry and romance, this essay does warn against one of the dangers of excessive mannerism, as practised in earlier Scottish writings. Alexander urges that an interest in style should not be divorced from an interest in the thought clothed by that style. "Language is but the apparel of poesy, which may give beauty, but not strength, and when I censure any poet, I first dissolve the general contexture of his work in several pieces, to see what sinews it hath, and to mark what will remain behind, when that external gorgeousness, consisting in the choice or placing of words, as if it would bribe the ear to corrupt the judgment, is first removed, or at least only marshalled in its own degree." This strikes a happy mean between the stylistic virtuosity of some of the minor lyricists, and the growing band of covenanting writers, who believed with William Mure, that the message should be expressed directly, for fear that poetic means might disguise or pervert it. Aware of these opposing viewpoints, Alexander concludes with a memorable and fairminded antithesis: "The treasures of poesie cannot be better bestowed than upon the apparelling of Truth, and Truth cannot be better apparrelled to please young lovers than with the excellencies of poesy."

James's *Reulis and Cautelis* had only been concerned with

poetry. Alexander's *Anacrisis* discusses prose as well. This is because the intervening period had seen a revival of interest in literary prosewriting among Scotsmen. For the purposes of this introduction let us discuss the very varied forms it took under the headings of Translations, Romance and Essays.

Adaptation and imitation were clearly encouraged by James VI and many of his Castalian band did render foreign masterpieces into Scots or English. Most however, were poems. James himself produced a clumsy version of Du Bartas' *Uranie*, Thomas Hudson translated the *Judith* and John Stewart's *Roland Furious* derives ultimately from Ariosto, although Desportes and the French translator Jean Martin are intermediaries. William Fowler, who started by translating Petrarch's *Trionfi*, however, progressed to the prose of Machiavelli's *Il Principe*. He appears to have embarked on this project, while also aiding James with his own political treatise, the *Basilicon Doron*, and his motives are thus partly those of political advancement. Nonetheless, his translation is infinitely superior to that of the *Trionfi*, which had suffered from being set in a ludicrous metre. Like Stewart he uses a French intermediary, *Le Prince* of Gaspard d'Auvergne (1553). Additions to the Italian text can be traced to this source, as in Chapter 26, where Fowler has "a new forme" and D'Auvergne "une nouvelle forme", but Machiavelli simply "forma". Occasionally he combines French and Italian, as in Chapter 3, where the phrase "abbaissing and infebling" is obviously drawn both from Machiavelli's "abbassorono" and D'Auvergne's "affoblissans". Such diligence in searching out earlier translations is typical of the professionalism of the Castalians, and it has been demonstrated that in this instance, a Latin translation, by Sylvester Telius (1560) also occasionally determines the nature of Fowler's text.

Fowler's prose style too has progressed since the aggressive but somewhat loose rhythms of the *Admonition*. Sentences still tend to be overcomplex, despite the desperate strengthening of prepositional phrases. Yet, the rhythm, with its intelligent use of doublets and triads ("conquesed and obtened"; "governed, uphalden and conteneued") is controlled and dignified. In all this, as in the balanced phrases, the alliteration and the prevailing periodic structure, one can detect the influence of Hoby, whom Fowler greatly admired.

The art of the translator, as Alexander Gray noted in his introtion to *Arrows*, is often condescended to, yet the great ages of literature have all been the great ages of translation. Further, the problems besetting any translator are enough to daunt the stoutest heart. Even in the simplest prose, it is difficult to find a word, which is the exact equivalent of the one being translated and almost impossible to find such a synonym with the same associative range in English as the original had in French or Italian. Even in prose (though more so in poetry) there is the additional problem of retaining not only the meanings but the rhythms of the passage being adapted. Should one's priorities be for a close rendering, or for the retention of stylistic devices like assonance and alliteration, although this might imply departing from a strict translation? This is why every translation in the strict sense is doomed to failure from the outset.

Fowler, in his *Prince* aimed primarily for a close literal rendering of *Il Principe*. He made little or no attempt to catch the conversational tones of Machiavelli. This is perhaps why his translation is less exciting, less well known and less satisfying as literature, than the other major prose translation of our period. This is of course Thomas Urquhart's translation of Rabelais, fit surely to rank with the Bible and Florio's *Montaigne* as one of the finest translations ever. Urquhart is not nearly so accurate as Fowler, but he enters into the spirit of his author much better. For example, almost all later translators of Rabelais have tried to lessen the French writer's excesses, whether these be excesses of bawdry or of style. Urquhart alone realises that the translator, if he wishes to recreate this original enthusiasm, must increase rather than dilute. This he does. His lists are longer. At every turn his imagination strives to top Rabelais'. Even the bawdry is dealt with in greater detail. Thus Rabelais has, "que tous ses larrys tant feurent oppilez et reserrez que a grande poine, avecques les dents, vous les eussiez eslargiz". Urquhart expands this into, "whereby all her lorris, arsepipes and conduits were so opilated, stopped, obstructed and contracted, that you could hardily have opened and enlarged them with your teeth."

Likewise Urquhart is careful to echo rhythmic effects. A literal translation of "Je n'en scay rien de ma part et bien peu me soucie ny d'elle ny d'aultre" would not transmit the easy bounding rhythm as well as Urquhart's "For my part truly I cannot tell, neither do I care very much for her, not for any body else." Indeed no other translator known to me has the same unerring sense of when the literal translation would lose more through rhythmic or associative effects, than it would gain in exactitude of meaning. Urquhart is the only translator of Rabelais to render, "retournant à noz moutons" in Chapter 1 Book 1, as "to returne to our weathers". The meaning is different, but he retains the concrete associations of sheep and shepherd, which fit so well into the highly imaginative atmosphere already set in this opening chapter. In short he renders poetic prose with poetic prose and pays as much attention to the first element as to the second. In this and in sharing with Rabelais the adventure of words, he surpasses the efforts of later translators, who in concentrating overmuch on the meaning, fail to render that meaning in all its associative fullness.

In the History of Sixteenth and Seventeenth Century Scottish Prose, Urquhart ranks in stature with Knox. While the latter was the finest exponent of prose as persuasion, and led the way to increased anglicisation and control of the classical period, Urquhart provided the finest translation, and of the Scottish prose writers, most enthusiastically experimented with word forms, rhetorical tropes and the devices of the artificial prose style. In England a courtly prose style had been gradually evolving since the time of Caxton. It reached its fullest expression in John Lyly's *Euphues* and received further nourishment from the many rhetorical treatises composed in England in the mid or late sixteenth century, as well as from translations of foreign romances by Guevera and others. The culmination of this interest in romantic prose narrative came with Sidney's *Arcadia*. Although critical of earlier works like the *Euphues* Sidney was conscious of working in the same tradition of fictional romance and drew on earlier English and European

examples (e.g. *Amadis of Gaul*; *Arcadia* of Sannazaro; Heliodorus'
Aethiopica) for his inspiration.

He could not easily have employed Scottish examples, as there
were none. Before 1603, Romantic fiction, even with a didactic
function or with some autobiographical pretensions, could not rise
above three challenges. There was the challenge of Latin as a more
dignified medium than the vernacular. There was the challenge of
real historical and religious crises, having the authoritative stamp
of truth. Finally there was the challenge of James's Castalian
Renaissance, focusing primarily on music and poetry rather than
prose. After 1603, the Scots lacked a court in Edinburgh and felt
strangers at the court in London. They became aware of the
popularity of Sidney and Montemayor, as Alexander's *Anacrisis*
bears witness, but lacked the confidence to follow suit. The first
major stirrings of the Scottish romance form are delayed till
Urquhart's *Jewel* of 1652 and George MacKenzie's *Aretina* of
1663. Earlier only Barclay's *Argenis* represents a brave but unsuc-
cessful effort in the mode.

The Jewel, like all of Urquhart's work, defies classification of
any rigid kind. Reduced to its basic essentials it consists of an
extended discussion on Urquhart's proposed Universal Language,
a satire on Scots bankers, a series of military biographies, and
finally a consideration of Scottish writers in which James VI brings
up the rear. On the way Urquhart contrives side swipes at Presbyterians, 'national' morals and the church, yet still he finds time
to support the union of Scotland with England. If there be a
unifying thread to all this, it is identified near the end, where
Urquhart confesses that the 'prime scope of the treatise' is to pro-
cure his own liberty and urge the government to restore the family
estates of Cromarty, lost to him because he had been a devout
Royalist during the Civil War. This accounts for the many anecdotes
stressing the importance of liberty and property sprinkled at regular
intervals throughout the book. It also explains the poetic conclusion,

> Pity it were to refuse such,
> As ask but little, and give much.

The highlight of this hotchpotch of linguistic adventure, military honours lists, philosophical speculations, and potted biographies, is the "biography" of the Admirable Crichton, so exaggerated as to vie with the extremes of the Elizabethan Romance form; so stylistically mannerised as to rank with the most extreme examples of mannerised prose. From the fantastic succession of events, I have chosen those scenes, where Crichton displays his ability as an actor and lover. To a large extent these extracts must speak for themselves. Never before and never since have romance or mimicry been so treated, for like Rabelais and Sterne, Urquhart has so peculiar and yet so consistent a vision of the world, that no artist could recreate it or critic successfully analyse it.

Yet, while obviously thoroughly enjoying his chosen mode, it seems likely that Urquhart was also satirising the traditional biographical and didactic romance, which had grown out of works like Guevera's *Decada de las vidas de los x. Cesares*. The highly artificial style adopted in the *Jewel* mirrors the manneristic excesses of this type of Romance in the seventeenth century. Yet at the end, Urquhart ironically regrets that he had not decorated his book "with an inundation of greater eloquence: and that one way tropologetically, by metonymical, ironical, metaphorical, and synechdochical instruments of elocution, in all their several kinds." This can only be a satirical comment on those authors who composed with treatises of rhetoric at their elbow.

The lengthy genealogies, which often preface such Romances are equally carried to extremes by Urquhart, who takes the genealogy of his own house back to Adam and Eve. Their formlessness and haphazard digressions are parodied by the formlessness of the work as a whole, particularly as this very danger had been slyly noted in the "Introductory Epistle". There Urquhart defines the very error he himself is to commit, fearing that he "would, by outbulking the book with this Epistle, make the porch greater than the lodging; enter into a digression longer then the purpose, and outstrip the period with the parenthesis." Further, like the writers of many didactic romances, he introduces examples of certain virtues, without in any way linking these anecdotes to the tale. But with a deft satiric touch, he explains all this to his reader, as if he regarded it as some form of literary virtue: "These collateral instances I introduce, not for application, but illustration sake; not for comparison, but explication of the congruent adapting of necessary punctilio's for the framing of a vertuous action."

Like Sterne in *Tristram Shandy*, Urquhart satirises the weaknesses of a traditional Romance form, by presenting them in exaggerated form, by extending the parentheses until they threaten to become the major part of the book, by dislocating the moral examples more completely from the natural train of the narrative, by introducing a very discursive narrator and hinting at autobiographical tendencies. At the same time, like Sterne's, the governing artistic vision is so consistent and idiosyncratic, that one enjoys the world of Urquhart's imaginings as much in and for itself as for the satiric light it obliquely casts on the degenerate exemplars of the autobiographical romance tradition. Indeed, it is perhaps peculiarly fitting, that the first creative comment by a Scot on prose romance, should at once reflect serious reservations, yet express these through the almost wholly unrestrained flights of the Celtic imagination.

George MacKenzie's *Aretina* is a much more conventional Romance. In an interesting prologue, MacKenzie confesses debts to Sidney and de la Scuderie, while stressing an overall didactic function. Stylistically he analyses the four modes he considers most prevalent in mid-seventeenth century Scotland and England. The University style is too pedantic for his tastes, the philosophic is characterized by "strong" sense and short periods, while the courtly style seems exaggerated and selfconscious. Perhaps not surprisingly, lawyer MacKenzie prefers the style of barristers, on the grounds that it is "flourished with similes" and similitudes to him suggest harmony. Although he stands apart from all four styles as thus defined, and proclaims, "It was to form to myself a style, that I undertook this piece", he does make extensive use of similes and those "longwinded periods", which he also isolated as features of the legal mode.

Aretina is primarily concerned with a Sidneian world of heroes and lovers, but does contain as the third of its four books a lightly disguised allegory of the Civil War, overthrow of Charles I, rise

of Cromwell and return of Charles II. This includes many fine
passages and reveals no small degree of ingenuity on the part of
the author. The Romance itself, however, is artistically more satisfying. It deals with the long, precarious but eventually successful
wooings of Philarites for Aretina and Megistus for Agapeta. These
four are obviously modelled to some degree on Sidney's Pyrocles
and Musidorus, Philoclea and Pamela with Barclay's *Argenis* a
secondary influence. At the same time, MacKenzie's work seems
to me to fit most convincingly into a transitional position between
the *Arcadia* and the historical romances of Fielding or Smollett.
To begin with, MacKenzie like Fielding carefully inserts both
moral and anecdotal digressions, either to confirm his heroes in
some virtue or to illuminate their situation through comparison
with others in a similar or slightly differentiated position. This
Sidney had done to some extent, but the more formalised approach
of MacKenzie looks forward rather than back. His heroes like
Fielding's pause in their gigantic strides to discuss the fickleness
of courtly fame, the dangers of ambition and love in all its varieties.
On a par with the anecdotes of the Man of the Hill or Mr Wilson
are those related by MacKenzie's two hermits. Of these, the first
laments a wife who committed suicide, the second contemplates
the skulls of Alexander and Plato as part of his general contempt
for the world. Both the moralisings of major characters and the
tales related by minor ones are functional elements in the plot,
clearly motivated by the needs of character development or situation creation. The loose form of the prose romance is gradually
moving towards the greater control of the novel.

This parallel with Fielding can be overstressed, but it is noticeable that MacKenzie also introduces more realism into the rather
idealistic romance form, notably in the shape of cynical, materialis-
tic or even just witty innkeepers, who clearly anticipate figures like
Mr and Mrs Tow Wouse. Thus, while the predominantly idealistic
tone remains and women are still melodramatically chased by
would-be ravishers, the lower levels of society begin to play a
stronger part, and humour undercuts excesses of idealism. It is
this strange yet effective mixture which is later to be adapted by
Fielding, using a much simpler style. Even from this angle, Mac-

Kenzie's style, though artificial, is clearly less flamboyant than Sidney's or the followers of *Euphues*. MacKenzie's *Aretina* seems to me an overlooked link between the courtly romances of Sidney and the historical romances of Fielding. As such it may rightly claim to be the first Scottish work, clearly to anticipate the early novel.

While the works of Barclay, Urquhart and MacKenzie hesitantly adapted the traditions of Romance, another genre had already reached a much higher degree of sophistication in Scotland. The Essay was used to cover all sorts of topics. Those chosen here, (James VI on Tobacco, Drummond on Death, MacKenzie on Religious Sects and Kirk and Sinclair on the Supernatural) merely represent a small cross-section of the themes covered and the styles adopted. The reasons for this popularity are clear. The shorter form appealed to writers, as yet not wholly sure of prose as a medium. The sermon, often of about the same length and using clearcut headings could act as a guide, and indeed did especially influence early essay writing in Scotland. Printers in Scotland encouraged both pamphlets and essays on controversial topics. They could be quickly produced and to a degree played the part of newspapers. Thus a series of essays might appear on tobacco, each picking up the argument as assessed by the last contributor. Witchcraft and modes of irrigation are but two more of the varied subjects so treated within our period.

James's *A Counterblaste to Tobacco* was published in 1604. Drummond's *Cypresse Grove* appeared in 1630 and MacKenzie's *Religio Stoici* in 1663. As the two works on the supernatural are respectively dated 1685 and 1691, this presents us with a neat chronological progression throughout the seventeenth century. The approach and style adopted by each author may also be taken as fairly representative of the age in which he was writing. These selections may thus be taken as a fair guideline to the progression of the essay genre in seventeenth century Scotland.

A Counterblaste to Tobacco for example obviously owes much to the neat, orderly form of the sermon as preached by Robert Bruce. James had often expressed his great admiration for this preacher and employs a similarly clearcut division of argument.

The formal introduction of the topic is followed by two false arguments of "reason" and then two false arguments based on "experience". Reason suggests that the dry and hot fumes of tobacco will balance the wet and cold brains of men. James counters, that the mixture of humours is not equalised in all parts of the body, while tobacco adds certain "venemous faculties" to its basic dry and hot admixture. Reason then suggests, that smoke can purge the head of 'rheumes and distillations'. Yet the heat of the brain will turn this smoke to water, as the sun turns smoky vapours into rain. Experience is made to argue, that so many people would not naturally like it, if tobacco were not *per se* good. This, James indicates, is to discount fashion and novelty as motivations. Experience then advances a number of objections, all attributed by the King to the basic error of *non causam pro causa*. If one is cured, while taking tobacco, this does not imply that tobacco caused the cure. Having disposed of these arguments in favour of tobacco, James turns to the negative side and builds up a forceful case against this "precious stinke". It is linked with lust, drunkenness, impotence and waste, before the final forceful climax is reached. Tobacco is there rejected as "A custome lothsome to the eye, hatefull to the nose, harmefull to the braine, dangerous to the lungs, and in the blacke stinking fume thereof, nearest resembling the horrible Stigian smoke of the pit that is bottomlesse".

The influence of the sermon and the long periodic structure, heavily influenced by James's classical studies, make this an essay of its age. Note also how many devices of persuasion James shares with Knox. There is the subtle irony of pretending to support the target of one's satire—"Omnipotent power of tobacco!" Or again, "It helpes all sorts of agues. It makes a man sober that was drunke. It refreshes a weary man and yet makes a man hungry." As in Knox's pamphlets, all the damaging associations possible cluster round the object under attack. Tobacco is initially presented as connected with a filthy disease, the pox; a base race, the Indians; and a currently hated courtier, Raleigh. Like Calvin and Knox, James mocks his opponents' views in farcical tones but places the most dignified interpretation on his own. The protagonists of tobacco therefore argue with the voice of an old woman urging quack cures for the cholic, but the consequences of tobacco-taking are linked with the seven deadly sins and seen to weaken the nation's character at home and abroad. As this effective satire is further underlined by skilful rhetorical use of triads, climaxes and question-series, *A Counterblaste* must have a very real claim to rank as James VI's finest literary work.

The charms of unified form, skilful rhetorical argument and biting wit, which characterise this essay, are absent in Drummond's *Cypresse Grove*. There the form follows the vagaries of association and reflection. The argument is melancholic, sober and poetic. The major topic is death, a theme dear to Drummond's heart and considered also in *Exequies of Alexander* and the *Flowres of Sion*. By this time the powerful sermon influence on the essay form was on the wane, and there is little trace of it here, although Drummond does touch on many fundamental theological problems such as the relationship of body and soul, or man's longing for the infinite.

Indeed, although the thought progression in this essay is interesting, and confirms Drummond's poetic obsessions with mutability and contempt for the world, it is not there that the major attraction lies. Rather is it, that for the first time a Scotsman is using the Elizabethan copious style with confidence and originality. The obvious classical influence on James, is for Drummond only a vague general pattern in the background. The self-conscious use of balance, of climax, of extended syntax as exemplified in earlier writers, flows apparently without effort from Drummond's pen. To this he adds the powerful associative effects, culled from his vast reading in European poetics and from his own efforts as poet and adaptor: "This earth is as a table booke, and men are the notes, the first are washen out, that new may be written in. They which forewent us did leave a roome for us, and should we grieve to doe the same to these which should come after us? Who being admitted to see the exquisite rarities of some antiquaries cabinet is grieved, all viewed, to have the courtaine drawen, and give place to new pilgrimes? And when the Lord of this universe hath shewed us the various wonders of his amazing frame, should wee take it to heart, when he thinketh time to dislodge?" Like James, Drummond is persuasive, but his associations become part of his argument, rather than backing up the logic at one remove. The smoothness of his style contrasts with James's staccato rhythms. Each is admirable but each in his own way, and Drummond's more assured and poetic handling of prose does reflect the general trend of the 1630s in Scotland. A comparison between James's *Reulis* and Alexander's *Anacrisis* for example, would confirm this conclusion.

MacKenzie's *Religio Stoici*, as the name suggests, was written with Sir Thomas Browne's *Religio Medici* in mind, and frequently MacKenzie takes up points raised in the earlier discussion. The title itself suggests disagreement with the criticisms of stoical philosophy raised by Browne in Section 44. Similarly, Browne interprets "superstition" as referring to church rituals, or "those outward and sensible motions, which may expresse, or promote my invisible devotion". Entitling one of the essays in the *Stoic*, "Of Superstition", MacKenzie argues that superstition does not lie in excess of ceremony, for only infinite service is worthy of an infinite deity. Instead it consists of unlawful worship, such as the sacrificing of children. Another point of conflict is reached in the definition of God as I AM. Browne in Section 11 suggests that this implies that God's present is our past, present and future. MacKenzie in "Of Eternity", states that I AM means that man can only comprehend that God exists, not that he IS without past or future. This is not the place for an extended comparison of the two works, but MacKenzie does, time and again, return to problems raised by Browne and often takes over Browne's vocabulary, although adapting or challenging his ideas. Comparisons between their respective treatments of atheism, the authority of the scriptures and the beauty of apparent monsters of nature, are particularly fruitful.

The other major charm of MacKenzie's essays is the combination of legal skill in argument with the literary skills of epigrammatic expression and carefully chosen image. MacKenzie's is an original mind which does not take anything on hearsay. Even the mercy of God is challenged, as God represents perfect justice and all mercy is a receding from justice. The imagery often is biblical in basis, but with the addition of a single realistic touch, which forces one to see the old situation with new eyes; "Whereas we did see

God but in a glass formerly, that glass is now so misted and soil'd
by each pedant's flegmatic breath, that it is hard to see him at all."
All these skills were possessed to a higher degree by Voltaire, and
the *Religio Stoici* would certainly appeal to readers of the *Lettres
Philosophiques*. Though lacking the Frenchman's sophistication,
MacKenzie does anticipate some of his positions. This applies
particularly to his attitudes to fanatics, his belief that man would
have to invent God if he did not exist and his sympathy with the
stoical conception of God as watchmaker.

MacKenzie's style, while still complex, reflects a further move
away from the determined periodic rhythms of the early essayists.
His direct links are not with the classical writers, but with the
thriving English prose tradition. Clausal connections are looser
and short sentences are no longer avoided. The two paths opened
up by this development are exemplified in the later essays of Kirk
and Sinclair. Kirk is at times even more complex syntactically
than MacKenzie, but increases the use of the short sentence as a
variation technique. Sinclair on the other hand, uses the predominantly simple prose style, which was becoming very popular
at the end of the century, especially as vernacular prose became the
accepted medium for mathematical and scientific works.

LETTERS, DIARIES

The study of more personal prose in the form of letters and diaries
presents a conflicting conclusion. The letters which remain to us
are rather disappointing. Political letters such as those by James
VI or John Colville have much more historical than literary value.
The letters of Robert Baillie, Principal of Glasgow University have
been preserved and extend in an almost unbroken period from
January 1637 to May 1662, but these are hardly flourishing
examples of style. Indeed, the only major group which proved to
be impressive from a literary viewpoint were those by the preacher
Samuel Rutherford. As the vast majority of these were written,
while he was imprisoned in Aberdeen, and represent efforts to
maintain contacts with his friends and parishioners, they also have

the attraction of the autobiography or even of the epistolary novel. Equally, as many of them are used by Rutherford as vehicles for the sermons he was no longer allowed to preach, it is evident that this collection might have been considered in each of the previous sections to this Introduction.

Nonetheless the many private confidences imparted, the varying tones for dear friends or distant acquaintances and the honest soul-searching as religion meets the test of adversity, all justify us in seeing these letters primarily as private effusions. This accepted, it is rewarding to follow sets of letters to one person through the varied collection. There are those to Marion McNaught, the confirmed Christian; letters breathing joy in God, in her and in her home ("that little vineyard of the Lord's planting"). Or there are those to Alex. Gordon, tracing the disastrous changes in fortune which befall him, but also revealing a character given over to self-pity at times. This draws from Rutherford, one of the few letters which show impatience and despair at the preacher's own fate as he tops each of Gordon's catastrophes with one of his own. Even in the silences there is meaning, or in the succession of letters, begging replies from recalcitrant correspondents.

It is easy to understand the vast popularity enjoyed by these letters in earlier times. There is the full picture conveyed of this patient Christian man enduring with as much patience as possible, the long separation from his first love—preaching. There is the thrill of piecing together from his epistolary comments, the varying characters of his parishioners. There is the sane philosophising and simple yet forthright viewpoint, which permeates all And if this is not enough, there is that powerful, inimitable style. Always intent on rhythmic effects and skilfully using the long-short sentence variation favoured in the latter half of the seventeenth century, Rutherford may rise to a powerful rhetorical climax to express his awe of God "Alas, I wronged him in making the comparison this way! O black sun and moon, but O fair Lord Jesus! O black flowers and black lilies and roses, but O fair, fair, ever fair Lord Jesus! O all fair things, black and deformed without beauty, when ye are beside that fairest Lord Jesus! O black heaven, but O fair Christ! O black Angels, but O surpassingly fair Lord Jesus!" He may startle us with a daring image ("the saints are Gods threshing instruments") or extend a conventional one ("we creep in under Our Lords wings in the great shower"). With all these virtues, our current neglect of Rutherford seems to me a much more puzzling phenomenon, than his earlier fame.

While the letters were mainly a disappointment, one could only marvel at the extensive riches of diary literature in sixteenth and seventeenth century Scotland. Styles vary from the pious tone and highly complex syntax of Johnston of Warriston to the concise, matter of fact journals of John Turnbull. The Brodie and James Melville diaries were eventually chosen, as good representatives of the "personal, parenthetic" and "copious, rhetorical" styles respectively. While the Brodies' diaries are more intensely domestic, their authors like Melville are concerned with wider political influences and governed in all matters by religious conviction. In this admixture, the selections are representative of a very large percentage of the diaries in the period. In their pages domestic trials or affairs of state are usually referred to the overruling will of God; and the comforts of prayer or preaching never far away. Here, for example, is Johnston of Warriston receiving news of his son's death: "Quhyl I am thus speak my good brother, S. Hay, comes in and tels me that it had pleased the Lord to call my son James Johnston to himselth betwixt on and two hours in the morning, quhilk newes dasched me and confounded my wyfe. Immediatly thairafter in my chalmer schoe and I fell on our knees, confessed our sins, acknowledged al his mercies and blessed his naime for al the footsteps of his indulgent providence in al the alterations that ever had befallen us togither or apairt. We acknowledged Gods good providence against our wils in Mr. H. Rolloks sermon and in his exhortation about Benjamins refusal to give over the men of Gibeah."

Styles are too idiosyncratic, and the nature of the diaries so varied, that only the most general of patterns can be imposed upon them. Yet there is a noticeable simplifying of sentence structure as the period moves to its close, and passages from Turnbull's Journal (1657-1704) would not look out of place in a present day diary. The overall impression is one of infinite and thoroughly enjoyable variety, fortunately already more extensively anthologised in *Scottish Diaries and Memoirs*, ed J. G. Fyfe (Stirling, 1928), Vol. I.

R.D.S.J.

Edinburgh, 1971.

JOHN KNOX

KNOX has of course made his reputation as Scotland's major voice of the Reformation, but a study of his biography shows this voice to have been silent for the first forty years of his life. Born at Gifford, near Haddington in 1514, he is said to have studied under Major at Glasgow University, but more probably spent his student days at St. Andrews. He then took priest's orders and as late as 1543 was still an ecclesiastical notary in the Haddington district. By this time the Reformation movement was well advanced in Scotland, Patrick Hamilton having initiated it as early as 1527. What changed Knox's course was first of all growing belief in "election" and secondly the arrival at Leith in 1545 of the youthful, prophetic George Wishart. He joined Wishart and after Wishart's martyrdom and the murder of Cardinal Beaton, retreated to St. Andrews' castle, in fear of Catholic reprisals. This was in 1547, and during the siege he unwillingly became minister in the Castle. When the Protestants surrendered in June, Knox, with the other commoners, became a prisoner on the French galleys, enduring much indignity and privation for nineteen months. The reign of the Protestant Edward VI brought him back to power, as one of the King's chaplains, but on the King's early death, persecution of the Protestants began again and Knox after some travels on the continent became minister at Geneva, with the occasional return trip to Scotland punctuating his stay. In 1556, he married Marjory Bowes, to whose mother he was then giving spiritual comfort. Two sons, Nathaniel and Eleazar came from this match, but Marjory died in 1560, ironically the same year in which the Protestant religion was formally established in Scotland. Knox by now had returned and was minister of Edinburgh, but his troubles were not at an end. Mary reached Scotland in the following year

and after Rizzio's murder, Knox again fled from Edinburgh. He
went into England armed with a safe-conduct and there visited
his two sons, although by this time he had married a second wife,
Margaret Stewart, daughter of Lord Ochiltree. When James VI succeeded, however, Knox was again firmly in power, and preached
the coronation sermon. He continued his ministry, beset with ill
health till 1572. He is buried in St. Giles' churchyard, Edinburgh.

Knox wrote a lot and not always well. Of his works, the most
impressive from a literary point of view, are probably, *Epistle to
the Congregation of St. Andrews* (1548); *Letter to the Queen
Dowager, Regent of Scotland* (1556); *Letter of Wholesome Counsel, Addressed to his Brethren in Scotland* (1556); *The First Blast
of the Trumpet against the Monstruous Regiment of Women*
(1558); *On Predestination* (1560); *An Answer to a Letter written
by James Tyrie, a Scottish Jesuit* (1572); and of course his *History
of the Reformation in Scotland*. From the last-named I have
chosen the witty and dramatic passage leading up to and describ-
ing the murder of Beaton. The other text cited, *The First Blast*
was composed at a time, when Knox felt his ambitions to be
hampered on all sides by women. Mary Tudor, a Catholic ruled
in England and Mary of Guise, another Catholic was regent of
Scotland. Of these the first had driven him out of the country and
the latter had recently scorned one of his letters to her, as a
"pasquil".

As with Buchanan, critical opinion on Knox is markedly divided.
Saintsbury comments that "*The Historie of the Reformatioun* has
something of the quaintness but little of the attraction of its time;
his tracts and letters have small literary interest", yet C. S. Lewis
considers him the finest prose writer of all the sixteenth century
religious controversialists. G. Gregory Smith approaching him
from another angle, laments his anglicised language, the "occasional
shows of northern idiom and vocabulary, touching up the text like
trimmings on honest south-country cloth".

The best overall edition of Knox is still David Laing's for the
Wodrow Society in 1896, although W. Croft Dickinson's modernised edition (1949) is preferable for *The Historie of the Reformatioun*. I have based my text of *The Historie* on the 1566 MS in

Edinburgh University Library. *The First Blast* is based on the first
Geneva Edition, secretly published in 1558 and bearing no author's
name.

THE FIRST BLAST OF THE TRUMPET
AGAINST THE MONSTRUOUS REGIMENT
OF WOMEN

To promote a woman to beare rule, superioritie, dominion or
empire above any realme, nation or citie, is repugnant to nature,
contumelie to God, a thing most contrarious to his reveled will
and approved ordinance, and finallie, it is the subversion of good
order, of all equitie and justice.

In the probation of this proposition, I will not be so curious as
to gather what soever may amplifie, set furth or decore the same;
but I am purposed, even as I have spoken my conscience in most
plaine and fewe wordes, so to stand content with a simple proofe
of everie membre, bringing in for my witnesse Goddes ordinance
in nature, his plaine will reveled in his worde, and the mindes of
such as be moste auncient amongest godlie writers.

And first, where that I affirme the empire of a woman to be a
thing repugnant to nature, I meane not onlie that God, by the
order of his creation, hath spoiled woman of authoritie and
dominion, but also that man hath seen, proved and pronounced
just causes why that it so shuld be. Man, I say, in many other
cases blind, doth in this behalfe see verie clearlie. For the causes
be so manifest, that they can not be hid. For who can denie but
it repugneth to nature, that the blind shall be appointed to leade
and conduct such as do see; that the weake, the sicke, and im-
potent persones shall norishe and kepe the hole and strong; and
finallie, that the foolishe, madde and phrenetike shal governe the
discrete, and give counsel to such as be sober of mind? And such
be al women, compared unto man in bearing of authoritie. For
their sight in civile regiment is but blindnes; their strength, weaknes; their cousel, foolishenes; and judgement, phrenesie, if it be
rightlie considered.

I except such as God, by singular priviledge, and for certein causes, knowen onlie to himselfe, hath exempted from the common ranke of women, and do speake of women as nature and experience do this day declare them. Nature, I say, doth paynt them furthe to be weake, fraile, impacient, feble and foolishe; and experience hath declared them to be unconstant, variable, cruell and lacking the spirit of counsel and regiment. And these notable faultes have men in all ages espied in that kinde, for the whiche not onlie they have removed women from rule and authoritie, but also some have thoght that men subject to the counsel or empire of their wyves were unworthie of all publike office. For thus writeth Aristotle in the seconde of his *Politikes*: "What difference shal we put," saith he, "whether that women beare authoritie, or the husbandes that obey the empire of their wyves, be appointed to be magistrates? For what insueth the one, must nedes folowe the other, to witte, injustice, confusion and disorder." The same author further reasoneth, that the policie or regiment of the Lacedemonians (who other wayes amongest the Grecians were moste excellent) was not worthie to be reputed nor accompted amongest the nombre of common welthes, that were well governed, because the magistrates and rulers of the same were to muche geven to please and obey their wyves. What wolde this writer (I pray you) have said to that realme or nation, where a woman sitteth crowned in parliament amongest the middest of men? Oh fearefull and terrible are thy judgementes (O Lord) whiche thus hast abased man for his iniquitie! I am assuredlie persuaded that if any of those men, which, illuminated onelie by the light of nature, did see and pro-nounce causes sufficient why women oght not to beare rule nor authoritie, shuld this day live and see a woman sitting in judge-ment, or riding frome parliament in the middest of men, having the royall crowne upon her head, the sworde and sceptre borne before her, in signe that the administration of justice was in her power; I am assuredlie persuaded, I say, that suche a sight shulde so astonishe them, that they shuld judge the hole worlde to be transformed into Amazones, and that suche a metamorphosis and change was made of all the men of that countrie, as poetes do feyn was made of the companyons of Ulisses, or at least, that

albeit the outwarde form of men remained, yet shuld they judge
that their hartes were changed frome the wisdome, understanding,
and courage of men, to the foolishe fondnes and cowardise of
women. Yea, they further shuld pronounce, that where women
reigne or be in authoritie, that there must nedes vanitie be preferred to vertue; ambition and pride to temperancie and modestie;
and finallie, that avarice, the mother of all mischefe, must nedes
devour equitie and justice. But lest that we shall seme to be of
this opinion alone, let us heare what others have seen and decreed
in this mater. In the *Rules of the Lawe*, thus it is written: "Women
are removed frome all civile and publike office, so that they nether
may be judges, nether may they occupie the place of the magistrate, nether yet may they be speakers for others." The same is
repeted in the third and in the sextenth bokes of the *Digestes*,
where certein persones are forbidden, *Ne pro aliis postulent*, that
is, that they be no speakers nor advocates for others. And among
the rest are women forbidden, and this cause is added, that they
do not against shamefastnes intermedle them selves with the
causes of others, nether yet that women presume to use the offices
due to men. The lawe in the same place doth further declare,
that a naturall shamfastnes oght to be in womankind, whiche most
certeinlie she loseth, whensoever she taketh upon her the office
and estate of man. As in Calphurnia was evidentlie declared, who
having licence to speake before the Senate, at length became so
impudent and importune, that by her babling she troubled the
hole assemblie, and so gave occasion that this lawe was established.

In the first boke of the *Digestes*, it is pronounced that the condition of the woman in many cases is worse then of the man. As
in jurisdiction (saith the lawe) in receiving of cure and tuition, in
adoption, in publike accusation, in delation, in all popular action,
and in motherlie power, which she hath not upon her own sonnes.
The lawe further will not permit, that the woman geve any thing
to her husband, because it is against the nature of her kinde, being
the inferiour membre, to presume to geve any thing to her head.
The lawe doth more over pronounce womankinde to be most
avaricious (which is a vice intolerable in those that shulde rule or
minister justice). And Aristotle, as before is touched, doth plainly

affirme, that whersoever women beare dominion, there must nedes the people be disordred, livinge and abounding in all intemperancie, geven to pride, excesse and vanitie; and finallie in the end, that they must nedes come to confusion and ruine.

Wold to God the examples were not so manifest to the further declaration of the imperfections of women, of their naturall weaknes and inordinat appetites! I might adduce histories, proving some women to have died for sodein joy, some for unpaciencie to have murthered them selves, some to have burned with such inordinat lust, that for the quenching of the same, they have betrayed to strangiers their countrie and citie; and some to have bene so desirous of dominion, that for the obteining of the same, they have murthered the children of their owne sonnes; yea, and some have killed with crueltie their owne husbandes and children. But to me it is sufficient (because this parte of nature is not my moste sure foundation) to have proved, that men illuminated onlie by the light of nature, have seen and have determined, that it is a thing moste repugnant to nature, that women rule and governe over men. For those that will not permit a woman to have power over her owne sonnes, will not permit her (I am assured) to have rule over a realme; and those that will not suffer her to speake in defense of those that be accused, nether that will admit her accusation intended against man, will not approve her, that she shal sit in judgement crowned with the royall crowne, usurping authoritie in the middest of men.

But now to the second part of nature, in the whiche I include the reveled will and perfect ordinance of God; and against this parte of nature, I say, that it doth manifestlie repugne that any woman shal reigne or beare dominion over man. For God, first by the order of his creation, and after by the curse and malediction pronounced against the woman, by the reason of her rebellion, hath pronounced the contrarie. First, I say, that woman in her greatest perfection was made to serve and obey man, not to rule and command him. As Saint Paule doth reason in these wordes: "Man is not of the woman, but the woman of the man. And man was not created for the cause of the woman, but the woman for the cause of the man; and therfore oght the woman to have a power upon her head," (that is, a coverture in signe of subjection). Of whiche words it is plaine that the apostle meaneth, that woman in her greatest perfection, shuld have knowen that man was Lord above her; and therfore that she shulde never have pretended any kind of superioritie above him, no more then do the angels above God the creator, or above Christ Jesus their head. So I say, that in her greatest perfection, woman was created to be subject to man. But after her fall and rebellion committed against God, there was put upon her a newe necessitie, and she was made subject to man by the irrevocable sentence of God, pronounced in these wordes: "I will greatlie multiplie thy sorowe and thy conception. With sorowe shalt thou beare thy children, and thy will shall be subject to thy man: and he shal beare dominion over the." Here-bie may such as altogither be not blinded plainlie see, that God, by his sentence, hath dejected all woman frome empire and dominion above man. For two punishmentes are laid upon her, to witte, a dolor, anguishe and payn, as oft as ever she shal be mother; and a subjection of her self, her appetites and will, to her husband and to his will. Frome the former parte of this malediction can nether arte, nobilitie, policie, nor lawe made by man, deliver womankinde; but who soever atteineth to that honour to be mother, proveth in experience the effect and strength of Goddes word. But (alas!) ignorance of God, ambition and tryannie, have studied to abolishe and destroy the second parte of Goddes punishment. For women are lifted up to be heades over realmes, and to rule above men at their pleasure and appetites. But horrible is the vengeance, which is prepared for the one and for the other, for the promoters, and for the persones promoted, except they spedelie repent. For they shall be dejected from the glorie of the sonnes of God to the sclaverie of the Devill, and to the torment that is prepared for all suche as do exalte them selves against God. Against God can nothing be more manifest then that a woman shal be exalted to reigne above man, for the contrarie sentence hath he pronounced in these wordes: "Thy will shall be subject to thy husband, and he shall beare dominion over the." As God shuld say, "Forasmuch as thou hast abused thy former condition, and because thy free will hath broght thy selfe and mankind into the bondage of Satan,

I therfore will bring the in bondage to man. For where before thy obedience shuld have bene voluntarie, nowe it shall be by constreint and by necessitie; and that because thou has deceived thy man, thou shalt therfore be no longar maistresse over thine own appetites, over thine owne will nor desires. For in the there is nether reason nor discretion, whiche be able to moderate they affections, and therfore they shall be subject to the desire of thy man. He shall be lord and governour, not onlie over thy bodie, but even over they appetites and will." This sentences, I say, did God pronounce against Heva and her daughters, as the rest of the scriptures doth evidentlie witnesse, so that no woman can ever presume to reigne above man, but the same she must nedes do in despite of God, and in contempt of his punishment and malediction.

I am not ignorant, that the most part of men do understand this malediction of the subjection of the wife to her husband, and of the dominion which he beareth above her; but the Holie Ghost geveth to us an other interpretation of this place, taking from all women all kinde of superioritie, authoritie and power over man, speaking as foloweth by the mouth of Saint Paule: "I suffer not a woman to teache, nether yet to usurpe authoritie above man." Here he nameth women in generall, excepting none, affirming that she may usurpe authoritie above no man. And that he speaketh more plainlie in an other place in these wordes: "Let women kepe silence in the congregation, for it is not permitted to them to speake, but to be subject, as the lawe sayeth." These two testimonies of the Holy Ghost be sufficient to prove what soever we have affirmed before, and to represse the inordinate pride of women, as also to correct the foolishnes of those that have studied to exalt women in authoritie above man, against God and against his sentence pronounced. But that the same two places of the apostle may the better be understand, it is to be noted, that in the latter, which is writen in the First Epistle to the Corinthes, the 14. chapitre, before the apostle had permitted that all persones shuld prophecie one after an other, addinge this reason, "that all may learne and all may receive consolation." And lest that any might have judged, that amongest a rude multitude, and the pluralitie of speakers, manie thinges litle to purpose might have bene affirmed, or elles that some confusion might have risen, he addeth, "The spirites of the prophetes are subject to the prophetes;" as he shuld say, "God shall alwayes raise up some to whome the veritie shalbe reveled, and unto such ye shal geve place, albeit they sit in the lowest seates." And thus the apostle wold have prophecying an exercise to be free to the hole churche, that everie one shuld communicate with the congregation, what God had reveled to them, providinge that it were orderlie done. But frome this generall priviledge he secludeth all woman, sayinge: "Let women kepe silence in the congregation." And why, I pray you? Was it because that the apostle thoght no woman to have any knowledge? No, he geveth an other reason, saying: "Let her be subject, as the lawe saith." In which wordes is first to be noted, that the apostle calleth this former sentence pronounced against woman a lawe, that is, the immutable decree of God, who by his owne voice hath subjected her to one membre of the congregation, that is to her husband. Wherupon the Holie Ghost concludeth, that she may never rule nor bear empire above man, for she that is made subject to one, may never be preferred to many. And that the Holie Ghoste doth manifestlie expresse, saying: 'I suffer not that woman usurpe authoritie above man." He sayth not, "I will not, that woman usurpe authoritie above her husband," but he nameth man in generall, taking frome her all power and authoritie to speake, to reason, to interprete, or to teache; but principallie to rule or to judge in the assemblie of men, so that woman by the lawe of God, and by the interpretation of the Holy Ghost, is utterly forbidden to occupie the place of God in the offices aforesaid, which he hath assigned to man, whome he hath appointed and ordeined his lieutenant in earth, secluding frome that honor and dignitie all woman, as this short argument shall evidentlie declare.

The apostle taketh power frome all woman to speake in the assemblie. *Ergo*, he permitteth no woman to rule above man. The former parte is evident, wherupon doth the conclusion of necessitie folowe, for he that taketh from woman the least parte of authoritie, dominion or rule, will not permit unto her that whiche is greatest. But greater it is to reigne above realmes and nations, to publish and to make lawes, and to commande men of all estates, and finallie, to appoint judges and ministers, then to speake in the congregation. For her judgement, sentence or opinion proposed in the congregation, may be judged by all, may be corrected by the learned and reformed by the godlie. But woman being promoted in sovereine authoritie, her lawes must be obeyed, her opinion folowed, and her tyrannie mainteined, supposing that it be expreslie against God and the prophet of the common welth, as to manifest experience doth this day witnesse. And therfore yet againe I repete, that whiche before I have affirmed, to witt, that a woman promoted to sit in the seate of God, that is, to teache, to judge or to reigne above man, is a monstre in nature, contumelie to God, and a thing most repugnant to his will and ordinance.

And nowe, to put an end to the first blast, seing that by the ordre of nature, by the malediction and curse pronounced against woman, by the mouth of Saint Paule, the interpreter of Goddes sentence, by the example of that common welth in whiche God by his word planted ordre and policie; and finallie, by the judgement of the most godlie writers, God hath dejected woman frome rule, dominion, empire and authoritie above man; moreover, seing that nether the example of Debora, nether the lawe made for the doughters of Zalphead, nether yet the foolishe consent of an ignorant multitude, be able to justifie that whiche God so plainlie hath condemned; let all men take hede what quarell and cause frome hence furthe they do defend. If God raise up any noble harte to vendicat the libertie of his countrie, and to suppresse the monstruous empire of women, let all suche as shal presume to defend them in the same, moste certeinlie knowe, that in so doing they lift their hand against God, and that one day they shall finde his power to fight against their foolishnes. Let not the faithfull, godlie and valiant hartes of Christes souldiours be utterlie discouraged, nether yet let the tyrannes rejoise, albeit for a time they triumphe against such as studie to represse their tyrannie, and to remove them from unjust authoritie. For the causes [are known to God] alone, why he suffereth the souldiours to fail in batel, whome nevertelesse he commandeth to fight, as somtimes did Israel fighting against Benjamin. The cause of the Israelites was most just, for it was to punishe that horrible abomination of those sonnes of Belial, abusing the Levites wife, whome the Benjamites did defend; and they had Goddes precept to assure them of well-doing, for he did not onelie commande them to fight, but also apointed Juda to be their leader and capitain; and yet fell they twise in plain batel against those most wicked adulterers.

The secret cause of this, I say, is knowen to God alone. But by his evident scriptures we may assuredly gather, that by such means doth his wisdome somtimes beat downe the pride of the flesh (for the Israelites at the firste trusted in their multitude, power and strength,) and somtimes by such overthrowes, he will punish the offenses of his owne children and bring them to the unfeined knowledge of the same, before he will geve them victorie against the manifest contemners, whom he hath apointed neverthelesse to uttermost perdition, as the end of that batel did witnesse. For althogh with greate murther the children of Israel did twise fall before the Benjamites, yet after they had wept before the Lorde, after they had fasted and made sacrifice in signe of their unfeined repentance, they so prevailed against that proude tribe of Benjamin, that after 25 thousande strong men of warre were killed in batel, they destroyed man, woman, childe and beaste, aswell in the fieldes as in the cities, whiche all were burned with fier; so that onelie of that hole tribe remained six hundreth men, who fled to the wildernes, where they remained foure monethes and so were saved.

The same God, who did execute this grevous punishment, even by the handes of those whom he suffred twise to be overcomen in batel, doth this day retein his power and justice. Cursed Jesabel of England, with the pestilent and detestable generation of papistes, make no litle bragge and boast, that they have triumphed not only against Wyet, but also against all such as have entreprised any thing against them or their procedinges. But let her and them consider, that yet they have not prevailed against God. His throne is more high then that the length of their hornes be able to reache. And let them further consider, that in the beginning of this their bloodie reigne, the harvest of their iniquitie was not comen to full maturitie and ripenes. No, it was so grene, so secret I meane, so covered and so hid with hypocrisie, that some men (even the servantes of God) thoght it not impossible but that wolves might be changed in to lambes, and also that the vipere might remove her natural venom. But God, who doth revele in his time apointed the secretes of hartes, and that will have his judgementes justified even by the verie wicked, hath now geven open testimonie of her and their beastlie crueltie. For man and woman, learned and unlearned, nobles and men of baser sorte, aged fathers and tendre damiselles, and finallie the bones of the dead, aswell women as men, have tasted of their tyrannie, so that now, not onlie the blood of Father Latimer, of the milde man of God the Bishop of Cantorburie, of learned and discrete Ridley, of innocent Ladie Jane Dudley and many godlie and worthie preachers that can not be forgotten, such as fier hath consumed, and the sworde of tyrannie moste unjustlie hath shed, doth call for vengeance in the eares of the Lord God of hostes; but also the sobbes and teares of the poore oppressed, the groninges of the angeles the watchmen of the Lord, yea, and everie earthlie creature abused by their tyrannie, do continuallie crie and call for the hastie execution of the same. I feare not to say, that the day of vengeance, whiche shall apprehend that horrible monstre Jesabel of England and suche as maintein her monstruous crueltie, is alredie apointed in the counsel of the Eternall: and I verelie beleve, that it is so nigh, that she shall not reigne so long in tyrannie as hitherto she hath done, when God shall declare him selfe to be her ennemie, when he shall poure furth contempt upon her, according to her crueltie, and shal kindle the hartes of such as somtimes did favor her with deadly hatred against her, that they may execute his judgementes. And therfore let such as assist her, take hede what they do; for assuredlie her empire and reigne is a wall without foundation. I meane the same of the authoritie of all women. It hath bene underpropped this blind time that is past, with the foolishnes of people and with the wicked lawes of ignorant and tyrannous princes. But the fier of Goddes worde is alredie laide to those rotten proppes (I include the Popes lawe with the rest) and

presentlie they burn, albeit we espie not the flame. When they
are consumed, (as shortlie they will be, for stuble and drie timbre
can not long indure the fier) that rotten wall, the usurped and
unjust empire of women, shall fall by itself in despit of all man,
to the destruction of so manie as shall labor to uphold it. And
therfore let all man be advertised, for the trumpet hath ones
blowen.

Praise God, ye that feare him.

THE HISTORIE
OF THE REFORMATIOUN OF RELIGIOUN
WITHIN THE REALM OF SCOTLAND

In that day was wrought no less a wonder than was at the
accusatioun and death of Jesus Christ, when that Pilate and
Herode, who befoir war ennemyes, war maid freindis, by consenting of thame boith to Christis condempnatioun. Differris nothing,
except that Pilate and Herode war brethrene under thare father
the Devill, in the estaite called temporall, and these two, of whome
we ar to speak, war brethren (sonnes of the same father the Devill)
in the estaite ecclesiasticall. Yf we enterlase merynes with earnest
materis, pardon us, goode readar, for the fact is so notable that it
deservith long memorye.

The cardinall was knowin proude, and Dumbare, Archibischope
of Glasgow, was knowin a glorious foole; and yitt becaus some-
tymes he was called the Kingis Maister, he was Chancelour of
Scotland. The cardinall cumis evin this same year, in the end of
harvest befoir, to Glasgow, upoun what purpose we omitt. But
whill they remane togither, the on in the toune, the other in the
castell, questioun ryses for bearing of thare croces. The cardinall
alledgeid, by reassoun of his cardinallschip, and that he was
Legatus Natus, and Primat within Scotland, in the kingdom of
Antichrist, that he should have the pre-eminence, and that his
croce should not onlye go befoir, but that also it should onlye be
borne, wharesoever he was. Good Gukstoun Glaikstour, the foirsaid archibischop, lacked no reassonis, as he thought, for manten-

ance of his glorie. He was ane archibishchope in his awin diosey, and in his awin cathedrall seat and church, and tharefor aught to give place to no man. The power of the cardinall was but begged from Rome and apperteined but to his awin persone, and nott to his bischoprik, for it mycht be, that his successour should nott be cardinall. Bot his dignitie was annexed with his office, and did apperteane to all that ever should be Bischoppis of Glasgow. Howsoever these doubtis war resolved by the doctouris of divinitie of boith the prelattis; yitt the decisioun was as ye shall hear.

Cuming furth (or going in, all is on) att the qweir doore of Glasgow Kirk, begynnes stryving for state betwix the two croce beraris, so that from glowmyng thei come to schouldering; frome schouldering thei go to buffettis, and from dry blawes, by neffis and neffelling; and then for cheriteis saik, thei crye, "*Dispersit dedit pauperibus*," and assayis quhilk of the croces was fynast mettall, which staf was strongast, and which berar could best defend his maisteris pre-eminence; and that thare should be no superioritie in that behalf, to the ground gois boyth the croces. And then begane no littill fray, butt yitt a meary game; for rockettis war rent, typpetis war torne, crounis war knapped, and syd gounis mycht have bene sein wantonly wag from the one wall to the other. Many of thame lacked beardis, and that was the more pitie; and therefore could not bukkill other by the byrse, as bold men wold haif doune. Butt fy on the jackmen that did nott thare dewitie, for had the one parte of thame reacontered the other, then had all gone rycht. But the sanctuarye, we suppose, saved the lyves of many. How mearelye that ever this be writtin, it was bitter bourding to the cardinall and his courte. It was more then irregularitie; yea, it mycht weall have bene judged lease majestie to the sone of perdition, the Papes awin persone; and yitt the other in his foly, as proud as a packocke, wold lett the cardinall know that he was a bischop, when the other was butt Betoun, befoir he gat Abirbrothok. This inemitie was judged mortall and without all hope of reconsiliatioun.

Butt the blood of the innocent servand of God buryed in oblivioun all that braggine and boast. For the Archibischope of Glasgow was the first unto whome the cardinall wraitt, signifeing unto him what was done, and earnestly craving of him, that he wold assist with his presence and counsall, how that such ane ennemye unto thare estaite mycht be suppressed. And thareto was nott the other slow, but keapt tyme appointed, satt nixt to the cardinall, voted and subscrivit first in the ranck, and lay ower the East blokhouse with the said cardinall, till the Martyre of God was consumed with fyre. For this we man note, that as all thei beastis consented in harte to the slauchter of that innocent, so did thei approve it wyth thare presence, having the hole ordinance of the castell of Sanctandrose bent towardis the place of executioun, which was ney to the said castell, reddy to have schote yf any wold have maid defence or reskew to Goddis servand.*

After the death of this blissed martyre of God, begane the people, in plaine speaking, to dampne and detest the crueltie that was used. Yea, men of great byrth, estimatioun and honour, at open tables avowed, that the blood of the said Maister George should be revenged, or ellis thei should cost lyef for lyef. Amonges whome Johnne Leslye, brother to the Erle of Rothess, was the cheaf; for he, in all cumpanyes, spared not to say, "That same whingar (schawin furth his dager), and that same hand, should be preastis to the cardinall". These bruytis came to the cardinalles earis, but he thought him self stout yneuch for all Scotland, for in Babylon, that is, in his new blok-house, he was suyre, as he thought; and upoun the feildis, he was able to matche all his ennemies. And to wryte the trewth, the most parte of the nobilitie of Scotland had ether gevin unto him thare bandis of manrent, or ellis war in confederacye and promessed amitie with him. He onlye feared thame in whose handis God did deliver him and for thame had he laid his neattis so secreatlie (as that he maid a full compt) that thare feit could not eschap, as we shall after heare; and something of his formare practises we man reacompt.

After the Pasche he came to Edinburgh, to hold the seinye (as the Papistes terme thare unhappy assemblie of Baallis schaven sorte). It was bruyted that something was purposed against him,

*The account of Wishart's martyrdom which follows, is based on John Fox's *The Actes and Monumentes of Martyrs*, and has been omitted in this selection.

at that tyme, by the Erle of Anguss and his freindis, whome he mortally hated, and whose destructioun he sought. But it failled, and so returned he to his strenth, yea, to his God and only conforte, asweill in heavin as in earth. And thare he remaned without all fear of death, promissing unto him self no less pleasur, nor did the riche man, of whome mentioun is maid by our Maister in the Evangell; for he didd nott onlie rejose and say, "Eitt and be glade, my saule, for thow hast great riches laid up in store for many dayis;" bot also he said, "Tush, a feg for the fead, and a buttoun for the braggyne of all the heretikis and thare assistance in Scotland. Is nott my Lord Governour myne? Witness his eldast sone thare pledge at my table? Have I not the Quene at my awin devotioun? (He ment of the mother to Mary that now myschevouslie regnes.) Is not France my freind, and I freind to France? What danger should I fear?" And thus in vanitie, the carnall cardinall delyted him self a lytill befoir his death. But yit he had devised to have cutt of such as he thought mycht cummer him; for he had appointed the haill gentilmen of Fyff to have mett him at Falkland, the Mononday after that he was slane upoun the Setterday. His treasonable purpoise was nott understand but by his secreat counsall; and it was this: that Normond Leslie, Schireff of Fyff, and appearing air to his father, the Erle of Rothess; the said Johnne Leslye, father-brother to Normound; the Lardis of Grange, eldar and youngar; Schir James Lermound of Darsye, and Provest of Sanctandross; and the faythfull Lard of Raith should eyther have bene slane, or ellis tane, and after to have bein used at his pleasur. This interprise was disclosed after his slauchtter, partlye by letteris and memorialles found in his chalmer, butt playnlie affirmed by suche as war of the consall. Many purposes war devised, how that wicked man mycht have bene tackin away. But all failled, till Fryday, the xxviii of Maii, Anno 1546, when the foirsaid Normound came at nycht to Sanctandross. Williame Kirkcaldye of Grange, youngar, was in the toune befoir, awaitting upoun the purpoise. Last came Johnne Leslye foirsaid, who was most suspected. What conclusion thei took that nycht, it was nott knawin, butt by the ischew which followed.

But airlie upoun the Setterday, in the mornyng, the 29 of Maii,

war thei in syndree cumpanyes in the Abbay kirk-yard, not far
distant frome the castell. First, the yettis being oppin, and the
draw-brig lettin doun, for receaving of lyme and stanes, and other
thingis necessar for buylding (for Babylon was almost finished)—
first, we say, assayed Williame Kirkcaldy of Grange, youngar, and
with him sex personis, and gottin enteress, held purpose with the
portare, yf my Lord was walking, who answered, "No." (And so
it was in dead, for he had bene busy at his comptis with Maistres
Marioun Ogilbye that nycht, who was espyed to departe frome
him by the previe posterne that morning and tharefor quyetness,
after the reuillis of phisick, and a morne sleap was requisite for my
Lord). Whill the said Williame and the portar talked, and his
servandis maid thame to look the work and the workemen,
approched Normound Leslie with his company; and becaus thei
war in no great nomber, thei easilie gat entress. Thei address
thame to the myddest of the close, and immediatlie came Johnne
Leslye, somewhat rudlye, and four personis with him. The portar,
fearing, wold have drawin the brig; but the said Johnne, being
entered thairon, stayed and lap in. And whill the portar maid
him for defence, his head was brokin, the keyis tackin frome him,
and he castin in the fowsea; and so the place was seased. The
schout arises. The workemen, to the nomber of mo then a
hundreth, ran of the wallis, and war without hurte put furth at
the wicked yett. The first thing that ever was done, Williame
Kirkcaldye took the garde of the prevey posterne, fearing that the
fox should have eschaped. Then go the rest to the gentilmenis
chalmeris, and without violence done to any man, thei put mo
then fyftie personis to the yett. The nomber that interprised and
did this, was but sextein personis. The cardinall, awalkned with
the schouttis, asked from his windo, what ment that noyse. It
was answered, that Normound Leslye had tackin his castell. Which
understand, he rane to the posterne; but perceaving the passage to
be keapt without, he returned quicklye to his chalmer, took his
twa-handed sword, and garte his chalmer child cast kystes and
other impedimentis to the doore. In this meane tyme came Johnne
Leslye unto it and biddis open. The cardinall askyne, "Who
calles?" he answeris, "My name is Leslye". He re-demandis, "Is

that Normond?" The other sayis, "Nay; my name is Johnne". "I will have Normound," sayis the cardinall, "for he is my freind". "Content your self with such as ar hear, for other shall ye gett nane". Thare war with the said Johnne, James Melven, a man familiarlie acquented with Maister George Wisharte, and Petir Caremichaell, a stout gentilman. In this meanetyme whill thei force at the doore, the cardinall hydis a box of gold under coallis that war laide in a secreat cornar. At length he asked, "Will ye save my lyef?" The said Johnne answered, "It may be that we will". "Nay," sayis the cardinall, "swear unto me by Goddis woundis, and I will open unto yow." Then answered the said Johnne, "It that was said, is unsaid," and so cryed, "Fyre, fyre!" (for the doore was verray stark) and so was brought ane chymlay full of burnyng coallis. Which perceaved, the cardinall or his chalmer child, (it is uncertane), opened the doore, and the cardinall satt doune in a chyre and cryed, "I am a preast; I am a preast: ye will nott slay me". The said Johnne Leslye, (according to his formar vowes), strook him first anes or twyse and so did the said Petir. But James Melven, (a man of nature most gentill and most modest), perceaving thame boyth in cholere, withdrew thame, and said, "This worke and judgement of God, (although it be secreit) aught to be done with greattar gravitie;" and presenting unto him the point of the sweard, said, "Repent thee of thy formar wicked lyef, but especiallie of the schedding of the blood of that notable instrument of God, Maister George Wisharte, which albeit the flame of fyre consumed befoir men, yitt cryes it a vengeance upoun thee, and we from God ar sent to revenge it; for heir, befoir my God, I protest, that nether the hetterent of thy persone, the luif of thy riches, nor the fear of any truble thow could have done to me in particulare, moved, nor movis me to stryk thee; but only becaus thow hast bein and remanes ane obstinat ennemye against Christ Jesus and his holy Evangell". And so he stroke him twyse or thrise trowght with a stog sweard, and so he fell, never word heard out of his mouth, but "I am a preast, I am a preast: fy, fy: all is gone".

Whill they war thus occupyed with the cardinall, the fray rises in the toune. The Provest assembles the communitie and cumis

to the fowseis syd, crying, "What have ye done with my Lord
Cardinall? Whare is my Lord Cardinall? Have ye slayne my Lord
Cardinall? Lett us see my Lord Cardinall!" Thei that war within
answered gentillye, "Best it war unto yow to returne to your awin
housis, for the man ye call the cardinall has receaved his reward,
and in his awin persone will truble the warld no more." But then
more enraigedlye, thei cry, "We shall never departe till that we
see him." And so was he brought to the East blokhouse head
and schawen dead ower the wall to the faythles multitude, which
would not beleve befoir it saw. How miserably lay David Betoun,
cairfull cardinall! And so thei departed, with *Requiem aeternam*
and *requiescant in pace* song for his saule. Now, becaus the
wether was hote, (for it was in Maii, as ye have heard), and his
funerallis could not suddandly be prepared, it was thought best,
to keape him from styncking, to geve him great salt ynewcht, a
cope of lead and a nuk in the boddome of the Sea-Toore (a place
whare many of Goddis childrene had bein empreasoned befoir) to
await what exequeis his brethrene the bischoppes wold prepare for
him.

These thingis we wreat mearelie, but we wold, that the reader
should observe Goddis just judgementis and how that he cane
deprehend the worldly wyse in thare awin wisdome, mak thare
table to be a snare to trape thare awin feit and thare awin presupposed strenth to be thare awin destructioun. These ar the
workis of our God, wharby he wold admonish the tyrantis of this
earth, that in the end he wilbe revenged of thare crueltye, what
strenth so ever thai mack in the contrare. But such is the blyndnes
of man, (as David speakis,) "That the posteritie does ever follow
the footsteppes of thare wicked fatheris, and principallie in thare
impietie;" for how litill differres the cruelty of that bastarde, that
yitt is called Bischope of Sanctandross, frome the crueltie of the
formar, we will after heare.

The death of this foirsaid tyrant was dolorous to the preastis,
dolorous to the Governour, most dolorous to the Quene Dowager;
for in him perished faythfulnes to France and the conforte to all
gentilwemen, and especiallie to wantoun wedowis. His death most
be revenged.

THOMAS MAITLAND (?)

IN 1568 the followers of Mary, Queen of Scots feared the power of the Regent, James Stewart, Earl of Moray and so tried numerous schemes, aimed at discrediting him in the eyes of the public. It was suggested that he had a plan to dethrone the young King James and a pamphlet to this effect was drawn up and called "Ane Advertisement from the Court to a Friend of My Lordis". It does not appear to have been actively circulated till after Moray's death, but then it did have a powerful effect, largely due to the literary skill and satiric subtlety of its author. He pretends to have unwittingly overheard Moray plotting the downfall of James, with Lord Lindsay, John Knox, John Wishart of Pitarrow, James Haliburton (the tutor of Pitcur) and James McGill. By skilfully parodying these men's attitudes, style and even highlighting favourite gestures, he builds up an amusing and unforgettable picture of this "pretended conference". The extract covers the contrasted contributions of Lindsay and Knox. Scarcely less memorable is the learned Haliburton's suggestion that Moray should mimic Hannibal and Scipio by strengthening his armed forces, while Moray's secretary, Wood, advances a cunning Machiavellian policy involving foreign alliances and infiltration into public office.

The authorship of the tract is not established beyond doubt, but it seems nearly certain that it was composed by Thomas Maitland, the third and least famous of that family, which also produced Richard Maitland of Lethington and John, Lord Thirlestane. Calderwood in his *History of the Kirk of Scotland* recounts the anger caused when the work was first circulated and traces it from the hands of the Abbot of Kilwinning to the Earls of Argyll and Mar, then finally to Knox himself. Inevitably Knox preached on the subject, and Calderwood comments, "The author, Mr. Thomas Matlane, brother to Lethington, was present and heard. When he was going out at the kirk doore, he confessed to his sister, the Lady Trabrowne, that he had forged that letter". Little else is known of Thomas Maitland, though he also figures as the interlocutor in George Buchanan's *De Jure Regni Apud Scotos*. He died at an early age. Calderwood places his death in Italy and sees it as the outcome of Knox's prophecy that the pamphlet's composer would die abroad and far from all friends. In this, however, Calderwood may not be a wholly unbiassed reporter.

Apart from Maitland and Knox, the other major character introduced in the extract is Lord Lindsay, 11th Earl of Crawford. The bluntness and violence of his temper as depicted by Maitland are exaggerations with a firm base in truth. Born in the late 1540s Lindsay had been cupbearer at Mary's marriage to Darnley and initially sided with her against Moray. Yet he did not participate in the Battle of Langside, where her forces were destroyed and in May 1569 signed a bond of allegiance to Moray and the young King James. Throughout his life, he was connected with deeds of violence and bloodshed. The most notorious of these was the murder of the Lord Chancellor Glamis, for which he was generally held responsible. Lindsay died in 1607.

Most critics have been impressed by the *Pretended Conference*. Thomas McCrie in his *Life of Knox* comments, "The modes of expression peculiar to each of the persons, were carefully imitated in the speeches put into their mouths, to give it the greater air of credibility." The Bannatyne Club editor backs up and expands on this: "A good deal of talent is shewn, as well as some humour, in suiting the speeches to the persons of the drama, and contrasting the military rudeness of Lindsay with the hypocritical cant ascribed to John Knox, and the worldly wisdom of Pitarrow and McGill. Although drawn in derision ... the characters and language bear probably the same resemblance to the original, as the sketches of a caricaturist do to real portraits."

My text is based on that contained in MS Cotton Caligula B ix (British Museum).

THE PRETENDED CONFERENCE

The copey of ane bill of adverteisment send be ane friend out of court to ane kynisman of the Erle Argillis, the x of December 1569, disclosand the consall of sax personis.

Eftir maist hartlie comendatioune as I promeist to adverteise yow of the proceidingis heir in court, principallie safar as concernit my Lord your cousing, sa will I yow to understand that at this tyme thair is no hoipe of guid wayis for him. This I knaw as not only be dyvers raportts of courteouris as be sa mekill as I can persave my self be my Lord Regentis awin spekand; bot also be ane discussion and counsall haldin very secretly, quhairto I trust no man in this realm is previe bot thame that war callit warily thairto and I, quha was coverit.

Aboute four dayis syne, in this towne, my Lord Regent went unto ane previe chamber, and with him thir sax personis, my Lord Lindsay, the Laird of Petarro, Mr Jhone Woud, Jhone Knox, Mr James McGill, the tutor of Petcur, quhilk are the men in the warlde, he beleivis maist into. Quhen thay war enterit he desyrit thame to place thame selvis, for he wald retein thame the space of thrie or four houris. It chancit I was lyand sleypand in ane bed within the cabinet, sa weill hyd that no man culd persave me, and eftir I was walknit with the bruit quhilk thay maid at thair entrie, I micht esilye heir everie word that thay spak. Then first my Lord Regent sayis to thame, "I have convenit yow at this tyme as the men in the warlde in quhome I put greitest confidence and traist in to, and quhome I beleiv wald fainest have my estait standand, to gif me your faythfull advice familiarly, for my advancement and standing. Ye sie quhow mony lyis out frome me, and mony that war with me at the beginning of this actione are miscontentit of my proceidingis presently, quhairfor I wald desyr yow to declair to me your opyniones quhow I may best stand and sett furth the purpois ye wait of." Quhen eftir he haid this spokin, he comandit my Lord Lyndsay to speik first.

Quha sayis, "My lord, ye knaw of the ald that I was evir mair rashe nor wyse. I can nocht gif yow ane verray wittie consall, bot I luif yow weill aneughe.To be schort, quhat suld ye do, bot use counsall, quhilk ye did nevir yeit. Thairfoir I think the devill causit men cheis yow to be ane Regent. Yeit my Lord, mycht ye be quit of thir Machivellistes and thir bastard lordis, that will circumvein you with thair policie, and wrak yow with thair force. I wald have ane guid hoip of all materis, and quhen ye fall to thame, bourd not with thame, for be Godis breith, and I persave that, I will pass to the Byris and halk as I did the last tyme at your being in Streveling. Gif ye do weill, gar thame dance heidles, and than ilk guid fallow may get ane loump of thair landis, quhilk will gar them fecht lyke swein, and uther men wilbe warier of the spang of the taill. And gif thair be ony stout carle, set me till him, and I sall gif him ane callado with ane stokado. And gif he be ane het man, I sall lat him play him ane quhyle, and syne sall gif him, behynd the hand, ane coup de jarret, and lat him ly thair. And quhen the principallis are this wayis dispeschit, ye may do with the gogie Lordis quhat yow list. And we haid the auld Crage in oure hands I wald lyk materis the bettir, bot ye knaw I will nocht speik aganis Grange. Bot yeit, I think I wilbe evyn with him and gif him ane heill wage for takin part with the Erle of Rothes aganis me."

Ye will not belief quhen he pat on his bonnet, quhow gret ane lauchter was in the haill hous, and syne my Lord Regent sayis, "Yea weill Sirs, for all his raitlyng and raillyng he kennes weill quhat he wald be." And than thay sweir all with ane voce, the d(evill) speid thame, bot my Lord haid spokin weill.

Nixt my Lord R(egent) causit John Knox to speik, quha luikit up to the hevin as (if) he haid bene begynand ane prayer before the preching (for be (ane) hoill I mycht see and behold the continance and persave quhat th(ay) did). And eftir he haid keipit sylence ane guid quhill, he beginn(is) with ane stur and kroking voce, and sayis, "I pryss my God gretfuly that hes hard my prayer, quhilk oftymis I pourit furth bef(oir) the throne of his Majestie, in anguiss of my sorowful hart, and that he hes maid his evangell to be prechit with so notable succes, u(ndir) so waik instrumentis; quhilk in deid, culd nevir haif bene done, except your grace haid bene constitute rewlar over this kirk, specially indewit with ane singular and ardent affectione to obey the will of God and voce of his ministeris. In respect quhairof, I, as ane of the servandis of God, imbrace your grace's guid zeill to the promotione of Godis glorie, and as Johne Knox favoris your grace better nor ony man apone the face of the erth, accordingly sall explane to your grace, my jugement concerning your awin standing, quhilk is sa conjunit with the establishment of the kirk. Yea, the weilfair of Godis kirke so dependis apone your grace, that gif ye succumbe, it is not possible to it for to induir ony lang tyme. Whairfoir it semis to me maist necessar, bayth for the honour of God, confort of the puir bretherin, and utilitie of this commoun weill, that first your grace's lyfe, nixt your estait, be preservit in equalitie of tyme, and nocht to prescryf ane certane dyat of xvi or xvii yeris, lyving mair to the constitutioun of the politik lawis, than the sovran operatioun of the eternall God. And as I never culd away yet with thir jolie wittis and politik branis, quhilk my Lord Lindsay callis Machivellistes, sa wald I, that thay war furtht of the way, gif it war possibill. For I traist assuredly, gif first your grace and syne the rest of the nobilitie of oure societie haid passit to wark with als grete magnanimitie, as I utterit my jugement simply and syncerly in my sermondis, maid purposly for that causs, that mater had bene forthir avancit, nor it is, or salbe this lang tyme, gif God grant na haistiar succes nor my sorrowfull hart prejugis. Siclyk, thame of the nobilitie and uthiris, that wald hinder your just pretence, thocht thay seme nocht sa in the eis of the blind warlde, I have prechit oppinly, and yeit daly cravis of God, that thai may be confondit with that wikkit woman, quhome to thai cleif so obstinatlie; and that thair posteritie may drink of the cowpe preparit for the iniquitie and punisment of thair forfathers. And heir I agre with my Lord Lindsay, that spak immediatlie befoir; bot men suld, to establishe the trew religioun, have ane forther respect and consideratioun. That is, that the governement be establisht in your persone sa lang as ye leif, for quhen this barne, quhome we call king, sall cum to age, dois ony man think that he will leif of all his royall insolence and suffer him self to be rewllit according to the simplicitie of the evangell?

Quhat guid hoip can we have of the child, borne of sic parentis? I will nocht speik of the suspitioun concerning the man that was killit, bot thocht he be his quhois he is callit, quhat can we luik for, bot, as it war, the heretage of the fatheris lychtnes, and iniquitie of the mother. Gif Johne Knox counsall be followit, the estait of the evangell and professouris thairof sall never cum under suche ane hassarde. Bettir it is to content ourselfis with him of quhais modestie we have rycht guid experience, bayth in welthe and umbre, and not to change from that graftit and rowttit societie, with the intemperance of ane unbrydilt childe. Your grace hes persavit quhow my blast of the trumpet set furth aganis the regiment of wemen, is apprevit of all the godly. I have wrettin in lyk manner, and hes it redy for the prenting, ane buik, quhairin I preif by sufficient ressonis, that all kingis, princes, and rewlaris, gois nocht be succession, nor that birth hes strynth to promote, nor yeit bastardy to seclude men fra government. This will walkin utheris to pance mair deiply upoun the mater. Besyde this we sall set furth ane act in the Generall Assemblie on this mater, and bayth I and all the rest of the bretherin sall repett the same in oure daly sermondis, till it be mair nor sufficientlye persuadit to the pepill. This beand solemnally done and than the buik of God oppynit and laid befoir the nobilitie, quha will say the contrar thairof, except he that will nocht feir the wechtie hand of the magistratt strikand with the sword, nor yeit to be ejectit frome the flok as ane scabit scheip be exortatioun and wyse customes of the kirk. This sall also serv in aventure the king depairt of this lyf as we ar all mortall, to keip us furth of the handis of the houses of Lennox and Hamiltoun, quhais imperfectionis are to us contrarious. Then your grace, whan avancit be God, we dout nocht bot ye salbe thankfull to all just deservers. Bot quha yow most offendit, we kurse or slay, as nocht the trew membris thairof and quhairby that the servandis of god may be sufficientlie interteineit according to their calling."* And so he held his pace.

Then my Lord Regent said, "Ye know that I was nevir ambitious and yeit I will not oppoise my self to the will of God reveallit be

---

*The writing of this sentence in the MS is almost illegible.

yow, quhilk are the trew ministeris. Bot Jhone, heir ye, for further-
ance of it, tell your oppynioun fra the pulpit."

GEORGE BUCHANAN

GEORGE BUCHANAN was born near Killearn in Stirlingshire in 1506, son of Robert Buchanan and Agnes Heriot. On the early death of his father, the family moved to lands in the vicinity of Cardross, when George was seven. Later, in 1520, the writer's uncle, James Heriot, seeing his talent, sent him to study at Paris. This was the time when the Sorbonne had taken up a firm position opposing the ideas of Luther, and it was in this atmosphere that Buchanan was educated. After two years the death of his uncle and his own failing health demanded a return to Scotland. The 1520s were a busy time for Buchanan. He accompanied Albany on his 1523 expedition into England; studied under Major at St. Andrews, returned to Paris to gain his M.A. and became Procurator of the German Nation in St. Barbe College in Paris. In 1531 he took up the post of tutor to the young Earl of Cassillis to whom he dedicated his Latin translation of Linacre's grammar. About 1535 he returned to Scotland and was arrested for heresy, fled to England, then returned to France, where he became Regent of a new school in Bordeaux, numbering Montaigne among his students. He enjoyed life at Bordeaux but due to pressure placed on him by Cardinal Beaton, still anxious to convict him of heresy, he was forced to move again. Guevea, a colleague at St. Barbe persuaded him to take up a post in a new Portuguese college, controlled by the University of Coimbra. All went well until Guevea's own death, when the Jesuits took control and Buchanan found himself imprisoned in a monastery after trial by the Inquisition. He left Portugal after his release in 1552 and for five years from 1554 was tutor to Timoleon du Cosse, son of the Marshal of France. 1562 saw him back in Scotland and in daily attendance on Mary, though he made his opposition to her beliefs quite clear. His breach with Mary occurred after her marriage to Bothwell, by which time he was Principal of St. Leonard's College. He made out the Latin statement of the charges against her and went with other commissioners to place it before Elizabeth. In 1570 at the age of 64 he became tutor to James VI, and remained mentally alert until his death in 1582. He is buried in Greyfriars' Churchyard, Edinburgh.

Buchanan's best works are of course written in Latin, in which medium he was the acknowledged master of his day throughout the world. He composed four plays of which *Medea* and *Alcestis* are Euripidean translations, but *Jephthes* and *Baptistes*, original. Of his poems, *Franciscanus* was an effective satire on the Scottish Clergy, while *De Sphaera* although a text book composed for Timoleon, is also a wider attack on false approaches to science. His longer works include the *De Iure Regni Apud Scotos* and a twenty volume history of Scotland written when age had broken his health. His two vernacular works however were both composed in the same year, 1570, and refer to the same political situation. After the deposition of Mary, Buchanan supported the Regent Moray. His rule however was opposed on one side by the Hamilton family, who were heirs presumptive, and on the other by Maitland of Lethington, a powerful figure as secretary, but in the words of James Melville, one of the "secret favourers of the queen". The Hamiltons are attacked in *Ane Admonitioun to the trew Lordis* and Maitland's macchiavellianism exposed in the more poetic *Chamaeleon*.

Buchanan's prose has divided critics. Some like Hume Brown believe, that "of all prose writers of the Scots dialect, Knox alone is to be named with him for vigour of thought and incisiveness of phrase". Others join with Principal Lindsay in seeing his vernacular efforts as "nervous" and not in the same class as his Latin. Finally others, like D. MacMillan sit on the fence and accept the Latin bias of his vernacular prose, aiding clarification, but depriving him of an independent style such as Knox's.

My text of the *Chamaeleon* is based on MS Cotton Caligula C.iii.265.

CHAMAELEON

Thair is a certane kynd of beist callit chamaeleon, engenderit in
sic cuntreis as the sone hes mair strenth in than in this yl of
Brettane, the quhilk, albeit it be small of corporance, noghttheless
it is of ane strange nature, the quhilk makis it to be na les celebrat
and spoken of than sum beastis of greittar quantitie. The proprietie is marvalous, for quhat thing evir it be applicat to, it
semis to be of the samyn cullour and imitatis all hewis except onelie the quhyte and reid, and for this caus ancient writtaris com-
mounlie comparis it to ane flatterare, quhilk imitatis all the haill
maneris of quhome he fenyeis him self to be freind to, except
quhyte, quhilk is takin to be the symboll and tokin gevin commoun-
lie in divise of colouris to signifie sempilnes and loyaltie, and reid
signifying manlines and heroyicall courage. This applicatioun,
being so usit, yit peradventure mony that hes nowther sene the
said beist, nor na perfyte protraict of it wald beleif sic thing not
to be trew. I will thairfore set furth schortlie the descriptioun of
sic ane monsture not lang ago engendrit in Scotland in the cuntre
of Lowthiane not far frome Hadingtoun to that effect that, the
forme knawin, the moist perstiferus nature of the said monsture
may be moir easelie evitit: for this monstre being under coverture
of a mannis figure, may easeliar endommage and wersid be
eschapit, than gif it wer moir deforme and strange of face, behaviour, schap and memberis. Praying the reidar to apardoun the
febilnes of my waike spreit and engyne, gif it can not expreme perfytelie ane strange creature maid be nature, other willing to schaw hir
greit strenth or be sum accident turnit be force frome the commoun
trade and course.

   This monstre, being engendrit under the figure of a man chyld,
first had ane proprietie of nature, flattering all manis ee and sensis
that beheld it, so that the commoun peiple wes in gude hoip of
greit vertue and to prosper with the tyme in it; other ferdar seing
of greit harmes and dampnage to cum to all that sould be familiarlie acquentit with it. This monstre, promovit to sic maturitie of

aige as it could easelie flatter and imitat every manis countenance, speche and fassoun, and subtill to draw out the secreittis of every mannis mynd, and depravat the counsellis to his awin propir gayne, enterit in the court of Scotland the ... and having espyit out not onelie factionis bot singular personis, addressit the self in the begyning to James efter Erll of Murray, and Gilbert than Erll of Cassillis, men excellent in the tyme, in all vertuus perteining to ane nobill man and speciall in lufe of the commoun welth of thair cuntre. And seeing that his nature could not bow to imitat in veritie, but onelie to contrafat fenyeitlie the gudnes of thir two personis, nor yit change thame to his nature, thocht expedient to leane to thame for a tyme and clym up be thair branches to hiear degre, as the wod bind clymeth on the oik and syne with tyme distroyis the tre that it wes supportit be. So he, having cum to sum estimatioun throw hanting of thir nobill lordis (quha wer than estemit of every man as thair vertuus meritit), wes sone be gud report of thame and ane fenyeit gudnes in him self put in credeit with the quene regent, verelie ane nobill lady and of greit prudence bot yit could not espy the gilt vyces under cullour of vertew hid in the said monster, specialie being clokit be favour of the two foirsaid lordis, in quhais company hir grace wald nevir have belevit that sic ane pestilent venum could have bene hid.

The first experience the said quene had of him wes in sending him to France for certane bissines occurrent for the tyme, quhair he did his commissioun sa weill to his awin intentioun, and sa far frome the quenis mynd, that he dissavit the cardinall of Lorayne, quha ontill that day thocht him self not onelie auld practicien bot als maister, yea doctour subtilis, in sic materis of negociatioun. His fals dealing being sone persavit and he greitlie hatit, yit scho being ane lady of greit prudence could not defend hir self frome subtilltie, bot within schort tyme be meanis of sic as belevit him to be thair freind, he crap in credence agane be ane other dur, and under ane other cullour, bot yit could not so weill as he wald, invent new falshead because of the auld suspitioun. And being of auld suspectit, sone persavit, and in dangerie to be taken reid hand and puneist efter his meritis, he fled out of Leyth and coverit him self with the cloik of religioun salang as it could serve, bot nevir sa close bot he keepit ane refuge to sum sanctuarie of the papistis, gif the court had changeit, as to the bischoppis of Sanctandrois and Glasgow, and vyeris diverse quhais caussis wer in his protectioun. And thairfoir the haly Doctor Cranstoun depertit to him largelie of the spoyle of Sanct Salvatouris College, and wes manteinit be Chamaeleon aganis all law and ressoun, besyde that he wes ane man contaminat in all kynd of vycis.

How far afoir the cuming hame of the quene, the kingis moder, he wes contrary to all hir actiouns and favourabill to hir adversaries and inclynit to hir deprivatioun, it is notourlie knawin bayth in Ingland and Scotland to sic as mellit than with the affairis of the estait in baith the realmis. Efter the quenis cuming hame he enterit schortlie, be changeing of cullouris and turning out the other syde of his cloik, and halding him be the branches of the Erll of Murray and for ane tyme applying him to the quenis gracis heir, that he allone wes hard in all secreit materis, casting of lytill and lytill the Erle of Murray, and thinking that he wes strang enewch to stand by himself, on leaning to the Erle of Murray. And becaus the Erll of Murray plesit not mony interprysis of mariage than attemptit, as with the princes of Spayne, with the Duke of Anjou, with the empriouris brother, the said Chamaeleon applyit himself to all thir parteis, and changeing hew as the quene sweyit the ballance of hir mynd and followit the appetyte of hir lust. And at lang the quene be avyis of hir oncles, devysit to destroy the Erl of Murray, thinking him to be ane greit brydill to refrane hir appetitis, and impediment to leif at libertie of hir plessure; not that evir he usit ony violence anentis hir, bot that his honestie wes sa greit that scho wes eschamit to attempt ony thing indecent in his presence. Scho than being deliberat to distroy him be the Erll of Huntlie, went to the north and he in hir cumpany; and howbeit the tressoun was oppynnit planelie, and Johnne Gordoun lying not far of the town* with a greit power, and the Erl of Murray expresslie ludgeit in ane hous separate fra all uther habitatioun and his deid be diverse wayis socht, this Chamaeleon quhether of sempilnes or for layk of foirsicht or for

*(of Aberdene)—added in margin by later hand.

bauldnes of courage, I refer to every manis conscience that doith knaw him, he alone could se no tressoun, could feare no dangear, and wald nevir beleif that the Erll of Huntlie wald take on hand sic ane interpryis. Howbeit thair wes gevin advertisement of it out of Ingland and France, letteres taken declarand it and the mater manifest befoir all mennis ene, it wer to lang to reherse and not verie necessar for the present, it being knawin to sa mony quhat diverse purposis wer tane, quhat dangearis eschapit all the tyme of that voyage, ontill the quene came to Aberdene agane and how miraculous wes the victorie: bot ane thing is not to be pretermittit, that the said Chamaeleon wes ane of the reddiest to gnaw the bainis of the deed, to spoyle the quyk, and mak his proffeit at that marcat.

Efter this the oursey trafficque of mariage growing cauld, the said Chamaeleon going in Ingland, delt sa betwix the protestantis and papistes that he changeit dailie colouris, sumtyme flattering the ane, sumtyme the other, and making every ane of thame beleif that he laubourit onelie for thame; and amangis other thingis be ane prevy intelligence with the quene and verie few of the nobilitie, practizit the mariage of the quene and Henry Lord Dernlie, of the quhilk he maid nevir the Erll of Murray prevy, untill all wes endit. Howbeit the Erll of Murray did nevir thinge nor tuke nevir propose without his advise and counsale. Heir the mater, quhilk he had raschelie brocht on, wes neir the point. Seing that the quene of Ingland disagreit with it for certane respectis, and the lordis of Scotland for the caus of the religioun, to the mainteinance of the quhilk thay desyrit ane promeis of the quene and the said Lord Dernlie, the Chamaeleon in secreit flatterit the quene and opinlie tuke the colour of the religioun and at the lang (seing my Lord of Murray for being precise and plane in all doingis cast out of court) cled him self onelie in the quenis colouris untill that David prevalit aganis him and had in a maner the haill credeit of all wechtie materis. At this poynt, thinking him selfe in werse caise than he belevit, socht to mak ane other change of court, and set up new play agane, awaytit on the court sumpart disgracit, louking for sum new cullour to apply him self to.

In this mene tyme the quene seking to move sum thing in the
religioun, maid ane querrell aganis certane lordis of the principallis of Scotland, the quhilkis, albeit that ane ressonabill power
faillit thame not, and that the favour of the cuntre wes for thame,
yit to schaw thair innocency, quhen thai could not brek the quenis
obstinat mynd of thair distructioun be prayer and sollicitatioun
of freindis, thay left the cuntre and went in Ingland. Yit, Chamaeleon held the small grip that he had in court secunding to David.

In this menetyme the parliament set to forfalt sic lordis as had
fled in Ingland, except the duke quha did be intercessioun of
silver by his remissioun fra David. The rest of the lordis, quhilk
were of wisdome or estimatioun, partlie requirit be the king, quha
wes in na credeit in respect of David, partlie for thair awin
libertie, conspyrit the deid of the said David, and executit the
same. Chamaeleon, cheifest ennemy to David eftir the kingis grace,
yit not being advertisit be the lordis of thair interpryise and suspectit of the quene, knawing his doubilnes, quhyther for verie
feare or preparing ane entre to the quenis favour, fled as utheris
did and eftir lang fetchis brocht agane to the court, kest clene
fra him all colouris of the kingis and cled him agane in the quenis
colouris, and wes ane of the principal instrumentis that nurissit
dissensioun betwix hir and the king. The quhilk practize, howbeit
he wald have dissimulatit, sumtyme brak out with him: as to
ane nobill woman, praying God to gif the king and the quene grace
to aggre, he answerit, "God let thame nevir aggre". For thay leving
in dissensioun, he thocht that his doubilnes could not be espyit
out. And than, seing the Erll Bothwile cum in credeit, he flatterit
him and evin as thai aggreit in all poyntis to put doun the king,
seing that he prospering thai could have no lyf, sa eftir the king
deid, the Erll Bothwile, having in that practize knawin his falset,
and fearing his inconstancy and desyring to be deliverit of sic an
witnes socht his deid: and he having na refuge to the quene for
the saymn cause tuke for a tyme the Erll of Mortonis colouris
and being borne furth be him agains.... the Erll Bothwiles power
and hatrent sa lang as he wes in fear ... under the Erll of Mortonis wingis and, the feir past, schew him self the said erllis
ennemy. And having no sufficient caus, nor appearand indice of

separatioun of cumpany and kyndnes, he fenyeit that the said
Erll of Mortoun had conspyrit his deid to be execute be sum
of the erllis freindis, and to prove the said conspiracy, allegit ane
famous witnes, (*maiorem omni exceptione*) the nobill and vertuus
Lady Gyltoun.

Now to returne agane to our propose- efter the deid of the king,
devysit be him, executit be the Erll Bothwile, for feir of the said
erll he lurkit a quhile out of court untill the tyme the quene at
Carberrie Hill come to the lordis, and the Erll Bothwile fled to
Dunbar. Than he come to parliament and, with sum otheris par-
ticipant of the kingis slaughter, wald haif had the quene slane
be act of parliament. And not finding mony consenting thairto and
specialie the Erll of Murray, than chosen regent, being in the
contrair, he sollicitat some previe men to gar hang hir on hir bed
with hir awin belt, that be that way he and his partinaris in the
kingis murthour mycht be deliverit of an witnesse; knawing weill
the quenis nature, that quhen sho wes misscontent of ony man,
scho wald tell all sic secreittis as scho did knaw of him. This propose not proceeding as he desyrit, he turnit him first in flattering
with the quene and send to hir, being in Lochlevin, ane picture of
the deliverance of the lyoun by the mouse; and nixt turnit his
haill wit to the distruction of the Erll of Murray, thinking that
the wickit could not proffeit greitlie, so just a man having the
supreme power, and als seing that the quenis craftines wes abill at
the lang to overthraw the Erll of Murrays sempilnes.

So he bendit all his wittis to the said erllis eversioun and the
quenis restitutioun and procedit in this caise, partlie be making
ane factioun of the counsalleris, and partakeris of the kingis
murthoure, of men lycht of fantase and covatous of geir, partlie
be corrupting of my Lord of Murrayis freindis and servandis and
travellit principallie with the Laird of Grange, thinking that it
sould be ane greit strenth to the factioun to have the castell of
Edinburgh at thair command. The regent, being divers tymes
advertisit of thir practizis, wes of so upricht nature that he wald
beleif na thing of ony that he had takin in freindschip, quhilk
he wald not haif done him self; and als mony of the factioun in

the begynning thocht it had bene bot ane ligue defensive aganis the power of the greate, that is accustumat to overthraw the small in tyme of troubill.

In this menetyme come the deliverance of the quene out of Lochlevin, the quhilk he wes not ignorant of, and specialie be the meanis of his cousing Johnne Hamiltoun of the Cochuoch. Yit he tareit with the regent to keip ane cullour of honestie and that with the quenis consent, quha had gevin him and diverse otheris, that wer in my Lord of Murrayis cumpany, fre remissioun for all bipast.

Bot the battele chansing vyerwayis than he desyrit and belevit, yit he persistit in his propose to distroy the regent not opinlie bot be secreit meanis, as being sent diverse tymes to commoun with the Lord Flemyng, evir did the contrair of the propose that he wes send for, and evir tendit to hald the cuntre in unquietnes; and in all assembleis for appointment, tendit to have all bipast remittit to keip ay thevis and revaris in courage and to abase the hartis of trew subjectis, that sould haif na hoip of redresse of wrangis done to thame be the kingis rebellis. Eftir that, be the diligence and wisdome of the regent the cuntre wes brocht to sum stay, and justice lyke to haif the over hand. The kingis rebellis purchessit at the quene of Inglandis handis, that scho sould considder the greit wrangis (as thai said) done to hir nixt nychtbour, being nixt of blude to hir, and other be hir requeist or puissance caus hir be restorit agane to her former authoritie. The quenis majestie of Ingland having yit no les regaird to justice nor to consanguinitie, desyrit sum of the principallis of the nobilitie to repair to hir or hir deputtis for thir requeistis and complayntis; and my lord deliberat to go in persoun wes in doubt, having ellis enterit in sum suspicions of this Chamaeleon quhethir he sould tak him with him self, or leif him beheind, for taking him he doubtit not bot he wald hinder the actioun in all maner possibill, and leaving him behind that following his naturall complexioun he wald troubill the cuntre in sic maner that it sould not be easelie in long tyme brocht to rest agane. At lang having deliberat to tak him with him, and persuadit him bayth be giftis of landis and money, he fand to be trew in deid all that he suspectit afoir; for every nycht in a maner he communicat all that wes amangis us with sum of our adversaries and armit thame safar as he could agane the said regent. Bot the force of the ressonis and cleirnes of the haill deductioun of the caus that my lord regent usit, wes sa persuasive to the auditouris, that be Chamaeleonis advertisement the kingis mother dischargeit hir commissiouners to proceid forther and differrit to ane mair commodious tyme for hir, for it wes weill knawin to hir that the quenis majestie of Ingland and hir counsall had allowit the said regentis proceidingis; and the ambassadour of Spaine seing the horribill cryme, sa abhominabill to all honest men, refusit to speik ane word in the mater, and the Frensche ambassadour excusit him self that he spak be command of his maister ...

And sens that tyme as afoir this gude subject and servand to the kingis grace confortit with counsale and conveying out of the cuntre the rebellis of Ingland the samyn being ennemeis to the king of Scotland and prattit proudlie vantyng that his pen sould be worth ten thousand men and threatnit schamefullie (gif he had reservit any schame) the quenis majestie of Ingland with wordis of quhilk the memory sould be rather abolissit be punitioun of him than rehersit for thair impudency; and fearit not to mak sa oppin a leye to nobillmen of Ingland as that the kingis trew subjectis acknawlegeing his authoritie wer not abill to assembill togidder fyve hundreth hors, quhair thai saw within four dayis moir than fyve thousand assemblit out of ane cornar of Scotland. And ay sensyne he hes bene at all convocatiouns of the kingis professit ennemeis in Scotland, in Dunkeld, in Athol, in Strabogy, in Braid-albin, and other quhair, and kepis contrebank to Mr Johnne Leslie of Kingusie, in all directionis to put the king out of his estait, his realme and at lenth out of this erdlie lyf.

Now, I pray yow espy out quhat proffeit the quene, our kingis moder, sall gadder of him that hes bene (as scho knawis) sa oftentymes traitour to hir moder, to hir selfe, to hir sone, to hir brother, and to hir cuntre. Scho will be exemplis consider that how mony colouris that evir this Chamaeleon change, that it can nevir aganis the nature of it, turne perfytelie quhyte.

Respice Finem,
Respice Funem.

JOHN LESLIE was born on the 27th September, 1526, an illegitimate member of the Cults branch of the Leslie family. His bastardy was not to prove a great hindrance to his ambitious nature, although John Knox referred to him contemptuously as a "priest's gett". From an early age he proved anxious to enter holy orders, and indeed received the necessary Papal dispensation in July 1538. After studying at the University of Aberdeen he gained the degree of Doctor of Laws from Paris in 1553. Soon his ability gained him various distinctions. In 1560 the Lords of the Congregation named him as one of the two Catholics to argue points of belief with Knox and Willox, the debate taking place in the following year. In 1561 also he tried to urge Mary to return from France to Scotland after the death of her husband Francis II, and while there won the high esteem of the young queen. Once she did take over the reins of office, Leslie soon became a member of the Privy Council, gained the vacant bishopric of Ross and led a commission engaged in revising the laws of Scotland. After Mary's escape from Lochleven in 1568, he returned to her side as commissioner and confidential agent but was eventually imprisoned by Elizabeth for taking part in the secret plot to unite Mary and the Duke of Norfolk. Threatened with the rack, he confessed his guilt and pretended to turn against Mary, although he attributes this to policy and the necessity for making an early escape. Released in 1573 he was banished to the Netherlands. For a while he toured France, Germany and Spain but eventually settled down in Rome for four years. Other stays in Prague and Rouen followed but when he heard of Mary's execution in 1587, he retired to an Augustinian monastery near Brussels, there spending the last nine years of his life till his death in 1596.

The *Historie* first of all covered the period from James I to Mary's accession, and was presented to the young queen in 1571. At Rome he added seven earlier books and a geographical description of Scotland, as well as making extensive alterations to the original and composing the whole in Latin. As the *De Origine Moribus et Rebus Gestis Scotorum* it was presented to Pope Gregory XIII and later translated back into Scots by Father James Dalrymple, a monk of Ratisbon, in 1593. Leslie's other works include, *A Defence of the Honour of the Right Highe, Mightye, and Noble Princesse Marie, Queene of Scotlande and Dowager of France,* 1596 (almost immediately suppressed); *Pro Libertate impetranda, Oratio, ad serenissimam Elizabetham Angliae Reginam,* 1574 (his appeal from the Tower during imprisonment); and *Piae afflecti Animi Consolationes, divinaque Remedia,* 1574 (translated into French in 1590).

His prose has generally received a mixed reception from critics. C. S. Lewis's tempered praise may be taken as typical, "His builded periods are those of a judicious classicist. His manner is, however, hardly maintained after he gets to business; his narrative is free from rhetoric and not very typical either of the medieval or the humanist kind of history. The truth is that he writes primarily as a man of affairs; he has read too many state papers and sat on too many committees to be either affected or racy."

The Dalrymple translation is not impressive. The Father's prose style is unmemorable and his Latin inaccurate. I have based my text on the earlier MS preserved among the Leven and Melville Collection; H.M. General Register House Edinburgh, GD 26/13/266.

THE HISTORIE OF SCOTLAND

QUENE MARIE

All thingis ncessarie for the mariage of the Quene of Scottis with the Dolphine being prepared, and the hoill nobilitie and estatis of the realme of France being convenit at Paris, apoun the xx day of Aprill 1558, in the gret hall of the palice of the Louver, in presens of Kinge Henry of France, of the Quene his wyfe, and gret nomber of cardinallis, duikis, erlis, bischoppis and nobill men, the fianzeillis, utherwyis callit the hand fastinge, was maid with gret triumphe be the cardinall of Loran, betwix the excellent young prince Frances, eldest sone to the most vailyeant, curageous and victorious prince Henry King of France, and Marie Quene, heritour of the realme of Scotlande, ane of the farest, most civile and verteous princes of the hoill world, with gret solempnitie, triumphe and banquating; and upoun the nixt Sonday, being the xxiiii of Aprill, the mariage was solempnizat and compleit betwix thame be the Cardinall of Burboun, Archebishop of Rouen, in Noster Damis kirke of Pareis; quhair the bishop of Paris maid ane verrey lerned and eloquent sermon, in presens and assistance of the King, Quene, and money prelattis, nobill men, ladeis and gentill men of all estatis and calling, with most excellent triumphe, and the herauldis crying with loude voces thrie sindre tymes, 'larges'; casting to the people gret quantitie of gold and silver of all kinde of sortes of conye, quhair thair was gret tumult of peple, everie one trubling and pressing utheris for gredines to get sum parte of the money. Eftir the quhilk thair was als gret magnifique solempniteis used in the kirke, with als gret dignitie and reverence as was possible; quhilk being done, thay entered in to the bishoppis palice, quhair thair was ane sumpteous and princelie denner prepared to the hoill cumpanie; and eftir thay had dyned, thair was used a princelie dansinge, called the ball royall, to the gret confort and pleasour of all being thair presente and quhosone the balling was endit, thay passit to the gret hall of the pallice royall, quhair thay suped with so gret magnificence, pompte and triumphe, that none of the assistance thair had evir sene the lyke; and thair presentlie was gevine to the Dolphine the tytle of King Dolphine, swa that he and the Quene was called thaireftir King and Quene Dolphine. The nixt day thay dyned in the same palice, and eftir denner retired to the Louver, quhair the banquatinge and triumphe was contenowed money dayes thaireftir; during the quhilk tyme thair was sindre gret mariages maid in the court.

During this hoill symmer, the warris continowit still betwix France and Flanders very hoit, and lykwyse betwix Scotlande and Inglande, quhair Monsieur Dosell and the Frenche men maid continowall incursionis, and the hoill nobill men and gentill men and substancious yemen keped the bordouris, and accompaned the Frenche men be quartaris, as use is of the realme; and thair was mony gret scarmishis maid with Ingland, quhair sindre was slayne and mony taikin on boith the sydis.

Quhill the realme was in this maner trubled with the warris, thay quha had invented of befoir, at Maxwell heuch, to steir up sum comotione and seditione aganis the Quene Regent and the Frenche men, begane to put thair practise to executione, and caused certane preachers cum within the realme, principallie Paule Messen, Johne Willox, Johne Douglas and certane utheris, quha in divers partis of the realme preached privatlie, and maid sic tumulte and uproir amangis the peple, that thay culd not be conteaned within the boundis of lauchfull obedience. Bot sindre of thame spak verrey sklanderouslie aganis the sacramentis, the authoritie of the kirk and utheris articles of the Catholique religeone; for the quhilk caus thair was ane conventione or provinciall counsall of the hoill prelattis and clargie of the realme assembled at Edin-burgh, aboute the ende of the monethe of Julii, quhair sindre was accused for heresie, bot nane was executed or punished in thair bodeis, bot ordanit to abjure thair arrouris at the marcatt croce of Edinburgh, apoun Sainct Gelis day the first of September; bot thair was so gret a tumult rased that day on the hie stret of Edin-burgh, that thay quha was appointed to do opin pennance war suddantlie careid away, and the hoill processione of the clargie disperced; the image of Sanct Geill being borne in processione, was taikin perforce fre the beraris thairof, brokin and distroyed; quhairwith the Quene Regent was hiechlie offendit, and for stanchinge of the lyk truble in tyme cuming, sho appointed the Lorde Setoun to be provest of the toun of Edinburgh, quha keped the same in resonable guid ordour quhill the nixt symmer thaireftir.

Quhen the ambassadouris and commissioners of Scotlande had tareit in the courte of France quhill the monethe of August, thay tuik thair leif of the Kinge, the Quene thayre owin Soverane, and of all the nobilitie, being richelie rewardit and propyned with copburdis of silver pairtlie gilt, of sindre sortes, to everie ane of thame, of sic quantitie as was convenient to thair estate and calling. And being honorablie dimished, taiking thair jornay frome Paris, thay come to Deip about the ende of the said monethe, quhair suddantlie all the principall nobill men and prelatis become seik. Bot shortlie thaireftir the most of thame, being of the wysest and most vailyeant of the realme of Scotland, deceisset thair, to the gret hurt of the commoune weill of the realme; for the bishope of Orknay, president of the College of Justice, of singuler wit, jugement, guid lerning and lyve, with lang experience, decessed in Deip the sixt of September. The Erle of Rothes, ane wyse nobill man and a counsalor of longe tyme, deit also thair the ix of November; and the Erle of Cassillis, Lord Thesaurer of Scotland, quho was boith wyse and vailyeant, deit thair the xiiii daye of the same monethe. And my Lord Fleming, a nobill young man of guid curage and jugement, deceissed at Paris the xviii day of September thaireftir. And swa thair returnit in Scotlande the archebishope of Glasgow, priour of Sanct Androis, the Lord Setoune, and laird of Dun, quha landit at Monros in the monethe of October; eftir quhais arryving, the Quene caused proclame a parliament to be haldin in Edinburgh in December followinge.

In the monethe of August in this yeir, ane nobill and wyse man, Archebalde Campbell Erle of Argyle, Justice Generall of Scotlande, and knycht of the ordour of Sanct Michaell in France, deit; and about the samyn tyme, the bishop of Breachin deceissit, and the abbot of Cuper was nominat to the bischoperike be the Quene; and Andro Durie bishope of Gallowaye deit lykwyse, and Maister Alexander Gordoun archebishope of Athenis, was nominat to the same; and David Panter bishope of Ros, and secretar of Scotland deceissit, and Maister Henry Sinclair dein of Glasgow and president of the College of Justice, was nominat thairto; and the abbayis of Melros and Kelso wes gevin to the cardinall of Gueis in France, be vertue of the acte of naturalizatione foirsaide; quhilk abbayis was than vacande be the deceis of the Lord James, eldest of the Kingis bastarde sonis, quha deceissed about the same tyme the abbot of Bamurinoche deceissit, quhilk was gevin to Maister Johne Haye.

About the middis of the monethe of November, Marie Quene of Inglande, pairtlie throuche gret maloncolie for the lose of Calice, and pairtlie throuch consumptione of seiknes, endit hir lyfe the xvii day of the same monethe, and in hir place ane beutifull and verteous princes, Lady Elizabethe, was proclamed Quene of Inglande, quha joyses the same to thir dais.

At the tyme appointed, the parliament was convenit at Edinburgh in the monethe of December, quhair the estatis of the realme, ondirstandinge the procedingis of the ambassadouris and commissioneris for thame in France, in contractinge and assistinge to the Quenis mariage with the Dolphin, thay approved and confermit the samin be universall consent, finding guid all that the ambassadours and commissioners had done thair intill. Thaireftir, in the same parliament, the Quene regent proponit to the estatis, desyring thame to grant ane crowne matrimoniall to the Dolphine of France, swa that he mycht be called and intitulat, King of Scotlande, duringe the matrimonie betwix thame; quhilk was aggreit, and act of parliament maid thairupoun, and all lettres in Scotlande styled "Frances and Marie, be the grace of God, King and Quene of Scotland, Dolphyne and Dolphines of Vien," and the seales and conye irnis changed in lyk maner. And the Erle of Argyle, and priour of Sanct Androis, was chosin be the estatis to pas in France with declaratione of the samin, quha eftir the parliament maid sum licklie preparatione to that effect; bot yeat, be counsall of sum utheris, seing a wechtier bissines abill to be shortlie in hande within the realme, quhairunto thay war cheiflie employed, apoun that respect stayit thair jornay and past not in France at that tyme.

The King of France, hering of the deathe of Quene Marie of Ingland, and of sic actis of parleament and statutes as sho had maid aganis hir sister Lady Elizabethe, to debar hir frome the successione of the crowne, considering thairfoir that the Quenis majestie of Scotlande being laitlie mareit to the Dolphine his eldest sone, was just heritour of the realme of Inglande, as nerrest and lauchfull to the croun thairof, being onelie dochtir to King James the Fyft of Scotlande, quhois moder Quene Margaret was eldest sister to King Henry the viii; and thairfoir caused make publict proclamatione in Paris, publishing the Quenis majestie of Scotlande to be Quene of Inglande, Scotlande and Ireland, and caused hir and the dolphin hir husbande tak the armes of Inglande and jone with the armes of Scotlande and France, and make all thair seales conforme thairto, and mark thair silver plait, brodir thair tapistries, hingers and all uthers thingis with the samyn. And King Henrie being a prince of hiech and magnificque curage and weill animated and incouraged be the vailyeant Duike of Gueis and his frendis, intendit to recover and obteane the realme of Inglande, as justlie pertening to the Quene of Scotlande; quhilk was the caus of gret truble betwix the Frenche men, Scottismen, and Inglismen, in Scotlande, the nixt twa yeares following, quhill the hoill controversie was aggreit at the seige of Leith, as eftirwart shall appeare.

In this meinetyme the tumult incressed dalie within the realme of Scotland, quhill at last the precheours begouth to preche opinlie in divers partis, and principallie within sum housis of the toun of Edinburgh; and sindre Inglis buikis, ballettis and treateis was gevin furth be thame amangis the people, to move thame to seditione. The Quene regent perceaving the tumult incres, past all the rest of that winter in sumpteous and magnificque banqueting, quhilk sho caused the lordis make severalie in Edinburgh, thinking be that and siclike familiar intertenement to have stayed all thair interprices; bot nothing culd stay thame frome the same. Thairfoir, at the desyre of sum temporall lordis and barronis, sho caused all the hoill prelattis and principallis of the clargie convene and begin a provinciall counsall in Edinburgh, the seconde day of Merche, quhilk continowit to the x day of Aprill thaireftir; and

send to thame with the Erle of Huntlie certane articles presented
to hir be the lordis and barronis; and thaireftir sho departed to
Striveling, leaving the Lord Setoun provest of the toun, to await
apoun the prelattis. Quhilkis articles war in effect as followis: —

First, that the commone prayers shuld be permitted to be used
publiclie in the parryshe kirkis, and the ministratione of the sacramentis, in the Inglis toung.

Secoundlie, that all bischoprikes and uther benefices should be
disponit to qualifeat men, to be chosin thairto be the electione of
the temporall lordis, and people of thair dyoseis and parochynns.

Thirdlie, that all bishoppis and utheris benefest men suld make
residence at thair kirkis, and preche be thame selfes, conforme
to thair calling; or utheris to be placed, quho culd best do the
samyn.

Fourtlie, that none shuld be admittit in tymes cuming to anye
benefice, bot these quha war of sic lerning and utheris qualiteis,
as thay culd be thame selfes but helpe of utheris execut thair
charge in precheing and ministratione of the sacramentis, with
sindrie utheris articles to this effect.

Eftir the prelattis had consulted lang thairupoun, thay gaf
answer to the Quene in this maner. As to the first, they had no
power to alter the ordour of publique prayers and administratione
of the sacramentis, prescryved and observed so mony yeiris be the
Catholique kirke, and thairfoir wald not agre that any prayers war
used publicklie in the volgar tounge, leaving to everye manis dis-
cretione to use his private prayers in quhat toung pleased him
best. And as to the electione of bishoppis and utheris benefest
men, thay walde wishe that the same ordour, quhilk is prescrivit
be the cannoune law in the electione of bishoppis and utheris
ministers of the kirke, war observed. Bot becaus the nominatione
of the prelattis of the realme pertenis principallie to the prince,
thairfoir thay remit the answer thairof to be gevin be the prince
hir self with hir counsall. As to the uther twa articles, tueching
the residence of benefest men in executione of thair office in
preching and ministratioun of the sacramentis, and that none suld
be promoved to benefices bot thay that are weill qualifeit thairfoir, thay affirmed that thair was no bettir ordour culd be devised

nor was prescrivit alreddy be the cannone law and statutes of
thair provinciall counsall to that effect; and thairfoir thay promesed
to caus the same be put to dew executione in all pointis. And
than presentlie thay maid mony sharp statutes, and commandit all
the bischoppis, abbottis, prioris, deanes, archedeanes and all the
rest thair presentlie assembled, and utheris throche all the partis
of the realme, to mak thame selvis able, and use thair awin offices
according to thair fondationis and callingis, within the space of
sax monethes, onder the pane of deprivation; quhilk was the
princepall caus that a gret nomber of younge abbottis, priors,
deanis and benefest men assisted to the interprice and practise
devysed for the ourthrow of the catholicke religeon, and tumult
aganis the Quene and Frenche men, fearing tham selvis to be put
at, according to the lawis and statutes. And so the counsall was
endit apoun the x daye of Apryle.

ROBERT LINDSAY OF PITSCOTTIE

THOUGH little is known of his life, it is generally assumed that Pitscottie was born about 1532. Certainly in 1553 Queen Mary granted him an "escheat" on "all the goods movable and immovable of the late Andrew Lindsay, burgess in Edinburgh." As such a grant would not be made to anyone under 21, this places his birth at a date not later than 1532. On the other hand his father, William Lindsay of Pyotstoun, married Isabella Logan in 1529, and as Robert seems to have been the third child, any date prior to 1532 is unlikely. The historian probably spent the majority of his life in the old Pitscottie farmhouse, situated on the Cupar to St. Andrews road, about three miles from the former and seven from the latter. He did not own the farm but was a tenant to the Scotts of Balwerie and (possibly) to the Melvilles of Raith. As his name does not appear in the *Acts of the Parliament of Scotland*, the *Calendar of Scottish Papers* or other primary sources, little else is known. Lindsay must however have died before 1592, as in that year his son Christopher married Christian Scott and is described in the contract as "lawful heir to the late Robert Lindesay of Pitscottie".

The Historie and Cronikles of Scotland in Lindsay's only known work and generally regarded as the Protestant equivalent of Leslie's *Historie*. Lindsay regards it as a continuation of Boece and his first chapter is actually a translation of Boece's eighteenth. None of the *Historie* can have been composed after 1579, as the author directs that the manuscript be passed on to the Earl of Athole, who died in that year. Equally from internal evidence, it is clear that much of the writing was done before 1577. Lindsay did intend it for publication, but in the dedicatory verse to the Bishop of Caithness, suggests this be delayed until Morton loses power, as it "mellis with authoritie". The delay however was to be much longer than he anticipated and the first edition appeared in 1728.

Critics have generally been impressed by the *Historie*. Kurt Wittig terms it the "high-water mark" of early Scottish prose, while C. S. Lewis comments: "It is in Pitscottie that we find a worthier specimen than Major of that old school of chronicling which the rhetorical histories of the humanists displaced; the kind of history which is still saga, full of the sharp sayings and tragic deaths of great men, and which can boast Herodotus, Snorri, the *Gesta Francorum*, and Froissart among its glories."

The best edition to date is that of Aeneas Mackay for the Scottish Text Society. His readings in the passages chosen are based on MS Laing. III. 218 (Edinburgh University Library). My text is also based on this MS.

THE HISTORIE AND CRONIKLES OF SCOTLAND

BOOK XX: THE SIAMESE TWINS

In this meane tyme thair was ane great marvell sene in Scotland. Ane bairne was borne, raknit to be ane man chyld bot frome the waist upe was two fair, fair persouns witht all memberis and pro-tratouris perteinand to twa bodyis, to wit twa heidis weill eyit, weill eirit and weill handit be twa bodyis. The on bak was to the utheris, bot frome the waist done they war bot on personage and could not weill knaw be the ingyne of man quhilk of the twa bodyis the legis and previe memberis proceidit. Nothwithtstanding, the kingis majestie gart tak great cure and deliegence upoun the upbringing of thir two bodyis in ane personage, gart nurische them and leir them to pley and singe upoun the instrumentis of musick, quho war become in schort tyme verie ingeneous and cunning in the art of musick, quhairby they could pleay and singe two pairtis, the on the tribill, the uther the tennour; quhilk was very dulse and melodious to heir be the common pepill, quho treatit thame wondrous weill. Allso they could speik sindrie and dyviers langagis, that is to say Latine, Frinche, Italieans, Spanis, Dutch, Dens and Inglische and Earische. Thir two bodyis lang conteinuant to the aige of xxviii yeiris and than the ane depairtit lang befoir the uther, quhilk was dollorous and heavie to the langest levar. For quhilk men requyrit of him and bad him be mirrie, he answerit and said, "How cane I be merrie that hes my trew marrow as ane deid carreoun upoun my bak, quhilk was wont to singe and pleay with me to commone and talk in lyke maner? Quhene I was sade he wald gif me comfort and I wald do lyke-wise unto him, bot now I have no thing bot dollour of the beiring of so heavie ane burthine, deid and cald undesollvit on my bak, quhilk takis all eardlie plesour frome me in this present lyfe. Thairfoir I pray to allmightie god to delyver me out of this present lyfe, that we may be laide and dissolvit in the earth quhair fre we come."

BOOK XX: FLODDEN

This the king of Scottland beand so insolent, havand no forsight nor myans in the contrie, lay still, takand no thocht, as ane man unconsable quhilk wald do nothing for his lordis and captains for saifgaird of his ost and commonweill of his nobillis, nor yeit for obtening of victorie and defending of his awin honour, bot lyand still bydand the ladie of Furdis coming; bot all for nocht. Scho did nothing, but deceived him and come nocht agane quhill the Inglische airme com witht hir, so the king of Scottland knew never the coming of the airme of Ingland, quhill they war withtin the space of thrie mylis, arrayit in sevin great battellis. Quhene thir novellis war schawin to the king of Scottland he wald skantlie credit thame bot lape on horse and raid to the hills to vessie thame. Bot quhene he saw thame command so fast fordwart he caussit to sound his trumpitis and put his men in array and ordanit to charge his artaillye and mak all redy.

In this mean tyme the lordis passit to the counsall, thinkand

they wald nocht suffer the king to gif battell at that tyme to ane
mane of law degre.

Bot quhene the lordis past to the consall, as said is, the king
dissagyssed him self and come prevelie and hard everie lordis
vott and quhat was thair conclusioun towartis his proceidingis.
To wit, the lordis devyssit and chargit Lord Patrick Lyndsay of
the Byris to be chancelar and first vottar in the consall because
he was best leirnit and of greatest aige and had greatest experience
amangis thame all at that tyme. They requyrit of him, gif he thocht
it good that the king sould gif battell to Ingland at that tyme or
nocht. The Lord Lyndsay being ryplie advyssit in this matter,
seing the proceidingis and conversatioun and behavieour of the
king, answerit to the lordis in this maner as efter followis, sayand:
"My lordis, ye desyre my oppinioun and jugment, gif the king
sould gif battell to Ingland at this tyme or nocht. My lordis, I
will gif yow fourtht ane similetude, desyrand yow to knaw my
mynd be the samin heirefter. I compair your lordschips to ane
honest mearchand, quho wald in his woage go to the dyce witht
ane commone haschatur and thair to jeopardie in the play on ane
cast aganis a glied half penney, quhilk gif this marchand winnis it,
it wilbe comptit lyttill or nocht, bot gif he tynes, he tynes his
honour witht that nobill peace of gould quhilk is of mair vallour.
Sa my lordis, ye may under stand be this, ye salbe callit the marchandis and your king ane rose nobill and Ingland a common
haschatour that hes nothing to jeopard bot ane gleid halfpenney in
compariesone of our nobill king, and ane auld cruikit cairll liand
in ane charieot, and thocht they tyne him they tint bot lyttill.
Bot gif we jeopard our nobill king at this tyme witht ane simpill
wight and happin to tyne him, we wilbe haldin evill marchandis
and far war consallouris to his majestie. For give we tyne him,
we tyne the haill realme of Scottland and the haill nobilietie
thairof, for nane of my lordis is biddin at this tyme bot gentill
men. The commons is all depairtit frome us for lak of victuallis,
swa it is not decent nor semlie to that we sould jeopard our
nobill king and his nobilietie witht ane auld cruikit cairll and ane
certane sowtaris and taillyouris witht him in companie. Bot better
it war to cause the king to remove, and certane of the lordis witht

him, quhom he thinkis maist expedient, to take the matter in hand and jeopard thame selvis for the kingis plesour and thair awin honour and the commone weill of the contrie at this tyme, and gif your lordschipis will conclude in this maner, I think it best for my awin pairt."

Be this the Lord Lyndsay had vottit in this maner, the haill lordis was contentit of this conclusioun and thairto nominat certane lordis to tak the battell in hand, that is to say, the Earle of Huntlie in the northt, the Earle of Argyle, the Earle of Crawfurd, the Earle Marchall, and in the wast pairt of Scotland, the Earle of Glencairne, the Lord Ghrame, the Lord Maxwell, and in the southt the Earle of Angus, the Earle Bothwell, the Lord Home, thir to be rewlaris of the kingis ost, and to fight in battell against Ingland; and the king to pase witht ane certane of his nobilietie a lytill frome the airme, quhair he might sie the vallieant actis of baitht the sydis and being in saifgaird him self.

This being devyssit and spokin and finallie concludit witht all the haill lordis, the king being neir hand by, dissagyssit as I schew yow befoir, desyrand to heir thair consall and conclusioun and to be unknawin of them, burst fourtht and answerit unhappellie in this maner, as efter followis, sayand to tham in ane furieous rage, "My lordis, I sall fight this day witht Ingland and ye had all sworne the contrair; thocht ye wald all flie frome me and schame your selvis, ye sall nocht schame me as ye devyse, and to Lord Patrick Lyndsay that hes gevin the first vott, I vow to god, I sall never sie Scottland souner nor I sall hang him on his awin yett". This the lordis war astonischit at the kingis answer, (and) seand him in ane furie, was faine to satisfie his plesour and serve his appietyte in all thingis as he commandit.

Be this the watchis come and schew the king that the Inglisch airme was in sight, marchand fast fordwart withtin the space of ane Scottis myle. Then the king gart blaw the trumpitis and sett his men in order of battell, to wit, he gaif the vangaird to the Earle of Huntlie and to the Lord Home, quho was in number ten thousand men, and tuik the great battell in to him self witht all the nobilietie of Scottland, quhilk passit nocht abone xx thousand men, and marchit fordwart a lyttill in the syght of the

Inglischemen, quhilk was than passand ower the bridge of Till. Then the maister gounar come in presentis of the king and fell on his kneyis desyrand at the king that he might schott his artaillye at the Inglische ost, quhair they war command ower the brige of Till; for he promissit and tuik in hand, that he sould cut the brig at thair owercomming, that the king sould have no displesour at the on half quhill the other sould be devourit, for he staillit his artaillye for the brige and thai come thairon. The king answerit to Robert Borthwik his gounar lyk ane man that was bereft of his wit, sayand to him, 'I sall hang the, quarter the, and draw the gif thow schott ane schot this day, for I ame determinat I will have them all befoir me on ane plaine feild and say thame quhat they can do all befor me". The Inglische men war all come ower the brige and the vandgaird was neir mearchant togither. Then the trumpitis blew on everie syde and the vangairdis joynitt togither, to wit, the Scottis vangaird, the Earle of Huntlie, the Lord Home, witht the borderaris and contriemen to the number of ten thousand, and on the uther syde of Ingland, the Lord Percie and the Lord Wastmureland witht the haill bordararis and contriemen tharof in lyk maner, quho junitt cruellie on everie syde and faught cruellie witht uncertaine victorie. Bot at last the Earle of Hunttlieis hieland men witht thair bowis and twa handit swordis wrocht sa manfullie that they defait the Inglischemen bot ony slaughter on thair syde. Then the Earle of Huntlie and Lord Home blew thair trumpittis and convenitt thair men agane to thair standartis. Be this the twa great battellis of Ingland come fordward upoun the kingis battell and joinitt awfullie at the sound of the trumpit and faught furieouslie and lang quhill. Bot at last the king of Scottland defaitt them both.

Then the great battell of Ingland led by the Lord Halbert, quho was under his father the Earle of Surray governour in that battell, quho come furieouslie upoun the king to the number of twentie thousand men; bot the kingis battell inconterid him cruellie and faught manfullie on both the saydis witht uncertane victorie, quhill that the stremeis of blude ran on ather syde so aboundantlie, that all the feildis and watteris was maid reid witht the conflewence thairof. The Earle of Huntlie then and the Lord of Home standand in ane rayit battell quho had win the vangaird afoir and few of thair men ether hurt or slaine, the Earle of Hunttlie desyrit at the Lord Home that he wald help the king and reskew him in his extremmetie, for he said he was over sett witht multitud of men. Nochtwithtstanding, the Lord Home answerit the Earle of Huntlie in this maner, sayand, "He dois weill that dois for him self. We have faught our vangaird ellis and win the samin. Thairfoir lat the laif do thair pairt as we". The Earle of Huntlie answerit againe and said he could nocht suffer his native prince to be owercome witht his enemeis befoir his ene, thairfor callit his men togither be sloghorne and sound of trumpit to have passit to the king, bot, or he come, all was defait on ether syde that few or nane was levand, nother on the kingis pairt nor on the uther. Sume sayis thair come foure men upoun foure horse rydand to the feild witht foure speiris and ane wyspe upoun everie speir heid, to be ane signe and witter to thame, that everie ane of them sould knawe ane uther. They raide in the feild and horssed the king and brocht him fourtht of the feild on ane dune haiknay. Bot soume sayis they had him in the Merse betwix Dunce and Kelso. Quhat they did witht him thair I can not tell. Bot ane man ten yeir efter convickit of slaughter offeirit to the Duik of Albanie, for his lyfe, to lat him sie the place quhair the prince was endit, to the taikin he sould lat him sie his belt of irone lyand besyde him in the grave; bot nochtwithtstanding this man gat no audience be thame that was about them the Duik of Albanie, quho desyrit not at that tyme that sic thingis sould be knawin.

Bot we will leif this and we will return to our porpois, to the feild as disconfeit on this maner on baitht the sydis, for nether Ingland nor Scottland knew who had the better in that battell, bot that the Scottismen mist thair king, for thair wer twa Inglischmen for ane Scottisman slaine, and sa money of the Inglischemen, that war on lyve reteirit to the Earle of Surray and Lord Halbert his sone and reteirit ane lyttill frome the feild and stude on thair feit that night, quhill on the morne at nyne houris, nocht knawand quho had win or tint the feild. And in lyke wyse the Lord Home stude all that night on his futte witht the number of ten M. men, quhill on the morne that the sone raise, he, seand of nowyse nether of Inglischemen nor Scottis, depairtit his way and left the kingis artaillye behind him, quhilk he might have reskewit and brocht witht him gif he had pleissit; for I hard say, upoun the morne at ten houris, that I^c Scottismen might have broght away the kingis artaillye saiflie withtout ony stope of Inglischemen. Bot the Inglischemen suin efter, heirand the Lord Home was reteirand frome the feild come soune togither witht the number they be and cairttit the artaillye and had it away to Berwick, quhair mikill of it remanis to this day; syne went throw the feild seikand the nobill men quho was slaine and in spetiall the kingis grace, quhome they fand money lyke him clade in his cott armor. Bot no man could say suirlie that it was hie, because the same day of the feild he caussit ten to be clad in his leifray, clad witht his cott airmor. Amang the rest thair was two of his gaird, the ane callit Alexander Makcullouck and the uther the Squyer of Clesche, quhilk was men of makdome baitht allyke to the king. Thairfoir quhene they war deid gottin in the feild and the kingis cott airmor upoun them, the Inglischemen beleivit that ane of thame was the king. Thairfoir they tuik ane of thame quhome they thocht maist peirandlie to have bene the king and caist him in ane cairt and had him away to Ingland with them. Bot yeit we knaw suirlie they gat not the king, because they had nocht the taikin of his irone belt to schaw to no Scottisman. This sorrowful battell strikin and endit on this maner at Flowdoun hillis in the monetht of September the nynt day, the yeir of god fre our redemptioun I^m v^c and xiii yeiris, and of his rigne the xxv yeir.

WILLIAM FOWLER

BORN IN 1560, he was the son of William Fowler, a burgess of Edinburgh. He studied at St. Andrews University from which he graduated in 1578. A period of legal study in France followed and there the poet was involved in hostilities with a group of Scottish Catholics, led by John Hay. One of those who threatened the poet at this time was John Hamilton, later Rector of the University of Paris. On his return to Scotland, Fowler replied to Hamilton's criticisms in a forceful tract, published by Lekprewick in 1581. After this, feigning dissatisfaction with Protestantism, he cultivated a friendship with Mauvissière the French ambassador, becoming a Protestant spy. In this rôle he gained valuable information for Walsingham, especially about La Mothe Fénelon's visit to Scotland in 1583. His subterfuge was eventually discovered and in 1584, he became pastor of Hawick, thus being a successor to Gavin Douglas. His introduction to court circles followed, when he went to Denmark to help organise marriage negotiations between James and Anne of Denmark. So much did he impress the authorities that he was appointed deputy Secretary to Anne. His superior, a Dane called Calixtus Schein, returned to Denmark shortly afterwards, and Fowler succeeded. Initially he was most successful. He arranged the grandiose festivities, preceding the baptism of Henry, Prince of Wales, to the satisfaction of all. But soon illness and his estates in Scotland made him virtually an absentee secretary. Despite this he held the post till his death in 1612. He was buried by a Protestant minister in St. Margaret's, Westminster. His will shows him to have been a man of wealth and property.

Fowler is perhaps better known for his poetry than his prose, though little known for either! His sonnet sequence, *The Tarantula of Love*, is the first in Scotland to profit from Italian literature and especially from the work of Petrarch and Castiglione. Fowler did spend some time in Italy and was befriended by Edward Dymok, the patron of Italian men of letters. This Italian bias accounts for his poetic adaptation of Petrarch's *Trionfi*, and his prose work, *The Prince*, a near translation of Machiavelli's *Il Principe*. This political work was probably composed during the late 1590s when Fowler was also aiding James VI, with his political manifesto, the *Basilicon Doron*. From *The Prince* I have chosen the chapter on Fortune, where Fowler shows some of the finest skills of Scottish prose translation. Of all Fowler's works, only two won their way into print. Both were prose tracts, but *A True Reportarie of the Baptisme of the Prince of Wales* (1594) is a catalogue of events, rather than a piece of entertaining prose. I have thus chosen instead an extract from Fowler's reply to John Hamilton, *An Answer to the Calumnious Letter and Erroneous propositions of an apostat named M. Io. Hammiltoun* (1581).

Fowler's critical fate has been to contribute briefly to paragraphs beginning, "Also writing at James VI's court were...." The only really valuable piece of comment to date is contained in John Purves's consideration of his works in the light of the growing Italian influence on Scottish literature at this time. This appears in Vol. III of *The Works of William Fowler*, ed. Meikle, Craigie, Purves, Scottish Text Society (Edinburgh and London, 1914-40). I have based my text for *The Prince* on Hawthornden MS Vol. 12 (National Library of Scotland). For *An Answer to Hammiltoun*, I have used Lekprewick's first edition of 1581.

AN ANSWER TO HAMMILTOUN

It is a saying na les commoun then commonly provit trew: he quha passes the bounds of schamefastnes and brekes the borders

of modestie, may ever afterwart lawfully be impudent. For the
nature of ungodly men, be raschful temeritie and insupportabill
audacitie, destitute of the feare of God, not retening in thair
actions ather honestie or just measure, but willingly despysing
reasoun, searches vitious extrimities, quhairby they endevoir thame
selves not only to put to executioun be violent force, all vice and
beastly crueltye, quhilk ather thairto be perverse mens counsal
are persuadit, or be thair awin cankred effectionis preassit. Bot
also fostering their foolishe foly with thair furious fantesies,
employes thair haill power, travel and diligence, calumniously to
sclander and sclanderously to blaspheme, partly thame, aganist
quhome injustly sic violent beastlines thai haif wrocht, partly
uthers be the lyke schameles impudencie to quhome sic outragious
mischeif and inhumane cruelty, justly is displesant. Quhilk of lait
be example mair nor manifest is ratifeit, and in experience be an
ungodlie apostat, an filthy and impure pest of man confirmit. Swa
it is (loving reader) I being in Paris inhumanlie invadit, and be
this bouchour (with uthairs accumpaneit) cruelly persecut, quhilk
unto thame, quha did behald sic outragious dealing gave ane large
mater of sorrow, and to uthair godly men in Scotland, an ampill
occasion of grit, grit greif, quhairof freindly being admonishit,
and be sum sharpely reprovit, despysing the ane, and contemning
the uthair, rejecting all admonitions quhairby to repentance he
micht bene brocht, now laitly agane, his evil wil not being changit,
nor his malicious mynd appaisit be a doggishe rage and enraged
dispite, as for his last dispair gevin a fairweil to al godlines and
honestie, nocht only my fame and honour (quhilk I micht sufferit
with pacience) bot Gods servants blasphemously hes defamit, and
his trew religioun sacrilegiously impugnit.

This evidentlie may apeir by his treatise an notabil act of
apostasy and the maist calumnious that ever was red, the injurious
superscription quhairof gave me not samekil the occasioun of
lauchter (being mair superstitious nor religious) then the contents
thairof ministred unto me the mater of mervel, quhilk men wald
beleif him for to have it written be an ardent desyre and zele of
veritie, then throuch ostentatioun or arrogancy, les nor his vitious
life and unbridelit behaviour war mair knawin, nor his devot affec-

tion manifest. Be the quhilk proudly puft up, and arrogantly inspyrit, mair aboundant he is in detracting nor in honoring and in defaming mair copious, then in deuly praysing. Althocht in it nathing he can crave, or justly to him vendicat thairin that is his, injuries, lies, calumnies, perjuries, and dispytefull invectives being exceptit (as rasche railars, seditious doctrene, vennom of intoxecat breists, flattring lyis, teuthles dogs, calumnious impostures, foolisch, mischeavous, dangerous errors, impoysonit breastis, hideous trumpeters of seditioun, affectionat ministers of lyes, raving headis abominabill, damnabill, detestabill, condemnabill heresies, theaves, revars, and stealers) with vyair infinite blasphemous wordis almaist the hail contents of his treatise, unwordy to be written, and uncumly to be rehearsit, gatherit out of the bordel, quhairin he ever maist hantit, to defame Christis servants, and to blaspheme his kirk. O iniquitie of tymes! O corruptioun of maners! O shameles malice that passis measure! Are thir the frutes of philosophie? Is this raving railing decent for an maister, quhais lyfe sould be ane example of modestie and gravitie, yit makes him selfe the mirrour of lyes, the trumpet of calumnies, and the roote of vanitie! Shameles foole, whair doth foly force thee, that thou sould be so immoderat in displaying filthely the force of thy venomful toung? Miserabill ar tha discipillis (monstrous heid) quha by thee are reuled and instructed, for quhat may thay els learne of the than that quhilk thai heare? Or how canst thou instruct thame verteously, quha sa vitiously dois lyve? Bot quhair honesties can have na swey, modestie can have na strenth. This thy writing, the umbre and shaddow of thy actionis is voyd of wit, and thy railing without ressoun, that gif be judgement punishment sould be decernit, with torments rather thou art to be confoundit, then with arguments confuted. Treuth it is indeid that from all replying my wil did mekil abhorre, willing to quenche the remembrance of sa immoderat injuries be forgetfulnes, and to burie the memorie of sa grit offences be oblivioun. Yit les, nor throuch my silence, his lyes perhappis sould have sic advantage of the treuth, that, that quhilk maliciously be writ and deade in effect he has performit, as rycht sould be receavit, I am forced to enter in defence, to satesfie be juste report thais quhais heartis are not preoccupat be

his false narratioun, nor myndes preventit by his feinyeid fals-
hoode.

How hard and difficil a thing it is unto thame, quha be the
singulare mercy of thair God, hes engravit in thair harts, an
detestatioun of erroneus doctrine, and superstitious idolatrie,
quyetly without dissembling grit cummer and perrelous danger, to
remaine in Paris the tresonabill treasons, the bloody massacars,
the unnaturall slauchters and horribill murders thair committit wil
testifie, and ma ages than this wil beir record. For Satan with sic
cruel rage hes swa enragit and enflamit his servantis aganist the
members of Christ, that nather thair untowardenes can be assuagit
by the feare of Gods punishments, nor malicious mindes repressit,
be his fearfull threatnings, nor thair wickednes coolit be his terri-
bill judgements. Yea thair ungodlynes hes sa far increassit, that
the hope of salvatioun can not alure thame from it, for sa grit hes
bene thair unbridelit fervencie to pleis thair maister, and sa lytil
thair thochtles cair to pleis our God; sa vehement hes bene thair
thrist efter the blood of Christs people, and yit not quenchit; sa
grit is thair drouth, but yit never slokned, seing that daylye the
devill movis the myndes of his awin to all horrible impietie, and
the harts of sic wood tygers to commit al wyld cruelty. Paris,
Rouen, Tholouse, Orleane, Burdeaux with vyair innumberabill
touns in France, may (allace) serve for overcertane proofe in this
mater, and my selfe for a witnesse. Swa the case is (gentill reader)
and so the mater standeth.

THE PRINCE

CHAPTER "25"

*How far fortoun hes pouar in mans affairs, and be quhat meanes
shee may be resisted.*

I am not ignorant that this opinioun hes bene and is maintened
be many, that the affairs of the warld ar in such wyes governed

and conducted by God and by fortoun that men with there wisdome
and forsight can not amend theme as things aboundoned of all
remeid, and for this cause they inferr this conclusioun, that it wer
great folye to brek or beate there brains or imploy any travel
heirin, bot leave there action and yssew thairoff to chanse and
adventur.

In our tyme, this opinion hes bene much belived and, be the
changes and vicissituds of all things, which hes bene and daylye ar
sene and remarked to occurr, surpassing all forsight and humane
conjectur, trusted very much unto. And quhils as I enter some-
tymes in the consideratioun therof, I enter and condiscendeth as
oft to almaist there opinioun. Nottheless, to the end our frie
will be not takken away and destroyed, I am of this judgment,
that it may (be) posseble that fortoun dispose upon the half part
of our actions and the other or litil les unto our government and
conduct. For I compair fortoun to a violent flood, rining from
the montains with impetuositie and ravishment, that whils as he is
swillted and deborded, overfloweth all the plane, drowneth the
nighbour banks, violentlye plucketh up the treis, and turneth away
the houses and forceablye caryeis and transporteth and heapeth an
part of earth til another ground, and so all pepill, giving place til
his furie, flyeth far off, having no meanes to withstand it.

Notwithstanding it be so, thair inlaiketh not sa far remedeis
bot that men in calmer and unstormyer tymes may mak gud provisioun to keip him in his naturel course with hight dykes and
rampiers, in such sort that quhen any tyme thairefter he beginneth
agane to wax great and to ryse in speat, he may be bonded in his
channell, or at the least, if he debord, his vehemencye sal not be
so hurtfull. The lyke falleth out with fortoun, quho then shaweth
her pouar maist, quhair shee finds and espyes least vertew to
resist her, and there turneth hir furie, quhair shee knaweth na
obstacles nor defenses ar maid to repress her.

And now if ye consider Italye, quha is the seat of sic mutable
changes, and is she that hes geven the beginings to the alterations, ye sal perceave her to be a waist feild, but banks, dykes
and rampiers, quha if she had bene fortefyed with convenient and
requeseit vertew, as Almaine, Spane and France ar, this inunda-

tioun and overflowing wald not have occasioned sic strange changes
as it is subject unto. And this sall suffice which I have spokken
touching the withstanding of fortoun in generall. Bot now purposing to condiscend to mair particuler discourse of her pouar, I
say that we behauld some prences to prosper this day and come to
ruyne the morrow, and by such causes as nane can be ascryved
ather to the change of his natur or government or any other his
condition; which change, I think, floweth fra the same things
which of before we have discoursed, to witt, that quhils a prence
steys and propps all his hap and courses upon fortoun, quha sa
sone agane as she altereth als suddenlye dois he perish. And I
judge him to be a happye prence, quhase consells in the conduct
of his affairs ar correspondent unto the tyme, and him unhappye
quhase proceidings and advyses disagrethe fra the season.

For we sie that men dois nocht proceid not after a sort in these
things that induces theme to the end of there courses, which ar
ather rychces or glorye; for some proceideth thairto slawlye and
with respect, others with rashnes and uncircumspectioun; some
with violence, some with subteltie, some with patience, some be
hir contrair, and everye ane of these men, nochtwithstanding thir
discordant moddes, may come to there awen end.

Morover, ye sal find that of twa cald and respecting humeurs,
ane of theme to attane the but and scope of his desyrs and the
other not; and lykwyse other twa quha baith alyke sal have a prosperous success in there ends, being of contrarye conceate and complexions, the ane being circumspect, the other unadvysed, the
causes quharof proceideth of the qualetie and condition of the
tyme, quhilk is ather aggreable to there fascons and maner of pro-
cedings or ells disconsformable. Of which consideration dois aryse
that which that I sayd alreddie, that twa be different and contrarious courses conveneth to a end, and agane other two be conformable moddes enjoyeth not the lyke effect.

And of this dependeth the vicissitud and variation of the end.
For gif he wha governeth his affairs by modestie and patience
rencontres and meiteth with sic season and tymes quhairin his
vertewes ar requeseit, he can not fail bot to prosper happelye in
his actions; bot if the tyme and things sal change, then dois he

perish, be reasoun he alters not his forme of proceeding. Yet not withstanding thair is na man to be found endewed with sic wisdome or sa parfitly accomplished, that can applye him self to all sic diversityes, be reasoun it is very difficill for ane to withdraw or devert his spreit fra his naturel inclinatioun, as also it wer very hard to dissuade a man fra that maner of course which he alwyes fallowed, and to leave that way as evil, which afore he found happie to the compassing of his actions. In consideration wharof, the person that is cald and circumspect, quhen tyme requyres him to be violent and vehement can not embrace that humeur, and so be his circumspectioun he cumeth to his ruyne, quha incace he had diversefyed and changed his nature according to the seasoun and occurrences, his guid fortoun had not decayed.

Pape Jule the 2 in all his actions proceded with vehemency and violent hastines, and fand the state of the tymes and the seasoun conformable to his maner of proceidings, which alwyes had there desyred and prosperous success. Consider a litill his first interpryses upon the cytie of Bologna, quhils John Bentivol the prence therof lived. The Venetians wer not contented that he suld attempt to tak it, and the kings of Spaine and France had a treatie together touching this expedition also. Yet notwithstanding, he with the fearsnes of his courage went personally to that enterpryse, which violent activitie held in suspense the myndes of Spaine and the Venetians, these for feare, the other for the desyre he had to recover the kingdome of Naples; and of the other part the king of France became to be in his partye, quha, seing him sa reddelye armed and marching fordward, thought it expedient for the easier overthrawn of the Venetians not to deny the Pape the help of his forces, incace he otherwyse had manfestlye offended him. And so the Pape by his promptenes and violent hastines compassed that which another Pape culd never by his wordlye wisdome have execut. For gif that he before his departeur furth of Rome had abidden upon ryte and advysed declaratioun and resolutioun of newe, as any other Pape have done, he suld never have brought that state to his obedience, for then the king of France wald have forged a thousand excuses and the others terrefyed him with als many feares. I will not waid farder in his actions which wer al efter an tenour, and all succeding happelye lykwyse. The schortnes of his lyfe suffered him not to feil a contrair fortoun, bot incace other tymes and occurrences had fallen out which wald have requyred slow advyse and circumspectioun, his ruine thairfrom sone had rissing, bycause he had never left off that faschon of proceiding, nor deverted fra ther meanes to which by nature he was enclyned. I conclud, thairfor, that quhils as mens obstinacye and complexions aggreeth with the varietye of fortoun, they ar happie, bot gif shee disagreeth fra there complexion, they come to destructioun. And I esteme it a far better adventurfull thing to be hate and hastie in execution than cald and fearful, be reasoun that fortoun is of the nature of wemen, which must be beaten and spurred to do the reason. And it is commonlye sene that shee suffers herself to be handled be these that ar hasardful and furthye then be these that ar respecting. And for this caus it is na mervell that she as a woman be inclyned towards yong men quha ar les respectful, mair fearles, and dois toward her with mair boldnes.

JAMES VI

THERE IS little point in retracing the well documented career of
James (1567-1625). In this context the important factor is that like
James I, James III, James IV and James V he had some claim to
both an interest and ability in the arts. As early as 1585, he published his *Essayes of a Prentise in the Devine Arte of Poesie.*
Among other things this contained the first Scottish treatise on
the theory of poetry, the *Reulis and Cautelis,* and a collection of
sonnets, which were to form the first impetus for the popularity of
that form in Scotland. As stated in the *Reulis,* James intended to
begin a revival of interest in Scottish vernacular literature, modelled
on the example of the Pléiade in France. To this end he formed a
group of poets and musicians centred at the Edinburgh court and
christened, by James, the Castalian band. Prominent in this group
were Alexander Montgomerie, John Stewart of Baldynneis, the
English brothers, Robert and Thomas Hudson, as well as William
Fowler, who is elsewhere represented in this anthology. Tragically,
James found affairs of state too onerous to allow him to continue
this early interest in literature and when he eventually moved
south at the Union of the Crowns in 1603, the Castalian band
broke up, with only Fowler following him to London. It is known
that when James came to revise his collected works for the London
edition of 1616 he and Charles went over the originals erasing
Scotticisms, but equally there is evidence to show that James,
unlike his son, did not advocate complete anglicisation, always
retaining his belief that some Scots words were untranslatable and
more effective than their English equivalents.

My choice of passages in the case of James may need some defence.
Particularly, I have omitted his major prose work, the *Basilicon*

Doron of 1598. Originally written as part of Prince Henry's educa-
tion, James and Fowler later expanded it and it was sent to various
European rulers as a statement of the King's governmental policies.
My reasons for excluding it, are: a) to provide variety in a short
anthology, which also includes Fowler's *Prince*, a work of somewhat similar scope; b) there is already a good Scottish Text Society
edition of the *Basilicon Doron*, while the same cannot be said for
A Counterblaste to Tobacco, the work chosen instead for major
representation. Equally I should perhaps account for basing my
text on the first (1585) edition of the *Reulis and Cautelis*, but preferring the 1616 London edition of James's Works, to the earlier
1604 edition, for the *Counterblaste*. The 1616 edition seemed
more reliable than the first edition of the *Counterblaste* and almost
certainly contains later authorial alterations. The intention is to
exemplify James's prose style and vocabulary in an early and a
late form.

THE REULIS AND CAUTELIS

THE PREFACE TO THE READER

The cause why (docile reader) I have not dedicat this short treatise
to any particular personis (as commounly workis usis to be) is, that
I esteme all thais quha hes already some beginning of knawledge,
with ane earnest desyre to atteyne to farther, alyke meit for the
reading of this worke, or any uther, quhilk may help thame to
the atteining to thair foirsaid desyre. Bot as to this work, quhilk
is intitulit, *The Reulis and cautelis to be observit and eschewit in
Scottis Poesie*, ye may marvell paraventure, quhairfore I sould have
writtin in that mater, sen sa mony learnit men, baith of auld and of
late hes already written thairof in dyvers and sindry languages.
I answer, that nochtwithstanding, I have lykewayis writtin of it,
for twa caussis. The ane is, as for them that wrait of auld, lyke
as the tyme is changeit sensyne, sa is the ordour of poesie changeit.
For then they observit not Flowing, nor eschewit not Ryming in

termes, besydes sindrie uther thingis, quhilk now we observe, and eschew, and dois weil in sa doing; because that now, quhen the warld is waxit auld, we have all their opinionis in writ, quhilk were learned before our tyme, besydes our awin ingynis, quhair as they then did it onelie be thair awin ingynis, but help of any uther. Thairfore, quhat I speik of poesie now, I speik of it, as being come to mannis age and perfectioun, quhair as then, it was bot in the infancie and chyldheid. The uther cause is, that as for thame that hes written in it of late, there hes never ane of thame written in our language. For albeit sindrie hes written of it in English, quhilk is lykest to our language, yit we differ from thame in sindrie reulis of poesie, as ye will find be experience. I have lykewayis omittit dyvers figures, quhilkis are necessare to be usit in verse, for twa causis. The ane is, because they are usit in all languages, and thairfore are spokin of be Du Bellay and sindrie utheris, quha hes written in this airt. Quhairfore gif I wrait of thame also, it sould seme that I did bot repete that, quhilk thay have written, and yit not sa weil, as thay have done already. The uther cause is, that they are figures of rhetorique and dialectique, quhilkis airtis I professe nocht, and thairfore will apply to my selfe the counsale, quhilk Apelles gave to the shoo-maker, quhen he said to him, seing him find falt with the shankis of the Image of Venus, efter that he had found falt with the pan-toun, *"Ne sutor ultra crepidam."*

I will also wish yow (docile reidar) that or ye cummer yow with reading thir reulis, ye may find in your self sic a beginning of Nature, as ye may put in practise in your verse many of thir foirsaidis preceptis, or ever ye sie them as they are heir set doun. For gif Nature be nocht the cheif worker in this airt, reulis wilbe bot a band to Nature, and will mak yow within short space weary of the haill airt; quhair as, gif Nature be cheif, and bent to it, reulis will be ane help and staff to Nature. I will end heir, lest my preface be langer nor my purpose and haill mater following, wishing yow, docile reidar, als gude succes and great proffeit by reiding this short treatise, as I tuke earnist and will-ing panis to blok it, as ye sie, for your cause. Fare weill.

CHAPTER VI

Ye man also be warre with composing ony thing in the same
maner, as hes bene ower oft usit of before. As in speciall, gif ye
speik of love, be warre ye descryve your loves makdome, or her
fairnes. And sicklyke that ye descryve not the morning, and rysing
of the sunne, in the preface of your verse; for thir thingis are sa
oft and dyverslie writtin upon be poëtis already, that gif ye do the
lyke, it will appeare, ye bot imitate, and that it cummis not of
your awin Inventioun, quhilk is ane of the cheif properteis of ane
poete. Thairfore gif your subject be to prayse your love, ye sall
rather prayse hir uther qualiteis, nor her fairnes, or hir shaip, or
ellis ye sall speik some lytill thing of it, and syne say, that your
wittis are sa smal and your utterance so barren, that ye can not
discryve any part of hir worthelie, remitting alwayis to the reider,
to judge of hir, in respect sho matches, or rather excellis Venus,
or any woman, quhome to it sall please yow to compaire her.
Bot gif your subject be sic, as ye man speik some thing of the
morning, or sunne rysing, tak heid, that quhat name ye give to
the sunne, the mone, or uther starris, the ane tyme, gif ye happin
to wryte thairof another tyme, to change thair names. As gif ye
call the sunne Titan, at a tyme, to call him Phoebus or Apollo
the uther tyme, and siclyke the mone and uther planettis.

CHAPTER VII

Bot sen Invention, is ane of the cheif vertewis in a poete, it is
best that ye invent your awin subject, your self, and not to compose of sene subjectis. Especially, translating any thing out of
uther language, quhilk doing, ye not onely essay not your awin
ingyne of Inventioun, bot be the same meanes, ye are bound, as
to a staik, to follow that buikis phrasis, quhilk ye translate.

Ye man also be war of wryting any thing of materis of commoun weill, or uther sic grave sene subjectis (except metaphori-
cally, of manifest treuth opinly knawin, yit nochtwithstanding

using it very seindil) because nocht onely ye essay nocht your awin
Inventioun, as I spak before, bot lykewayis they are to grave
materis for a poet to mell in. Bot because ye can not have the
Inventioun except it come of Nature, I remit it thairunto, as the
cheif cause, not onely of Inventioun, bot also of all the uther
pairtis of poesie. For airt is onely bot ane help and a remembraunce
to Nature, as I shewe yow in the Preface.

A COUNTERBLASTE TO TOBACCO

And now good cuntrey-men, let us (I pray you) consider, what
honour or policy can moove us to imitate the barbarous and
beastly maners of the wilde, godlesse, and slavish Indians, especially in so vile and stinking a custome? Shall we that disdaine to
imitate the maners of our neighbour France (having the stile of
the first Christian kingdome) and that cannot endure the spirit of
the Spaniards (their King being now comparable in largenesse
of dominions, to the great Emperour of Turkie); shall wee, I say,
that have bene so long civill and wealthy in peace, famous and
invincible in warre, fortunate in both, we that have bene ever
able to aide any of our neighbours (but never deafed any of their
eares with any of our supplications for assistance) shall wee, I say,
without blushing, abase our selves so farre, as to imitate these
beastly Indians, slaves to the Spaniards, refuse to the world, and
as yet aliens from the holy covenant of God? Why doe we not
as well imitate them in walking naked as they doe, in preferring
glasses, feathers, and such toyes, to gold and precious stones, as
they doe, yea why doe we not denie God and adore the divel, as
they doe?

The other argument drawn from a mistaken experience, is but the
more particular probation of this generall, because it is alledged
to be found trew by proofe, that by the taking of tobacco divers
and very many doe finde themselves cured of divers diseases as
on the other part, no man ever received harme thereby. In this

argument there is first a great mistaking and next a monstrous
absurditie, for is it not a very great mistaking, to take *non causam
pro causa*, as they say in the Logickes? Because peradventure,
when a sicke man hath had his disease at the height, hee hath at
that instant taken tobacco, and afterward his disease taking the
naturall course of declining, and consequently the patient of re-
covering his health, O then the tobacco forsooth, was the worker
of that miracle. Beside that, it is a thing well known to all physicians, that the apprehension and conceit of the patient, hath by
wakening and uniting the vitall spirits, and so strengthening
nature, a great power and vertue, to cure divers diseases. For an
evident proofe of mistaking in the like case, I pray you what
foolish boy, what sillie wench, what olde doting wife, or ignorant
countrey clowne, is not a physician for the toothach, for the
cholicke and divers such common diseases? Yea, will not every
man you meete withall, teach you a sundry cure for the same, and
sweare by that meane either himselfe, or some of his neerest
kinsemen and friends was cured? And yet I hope no man is so
foolish as to beleeve them. And all these toyes do only proceed
from the mistaking *non causam pro causa*, as I have already said,
and so if a man chance to recover one of any disease, after hee
hath taken tobacco, that must have the thanks of all. But by the
contrary, if a man smoke himselfe to death with it (and many
have done) O then some other disease must beare the blame for
that fault. So doe olde harlots thanke their harlotrie for their
many yeeres, that custome being healthfull (say they) *ad purgan-
dos renes*, but never have mind how many die of the pockes in
the flower of their youth. And so doe olde drunkards thinke they
prolong their dayes, by their swinelike diet, but never remember
how many die drowned in drinke before they be halfe olde.

And what greater absurditie can there be, then to say that one
cure shall serve for divers, nay, contrarious sorts of diseases? It is
an undoubted ground among all physicians, that there is almost
no sort either of nourishment or medicine, that hath not some
thing in it disagreeable to some part of mans bodie, because, as
I have alreadie said, the nature of the temperature of every part,
is so different from another, that according to the olde proverbe,

that which is good for the head is evill for the necke and the shoulders. For even as a strong enemy, that invades a town or fortresse, although in his siege thereof, he do belay and compasse it round about, yet he makes his breach and entry at some one or fewe speciall parts thereof, which hee hath tried and found to be weakest and least able to resist; so sickenes doth make her particular assault, upon such part or parts of our body, as are weakest and easiest to be overcome by that sort of disease, which then doth assaile us, although all the rest of the body by sympathie feele it selfe, to be as it were belayed, and besieged by the affliction of that speciall part, the griefe and smart thereof being by the sense of feeling dispersed through all the rest of our members. And therefore the skilfull physician presses by such cures, to purge and strengthen that part which is afflicted, as are only fit for that sort of disease, and doe best agree with the nature of that infirme part; which being abused to a disease of another nature, would prove as hurtfull for the one, as helpfull for the other. Yea, not onely will a skilfull and wary physician be carefull to use no cure but that which is fit for that sort of disease, but he will also consider all other circumstances, and make the remedies sutable therunto; as the temperature of the clime where the patient is, the constitution of the planets, the time of the moone, the season of the yeere, the age and complexion of the patient, and the present state of his body, in strength or weaknes. For one cure must not ever be used for the selfesame disease, but according to the varying of any of the foresaid circumstances, that sort of remedy must be used which is fittest for the same. Where by the contrary in this case, such is the miraculous omnipotencie of our strong tasted tobacco, as it cures al sorts of diseases (which never any drugge could do before) in all persons, and at all times. It cures all maner of distillations, either in the head or stomacke (if you beleeve their axiomes) although in very deed it doe both corrupt the braine, and by causing over quicke digestion, fill the stomacke full of crudities. It cures the gout in the feet, and (which is miraculous) in that very instant when the smoke thereof, as light, flies up into the head, the vertue therof, as heavy, runs down to the litle toe. It helps all sorts of agues. It makes a man sober that was drunk. It refreshes a weary man and yet makes a man hungry. Being taken when they goe to bed, it makes one sleepe soundly, and yet being taken when a man is sleepie and drowsie, it will, as they say, awake his braine and quicken his understanding. As for curing of the pockes, it serves for that use but among the pockie Indian slaves. Here in England it is refined, and will not deigne to cure here any other then cleanly and gentlemanly diseases. O omnipotent power of tobacco! And if it could by the smoake thereof chase out devils, as the smoake of Tobias fish did (which I am sure could smell no stronglier), it would serve for a precious relicke, both for the superstitious priests, and the insolent puritanes to cast out devils withall.

Admitting then, and not confessing, that the use thereof were healthful for some sorts of diseases, should it be used for all sicknesses? Should it be used by all men? Should it be used at all times? Yea, should it be used by able, yong, strong, healthful men? Medicine hath that vertue, that it never leaves a man in that state wherein it finds him. It makes a sicke man whole, but a whole man sicke. And as medicine helps nature, being taken at times of necessitie, so being ever and continually used, it doeth but weaken, weary and weare nature. What speake I of medicine? Nay, let a man every houre of the day, or as oft as many in this countrey use to take tobacco, let a man, I say, but take as oft the best sorts of nourishments in meate and drinke that can be devised, he shall with the continuall use thereof weaken both his head and his stomacke. All his members shall become feeble, his spirits dull, and in the end, as a drowsie lazie belly-god, he shall evanish in a lethargie.

And from this weaknesse it proceeds, that many in this kingdome have had such a continuall use of taking this unsavorie smoake, as now they are not able to forbeare the same, no more then an old drunkard can abide to be long sober, without falling into an incurable weaknesse and evill constitution, for their continuall custome hath made to them, *habitum, alteram naturam*, so to those that from their birth have bene continually nourished upon poison and things venemous, wholsome meats are only poisonable.

Thus having, as I trust, sufficiently answered the most principall arguments that are used in defence of this vile custome, it rests only to informe you what sinnes and vanities you commit in the filthie abuse thereof. First, are you not guiltie of sinnefull and shamefull lust (for lust may be as well in any of the senses as in feeling) that although you be troubled with no disease, but in perfect health, yet can you neither be merry at an ordinary, nor lascivious in the stewes, if you lacke tobacco to provoke your appetite to any of those sorts of recreation, lusting after it as the children of Israel did in the wildernesse after quailes? Secondly it is, as you use or rather abuse it, a branch of the sinne of drunken-nes, which is the root of all sinnes. For as the only delight that drunkards take in wine is the strength of the taste and the force of the fume therof, that mounts up to the braine (for no drunkards love any weake, or sweete drinke) so are not those (I meane the strong heate and the fume) the onely qualities that make tobacco so delectable to all the lovers of it? And as no man likes strong heady drinke the first day (because *nemo repente fit turpissimus*) but by custome is piece and piece allured, while in the ende, a drunkard will have as great a thirst to be drunke, as a sober man to quench his thirst with a draught when hee hath need of it, so is not this the very case of all the great takers of tobacco, which therefore they themselves do attribute to a bewitching qualitie in it? Thirdly, is it not the greatest sinne of all, that you the people of all sorts of this kingdome, who are created and ordeined by God, to bestow both your persons and goods, for the maintenance both of the honour and safety of your King and Commonwealth, should disable your selves in both? In your persons having by this continuall vile custome brought your selves to this shamefull imbecilitie, that you are not able to ride or walke the journey of a Jewes sabboth, but you must have a reekie cole brought you from the next poore house to kindle your tobacco with? Whereas he cannot be thought able for any service in the warres, that cannot endure oftentimes the want of meat, drinke and sleepe, much more then must he endure the want of tobacco. In the times of the many glorious and victorious battailes fought by this nation, there was no word of tobacco. But now if it were time of warres, and that you were to make some sudden cavalcado upon

your enemies, if any of you should seeke leisure to stay behinde
his fellow for taking of tobacco, for my part I should never be
sory for any evill chance that might befall him. To take a custome
in any thing that cannot be left againe, is most harmeful to the
people of any land. Mollicies and delicacie were the wracke and
overthrow, first of the Persian, and next of the Romane empire.
And this very custome of taking tobacco (whereof our present
purpose is) is even at this day accounted so effeminate among the
Indians themselves, as in the market they will offer no price for
a slave to be sold, whom they find to be a great tobacco taker.

Now how you are by this custome disabled in your goods, let
the gentry of this land beare witnesse, some of them bestowing
three, some foure hundred pounds a yeere upon this precious
stinke, which I am sure might be bestowed upon many farre better
uses. I read indeed of a knavish courtier, who for abusing the
favour of the Emperour Alexander Severus his master, by taking
bribes to intercede for sundry persons in his masters eare (for
whom he never once opened his mouth), was justly choked with
smoke, with this doome, *fumo pereat, qui fumum vendidit.* But
of so many smoke-buyers, as are at this present in this kingdome,
I never read nor heard.

And for the vanities committed in this filthy custome, is it not
both great vanitie and uncleannesse, that at the table, a place of
respect, of cleanlinesse, of modestie, men should not be ashamed,
to sit tossing of tobacco pipes and puffing of the smoke of tobacco
one to another, making the filthy smoke and stinke thereof, to
exhale athwart the dishes and infect the aire, when very often,
men that abhorre it are at their repast? Surely smoke becomes a
kitchin farre better then a dining chamber and yet it makes a
kitchin also oftentimes in the inward parts of men, soyling and
infecting them, with an unctuous and oily kind of soote, as hath
bene found in some great tobacco takers, that after their death
were opened. And not onely meate time, but no other time nor
action is exempted from the publike use of this uncivill tricke, so
as if the wives of Diepe list to contest with this nation for good
maners, their worst maners would in all reason be found at least
not so dishonest (as ours are) in this point. The publike use

whereof, at all times, and in all places, hath now so farre prevailed, as divers men very sound both in judgement and complexion, have bene at last forced to take it also without desire, partly because they were ashamed to seeme singular (like the two philosophers that were forced to ducke themselves in that raine water, and so become fooles as well as the rest of the people) and partly, to be as one that was content to eate garlicke (which he did not love) that he might not be troubled with the smell of it in the breath of his fellowes. And is it not a great vanitie, that a man cannot heartily welcome his friend now, but straight they must be in hand with tobacco? No it is become in place of a cure, a point of good fellowship, and hee that will refuse to take a pipe of tobacco among his fellowes (though by his owne election hee would rather feele the favour of a sinke) is accounted peevish and no good company, even as they doe with tipling in the colde easterne countreys. Yea, the mistresse cannot in a more manerly kind, entertaine her servant, then by giving him out of her faire hand a pipe of tobacco. But herein is not only a great vanity, but a great contempt of Gods good giftes, that the sweetnesse of mans breath, being a good gift of God, should be wilfully corrupted by this stinking smoke, wherin I must confesse, it hath too strong a vertue. And so, that which is an ornament of nature, and can neither by any artifice be at the first acquired, nor once lost, be recovered againe, shalbe filthily corrupted with an incurable stinke, which vile qualitie is as directly contrary to that wrong opinion which is holden of the wholesomnesse therof, as the venime of putrifaction is contrary to the vertue preservative.

Moreover, which is a great iniquitie, and against all humanitie, the husband shall not be ashamed, to reduce therby his delicate, wholesom and cleane complexioned wife, to that extremity, that either she must also corrupt her sweet breath therwith, or els resolve to live in a perpetual stinking torment.

Have you not reason then to be ashamed and to forbeare this filthy noveltie, so basely grounded, so foolishly received, and so grossely mistaken in the right use thereof; in your abuse thereof sinning against God, harming your selves both in persons and goods, and raking also thereby the markes and notes of vanitie upon you; by the custome thereof making your selves to be wondered at by all forreine civill nations, and by all strangers that come among you, to be scorned and contemned? A custome loath-some to the eye, hatefull to the nose, harmefull to the braine, dangerous to the lungs, and in the blacke stinking fume thereof, neerest resembling the horrible Stigian smoake of the pit that is bottomlesse.

WILLIAM DRUMMOND

WILLIAM DRUMMOND was born in 1585, the son of John Drummond, first Laird of Hawthornden. He attended the University of Edinburgh, graduating in 1605. As his father wished him to become a lawyer, he was then sent to Paris and Bourges to embark on a course of legal study. His father however died early and in 1610, at the age of 24, the youthful poet found himself lord of a comfortable estate near Edinburgh. This idyllic situation has tempted many biographers to turn the poet into a humour creation—that of the romantic hermit. Admittedly Drummond spent a large portion of his time in Hawthornden, surrounded by a library, which even in 1611 contained 552 works. On the other hand, he formed friendships with writers on both sides of the border, notably William Alexander and Michael Drayton. Such critics pass over, in addition, his ambiguous relationship with Euphemia Cunningham of Barns. Although there is now definite proof that she could not have been the major inspiration for his love poetry, Drummond certainly did have a strong affection for her. They ignore, or are ignorant of, the evidence that he fathered three illegitimate children. They forget those fifteen weapons of destruction he patented in September 1627. They forget his decision at the age of 46 to relinquish bachelorhood and marry Elizabeth Logan. Drummond's life may have been more sheltered than many of those examined in this anthology, but his interests were wider, his contacts outside Hawthornden more extensive than is generally allowed. On December 4th 1649 he died and was buried in Lasswade cemetery.

Like Fowler, Drummond is better known for his poetry, most of which relies heavily on foreign sources, most noticeably Sidney, Marino, Tasso and Pontus de Tyard. *A Cypresse Grove*, however, Drummond's semi philosophical prose speculation on death is one of the finest pieces of prose written in the seventeenth century. It appeared first in the *Flowres of Sion*, edition of 1630. From it I have chosen a number of passages, which illustrate Drummond's prose, both its quality and range, while affording the reader a fair idea of the general argument. In addition I have included a short portion of the work in its first form as *A Midnight's Trance*, published eleven years earlier. Intentionally one portion is allowed to overlap, so that the nature of Drummond's alterations may be illustrated.

Critics have generally been appreciative of Drummond, though anxious at the same time to emphasise the obvious "Englishness" of his muse. Thus C. S. Lewis comments "And of course there is always Drummond. But Drummond himself, when all's said, is a Scotchman only 'out of school'," while the editors of *The Oxford Book of Scottish Verse*, justify themselves for citing only one of his poems, with the remark that his work "seems to be more at home in the English tradition than in the Scottish". On the other hand, if Scottish writers are to be ignored whenever their interests merge with those of their English counterparts, then a strong case could be made for also ignoring Dunbar and others. On *A Cypresse Grove* specifically, perhaps the most memorable comment has come from David Masson. "Here, in a short series of prose pages, we have a meditation on Death by our poet of Hawthornden, which for its pensive beauty, its moral high-mindedness, and the mournful music that rolls through it, surpasses any similar piece of old English prose known to me, unless it be here and there, perhaps, a passage in some of the English Divines at their best, or Sir Thomas Browne of Norwich in the finest parts of his *Urn-Burial*."

My text for *A Midnight's Trance* is based on that of R. Ellrodt's reprint of the 1619 edition. The text for *A Cypresse Grove* is based on the Edinburgh edition of 1630.

A MIDNIGHT'S TRANCE

Though it hath beene doubted if there be in the soule of man such imperious and superexcellent power, as that it can by the vehement and earnest working of it, deliver knowledge to another without bodily organs, and by the only conceptions and ideas of it, produce reall effects, yet it hath beene ever and of all thought infallible and most certaine, that it often (either by outward inspiration, or some secret motion of it selfe) is augure of its owne misfortunes, and hath shadowes of comming dangers presented unto it, a while before they fall forth. Hence so many strange apparitions and signes, true visions, dreames most certaine, uncouth languishings and drowsinesse, of which to seeke a reason, unlesse from the sparkling of GOD in the soule, or from the God-like sparkles of the soule, were to make reason unreasonable, in reasoning of things transcending her reach.

Having often and divers times, when I had given my selfe to rest in the quiet solitarinesse of the night, found my imagination troubled with a confused feare, no, sorrow, or horror, which interrupting sleepe did confound my senses, and rouse mee up all appalled and transported in a suddaine agony and sad amazednes; of such an unaccustomed perturbation and nameless woe, not knowing, nor being able to imagine any apparent cause, carried away with the streame of my (then doubting) thoghts, I was brought to ascribe it to that secret foreknowledg and presageing power of the propheticke mind; and to interpret such an agonie to bee to the spirit, as a faintnes and universall wearinesse is to the body, a token of following sicknesse, or as the earth-quakes are to great cities, harbingers of greater calamities, or as the roring of the sea is, in a stil calme, a signe of some ensuing tempest.

Hereupon, not thinking it strange, if whatsoever is humane should befall me, knowing how providence abates griefe, and discountenances crosses, and that as we should not despaire of evils, which may happen us, wee should not trust too much in those goods we enjoy, I began to turne over in my remembrance all that could afflict miserable mortalitie, and to fore-cast every thing that with a maske of horror could shew it selfe to humane eyes, till in the end, as by unities and points, mathematicians are brought to great numbers and huge greatnesse, after many fantasticall glances of mankinds sorrow, and those incumbrances which follow life, I was brought to thinke, and with amazement, on the last of humane evils, or (as one said) the last of all dreadfull and terrible things, Death.

And why may wee not beleeve that the soule (though darkely) fore-seeing, and having secret intelligence of that sharpe divorcement it is to have from the body, should be overgrieved and surprised with an uncouth and unaccustomed sorrow? And at the first encounter examining their neere union, long familiarity and friendship, with the great chang, paine, and uglines, which is apprehended to bee in Death, it shall not appeare to be without reason.

They had their being together, parts they are of one reasonable creature, the hurting of the one is the enfeebling of the working of the other. What deare contentments doth the soule enjoy by the senses? They are the gates and windowes of its knowledge, the organs of its delight. If it bee grievous to an excellent lutanist to bee long without a lute, how much more must the want of so noble an instrument bee painefull to the soule? And if two pilgrims who have wandred some few miles together, have a hearts griefe when they part, what must the sorrow be at the parting of two so loving friends, as is the soule and body?

Death is the violent estranger of acquaintance, the eternall divorcer of marriage, the ravisher of the children from the parents, the stealer of the parents from the children, the intomber of fame, the only cause of forgetfulnes, by which men talk of them that are gon away, as of so many shadows, or ageworn stories....

A CYPRESSE GROVE

They had their beeing together, partes they are of one reasonable creature, the harming of the one is the weakning of the working of the other. What sweete contentments doeth the soule enjoye by the senses? They are the gates and windowes of its knowledge, the organes of its delight? If it bee tideous to an excellent player on the lute to endure but a few monethes the want of one, how much more must the beeing without such noble tooles and engines bee plaintfull to the soule? And, if two pilgrimes, which have wandred some little peece of ground together, have an hearts-griefe when they are neare to parte, what must the sorrow bee at the parting of two so loving friendes and never-loathing lovers as are the bodie and soule?

Death is the sade estranger of acquantance, the eternall divorcer of mariage, the ravisher of the children from their parentes, the stealer of parents from the children, the interrer of fame, the sole cause of forgetfulnesse, by which the living talke of those gone away as of so manie shadowes or fabulous paladines. All strength by it is enfeebled, beautie turned in deformitie and rottennesse, honour in contempt, glorie into basenesse. It is the unreasonable breaker off of all the actions of vertue, by which wee enjoye no more the sweete pleasures on earth, neither contemplate the statelie revolutions of the heavens; sunne perpetuallie setteth, starres never rise unto us; it in one moment depriveth us of what with so great toyle and care in manie yeeres wee have heaped together. By this are successions of linages cut short, kingdomes left heirelesse, and greatest states orphaned. It is not overcome by pride, smoothed by gaudie flatterie, tamed by intreaties, bribed by benefites, softned by lamentations, diverted by time. Wisedome, save this, can alter and helpe anie thing. By death wee are exiled from this faire citie of the world. It is no more a world unto us, nor wee anie more people into it. The ruines of phanes, palaces, and other magnificent frames, yeeld a sad prospect to the soule, and how should it consider the wracke of such a wonderfull maister-piece as is the bodie without horrour?

*

If thou doest complaine, that there shall bee a time in the which thou shalt not bee, why doest thou not too grieve, that there was a time in the which thou wast not, and so that thou art not as olde, as that enlifening planet of time? For, not to have beene a thousand yeeres before this moment, is as much to bee deplored, as not to bee a thousand after it, the effect of them both beeing one. That will bee after us which long, long ere wee were was. Our childrens children have that same reason to murmure that they were not young men in our dayes, which wee now, to complaine that wee shall not be old in theirs. The violets have their time, though they empurple not the winter, and the roses keepe their season, though they discover not their beautie in the spring.

Empires, states, kingdomes, have by the doome of the supreame providence their fatall periods; great cities lye sadlie buried in their dust; artes and sciences have not onelie their ecclipses, but their wainings and deathes; the gastlie wonders of the world, raised by the ambition of ages, are overthrowne and trampled; some lights above (deserving to bee intitled starres) are loosed and never more seene of us; the excellent fabrike of this universe it selfe shall one day suffer ruine, or a change like a ruine, and poore earthlings thus to bee handled complaine!

But is this life so great a good, that the lose of it should be so deare unto man? If it be, the meanest creatures of nature thus bee happie, for they live no lesse than hee. If it bee so great a felicitie, how is it esteemed of man himselfe at so small a rate, that for so poore gaines, nay one disgracefull word, hee will not stand to loose it? What excellencie is there in it, for the which hee should desire it perpetuall, and repine to bee at rest, and returne to his olde grand-mother dust? Of what moment are the labours and actions of it, that the interruption and leaving off of them should bee to him so distastfull, and with such grudging lamentations received?

Is not the entring into life weaknesse, the continuing sorrow? In the one hee is exposed to all the injuries of the elementes, and like a condemned trespasser (as if it were a fault to come to light) no sooner borne than fast manacled and bound. In the other hee is restlesslie, like a ball, tossed in the tinnise-court of this world. When hee is in the brightest meridiane of his glorie, there needeth nothing to destroy him, but to let him fall his owne hight. A reflexe of the sunne, a blast of winde, nay, the glance of an eye is sufficient to undoe him. Howe can that be anie great matter, of which so small instrumentes and slender actions are maisters?

His bodie is but a masse of discording humours, composed and elemented by the conspiring influences of superior lights, which though agreeing for a trace of tyme, yet can never be made uniforme and keept in a just proportion. To what sickenesse is it subject unto, beyond those of the other sensible creatures, no parte of it beeing which is not particularlie infected and afflicted by some one, nay, everie part with many, yea, so many, that the maisters of that arte can scarce number or name them, so that the life of diverse of the meanest creatures of nature, hath with great reason by the most wise, beene preferred to the naturall life of man, and wee should rather wonder how so fragill a matter should so long endure, than how so soone dissolve and decay!

Are the actiones of the most part of men, much differing from the exercise of the spider, that pitcheth toyles, and is tapist, to pray on the smaller creatures, and for the weaving of a scornefull webbe eviscerateth it selfe manie dayes, which when with much industerie finished, a little puffe of winde carrieth away both the worke and the worker? Or are they not, like the playes of children? Or (to hold them at their highest rate) as is a May-game, a maske, or what is more earnest, some studie at chesse? Everie day wee rise and lye downe, apparrell our bodies and disapparrell them, make them sepulchers of dead creatures, wearie them, and refresh them; which is a circle of idle travells and laboures (like Penelopes taske) unprofitablie renewed. Some time wee are in a chase after a fading beautie; now wee seeke to enlarge our boundes, increase our treasure, living poorelie, to purchase what wee must leave to those wee shall never see, or (happelie) to a foole, or a prodigall heire. Raised with the wind of ambition, wee courte that idle name of honour, not considering how they, mounted aloft in the highest ascendant of earthlie glorie, are but tortured ghostes, wandring with golden fetters in glistering prisones, having feare and danger their unseparable executioners, in the midst of multitudes rather guarded then regarded. They whom opacke imaginations and inward thoughtfulnesse, have made wearie of the worlds eye, though they have withdrawne themselves from the course of vulgare affaires, by vaine contemplationes, curious searches, thinke their life away, are more disquieted, and live worse than others, their wit beeing too sharpe to give them a true taste of present infelicities, and to aggravate their woes; while they of a more shallow and blunt conceit, have want of knowledge and ignorance of themselves, for a remedie and antidote against all the greevances and incombrances of life.

What camelion, what euripe, what rain-bow, what moone doth change so oft as man? Hee seemeth not the same person in one and the same day. What pleaseth him in the morning, is in the evening distastfull unto him. Yong, hee scorneth his childish conceits, and wading deeper in yeeres (for yeeres are a sea, into which hee wadeth untill hee drowne) hee esteemeth his youth unconstancie, rashnesse, follie. Old, hee beginneth to pittie himselfe, plaining because hee is changed, that the world is changed, like those in a ship, which when they launce from the shore, are brought to thinke the shore doeth flie from them. Hee hath no sooner acquired what hee did desire, but hee beginneth to enter into new cares and desire what hee shall never bee able to acquire. When he seemeth freed of evill in his owne estate, hee grudgeth and vexeth himselfe at the happinesse and fortunes of others. Hee is pressed with care for what is present, with griefe for what is past, with feare for what is to come, nay, for what will never come; and as in the eye one teare draweth another after it, so maketh hee one sorrow follow upon a former, and everie day lay up stuffe of griefe for the next.

*

If the bodie shall not arise, how can the onelie and soveraigne good bee perfectlie and infinitlie good? For how shall Hee be just, nay, have so much justice as man, if he suffer the evill and vicious to have a more prosperous and happie life, than the followers of religion and vertue, which ordinarlie useth to fall forth in this life? For, the most wicked are Lords and Gods of this earth, sleeping in the lee port of honour, as if the spacious habitation of the world had beene made onelie for them, and the vertuous and good are but forlorne cast-awayes, floting in the surges of distresse, seeming heere either of the eye of providence not pittied, or not reguarded; beeing subject to all dishonours, wrongs, wrackes;

in their best estate passing away their dayes (like the dazies in the field) in silence and contempt.

*

But it is not of death (perhaps) that we complaine, but of tyme, under the fatall shadow of whose winges, all things decay and wither. This is that tyrant, which executing against us his diamantine laws, altereth the harmonious constitution of our bodies, benuming the organes of our knowledge, turneth our best senses sencelesse, makes us loathsome to others and a burthen to our selves, of which evills death relieveth us. So that, if wee could bee transported (O happy colonie!) to a place exempted from the lawes and conditiones of time, where neither change, motion, nor other affection of materiall and corruptible things were, but an immortall, unchangeable, impassible, all-sufficient kinde of life, it were the last of things wisheable, the tearme and center of all our desires. Death maketh this transplantation; for the last instant of corruption, or leaving off of any thing to bee what it was, is the first of generation, or being of that which succeedeth. Death then beeing the end of this miserable transitory life, of necessity must bee the beginning of that other all excellent and eternall, and so causeslie of a vertuous soule it is either feared or complained on.

*

Heere is the Palace Royall of the Almightie King, in which the uncomprehensible comprehensiblie manifesteth himselfe; in place highest, in substance not subject to any corruption or change, for it is above all motion, and solide turneth not; in quantitie greatest, for if one starre, one spheare, bee so vast, how large, how hudge in exceeding demensions, must those boundes bee, which doe them all containe? In qualitie most pure and orient, heaven heere is all but a sunne, or the sunne all but a heaven. If to earthlinges the foote-stoole of God, and that stage which Hee raised for a small course of tyme, seemeth so glorious and magnificent, how highlie would they prize (if they could see) his eternall habitation and throne? And if these bee so dazeling, what is the sight of Him, for whom, and by whom all was created, of whose glory to behold the thousand, thousand part, the most pure intelligences are fully satiate, and with wonder and delight rest amazed; for the beauty of His light and the light of his beauty are uncomprehensible! Heere doth that earnest appetite of the understanding content it selfe, not seeking to know any more; for it seeth before it, in the vision of the divine essence (a mirour in the which not images or shadowes, but the true and perfect essence of every thing created, is more cleare and conspicuous, than in it selfe) all that is knowne or understood; and where as on earth our senses show us the creator by his creatures, heere wee see the creatures by the creator. Heere doth the will pause it selfe, as in the center of its eternall rest, glowing with a fervent affection of that infinite and all-sufficient good, which beeing fully knowne, cannot (for the infinite motives and causes of love which are in Him) but bee fully and perfectly loved. As Hee is onely true and essentiall bountie so is Hee onelie essentiall and true beauty, deserving alone all love and admiration, by which the creatures are onely in so much faire and excellent, as they participate of his beauty and excelling excellencies.

Heere is a blessed company, every one joying as much in anothers felicity, as in that which is proper, because each seeth another equallie loved of God. Thus their distinct joyes are no fewer, than the co-partners of the joye; and as the assemblie is in number answerable to the large capacitie of the place, so are the joyes answerable to the numberlesse number of the assemblie. No poore and pittifull mortall, confined on the globe of earth, who hath never seene but sorrow, or interchangablie some painted superficiall pleasures, and had but guesses of contentment, can rightlie thinke on, or be sufficient to conceive the tearmelesse delightes of this place. So manie feathers move not on birdes, so manie birds dint not the aire, so manie leaves tremble not on trees, so manie trees grow not in the solitarie forestes, so manie waves turne not in the ocean, and so manie graines of sand limit not those waves; as this triumphant court hath varietie of delights, and joyes exempted from all comparison. Happinesse at once heere is fullie knowne and fullie enjoyed, and as infinite in continuance as extent. Heere is flourishing and never-fading youth without age, strength without weaknesse, beautie never blasting, knowledge without learning, aboundance without lothing, peace without disturbance, participation without envy, rest without labour, light without rising or setting sunne, perpetuitie without momentes, for time (which is the measure of motion) did never enter in this shining eternitie. Ambition, disdaine, malice, difference of opinions, can not approach this place, resembling those foggie mists, which cover those lists of sublunarie things. All pleasure, paragon'd with what is heere, is paine, all mirth mourning, all beautie deformitie: here one dayes abiding is above the continuing in the most fortunate estate on the earth manie yeeres, and sufficient to contervaile the extreamest tormentes of life. But, although this blisse of soules bee great, and their joyes many, yet shall they admit addition, and bee more full and perfect, at that long wished and generall reunion with their bodies.

JAMES ROW

JAMES ROW, grandson of John Row the Reformer graduated M.A. from Edinburgh in 1618 and was admitted minister of Muthill in 1635. He attended the Glasgow Assembly of 1638 but was suspended in February 1645 for favouring tthe royal cause. He was reinstated by the Assembly on the recommendation of his Synod in 1650, whereupon he petitioned Parliament for exemption from public burdens on the grounds of extreme hardship, being unable to acquire the stipend and "having a wyff and eight children". He was admitted minister of Monzievaird and Strowan in 1655 and received £50 from Parliament in 1661 on account of his sufferings. He was still active in his ministry in January 1680.

His fame rests on this one famous sermon preached in 1638. Although Row opens with a long indictment of the Kirk's sins in the near past, his tone is optimistic. It must be remembered that this is a sermon preached shortly after the signing of the Covenant, and this is why Row sees the kirk not in shame, but "riding to Jerusalem in Triumph". The major purpose of the sermon is to encourage those in high position, who have not yet signed the Covenant, to do so without hesitation. It is thus part of the pressure applied by Scottish ministers at this time on the King, culminating in July 1638, with Charles revoking the Prayer Book, canons and Five Articles of Perth. Of particular interest is Row's final appeal to the Provost and Doctors of Aberdeen, for that city in particular had refused the Covenant and two months after this sermon a special mission was sent north to debate points of theology with the doctors there. It is recorded that the pro-Covenant mission was out-argued, and it is quite possible that Row was one of the ministers involved. Certainly he seems to have taken a special interest in the Aberdeen question, for in John Row's *History of Scotland*, we learn that "the Town of Aberdeen subscryved the Covenant, after Mr. James Row had preached on Acts V chp., 38, 39 verses".

The forceful style, imagery and effective use of Scots makes the sermon's fame readily understandable. My text is based on the London edition of 1642.

RED-SHANKES SERMON (OR POCKMANTY PREACHING)

The Red-Shankes Sermon: Preached at Saint Giles Church in Edenburgh, the last Sunday in April, by a Highland Minister.

Jerem. 30 "Sion is wounded and I will heale her, saith the Lord." "I need not trouble you to set forth, who is meant by Sion. Yee all know well enough, that it is the poore Church of Scotland, who is now wounded in her head, in her heart, in her hands and in her feet; in her head by government, in her heart by doctrine, in her hands by discipline and in her feet by worship. First, she is wounded in her head, where she hath got such a clash as hath made all her braines clatter again and almost put her beside her five senses. First in her seeing, for she could have seen as wel as any Christian Kirk, but now she cannot distinguish betweene blacke and white, for bring plaine popery before her and she cannot discerne between that and true religion. Secondly, she is wounded in her hearing. She could have distinguished the sound of the gospell and the rigor of the law, but now since the organes came in, she is growne as deafe as a doore naile. Thirdly, she could have smelled as well as any other Kirk, but now she hath smelt the whore of Babilon, she is so senselesse, as bring the stinking popish trash under her nose, and it will seeme as sweet as a rose. Fourthly, she could have tasted as well as the best, but now she hath so tasted of the Popes idolatrie, she cannot rellish her former food. Lastly, she was so pure and tender as shee would not touch any thing which had been corrupted, but now she hath toucht some popish pitch, and how can she but be defiled? The application followes.

"You see how she hath almost lost her senses, and you that are old men have seene her ministers, going in good old short cloakes with round black velvet capes, which little cloakes turned more soules to God then ever the long gownes did. You have heard such good ministers expound the law and apply the gospell in their pulpits, but now you may heare the proud prelates rumbling up and downe the streets in their coaches, in their long gownes, and if you would heare them speake, follow them to the Councell table, and there you shall heare more then you will be content to followe. For her smelling, I am sure she smels better then ever she did, for shee can smell a bishoprick, ten yeares before it fall, but it may be those that smell best shall never lay their fingers ends on it now. The Kirke tastes better then ever she did, for in old time shee would have beene content with a messe of milke and bread and such homely fare, but now they must feed on the finest and take a licke of the best liquor. Lastly, she touches now better then ever she did, for where she would touch nothing formerly but spirituall matters, now she will take upon her to handle the temporall businesse first and leave the other till they have leasure.

"I have now shewed you that the Kirk is wounded in her head and decay of her sences, and I will returne to show you the rest of her wounds. Secondly, she is wounded in her heart, which is by the doctrine of the Kirk through the aboundance of popery and Arminianisme, now common in our kirks and schooles. The Kirck of Scotland was once a bonny grammer school, and then shee was skilled in *Regimen et concordantia*, and could have made a pretty peece of Latin, for everie thing she did was forced *dare regulum*, and when she offended, was *pandere manum*, but afterward, when she went to the Colledge, shee either had, or would take, more liberty unto her. And then first of all shee began her rhetorick, and instead of true and proper speaking, she learned nothing but alegories and hyperbolies. Then she came to the logicke and instead of the true demonstration, shee learned nothing but homogenes and syllogismes. Afterward, she came to the ethicks, but she did not much trouble her selfe with them, but studied the politicks, where she prospered so well, as she turned true religion into state pollicy. And for the metaphysicks, ye know their ends, which should be *unum utrum et bonum*; so true religion must be one true and good religion. But this was too high and honest for them, too hard to learn, wherfore she studied no more the physick, but turned true religion into *materia prima*, and made it capable of any forme they pleased to impose upon it. So that, yee see, our Kirke is wounded in her heart, by the doctrine of the Kirk and teaching of the schooles, which have beene such, as I am sure that many of you that heare me at this time have wished a hundred times to have beene out of the Kirk, when you heard such paultry stuffe as came from them.

"Thirdly, the Kirk is wounded in her hands, which is the discipline of the Kirk, once famous by her reformation, after she ran away from Rome. But hard did they follow her. Faine would they have overtaken her, and if they had gotten her, they had given her the largest lash, but (God be thanked) shee ran too fast for them. But nowe of late shee hath gon pilgrimage to Rome, where shee was taken stealing of some of their trumperie. Yet, when they knew her mind, and saw it was but onlie a booke of Common prayer, and the Canons of High Commission, which they saw made much for their matter, therefore they let her goe and flatterred her to follow the order of the Mother Kirke in other kingedomes, which shee promising to doe, then they bound her hands with a silken cord of canonicall obedience to the ordinarie, and shee tooke much delight to be bound with so bonny a band. But after they got her fast, they made that silken band a cable rope, with which they have girded her so hard as shee cannot stirre, and so they will force us either to a blinde obedience, and to accept of such idolatrous and superstitious ceremonies on the one side, or els to be all forsworne fellowes on the other side, by which meanes the Kirke of Scotland hath beene so wounded and bound in her hands as, this 20. yeares by-past, the poore Kirke of Scotland could not have a meeting of her members in a lawfull assemblie.

"Now I come to tell you how shee is wounded in her feet—that is, in the worship of the Kirke. The office of the feet is to travell withall, and they have made a verie hackney of religion. The Kirke was once a bonny nag, and so pretty as every man thought it pitty to ride her, till at last the bishops, those ranke riding lowns, got on her back, and then she trotted so hard as they could hardlie at the first well ride her. Yet at last they so crosse legd her and hopshackled her, that shee became a pretty pacing beast, and so easie, that they tooke great pleasure to ride upon her. But now, what with their riding her up and downe betweene Edenburgh and London (and one journey to Rome too) they had given her sick sore heate, that wee have beene this twelvemoneth walking her up and downe to keep her from foundering.

"Nay, they have not onlie made a horse but an asse also of the Kirke of Scotland; yea an asse worse then Balaams was. Balaam, ye ken, was ganging a great way, and the errand ye ken too—to curse where the Lord had blessed. And the angell first met him in a broad way, and the asse bogled and startled, but Balaam beate the asse and got by the angell. And so was our Kirke beaten unreasonablie, when episcopacie came riding on her asse amongst us.

"Afterwards Balaam met the angell againe in a straiter way, and then the asse startled more then before. Balaam beat her againe, worse then he did before. So was our Kirke kickt and verie shrewdlie wounded, when the bishops brought in the 5. Articles of Perth amongst us. The third time the angell met Balaam in so strait a way as the asse could not passe by, and Balaam beate the asse againe, but the Lord made the asse to speake and reprove him for beating her, and then God opened Balaams eyes. So the bishops (being as blind as Balaam) have ridden and beaten our Kirke so long, and taken us such a strait, as wee were even ready to be destroied. But God hath heard our cry, and wee pray him also open the eyes of our adversaries, who were even as blind as Balaam, and were going as unlucky a way as hee; for they were posting to Rome with a poakmantie behind them. And what was in their poakmantie, trow ye? Marry, even the book of Common praier, the book of Cannons, and orders of the High Commission. Now, as sone as the asse saw the angell, shee falls to flinging and over goes the poakmantie, and it hung on the one side of the asse by one string, and the bishops hang by the hamme on the other side, so as they hang crosse the asse (like a paire of paniers) stuft full of popish trash and trinkets. Faine would the blind carle have beene on the saddle againe, but hee could not. Nay, so he might be but set to ride againe, he would be content to leave his poakmanty amongst us. But let me exhort yee, deare brethren, not to let such a swinger ride any more on your religion, for if he doe, he will be sure one time or other to get the poakmantie behind him againe.

"They have not onlie wounded the Kirke of Scotland, as I have tolde you, and made an horse and an asse of it, but they have betrayed it also for a some of money, as Judas did Christ. Yee ken, who betraid our Saviour, not onlie hee that tooke money to betray him, but also those that were silent in so good a cause, those that accuse him, those adjudged him, and those that forsooke him. And I fear me wee have them that betray our religion in all these waies, as I shall touch anon. But now I will see if I can find out the false Judas, that takes money or promotion to betray our religion. And I must now tell you a metaphoricall tale. I dare not say it is true, but you shall have it as I had it.

"When I was a little lad at schoole, there was a young hopefull theologue and expectant, who is now another manner of man (not such another in the land), and he being to preach of those words of Judas, '*Quid mihi dabitis etc,*' (what will you give me and I will deliver him into your hands?). The young man loved his text so well, as he tolde over and over againe, both in Latine and Scottish. There was a good olde man sitting neare him and hearing him still upon that text, thought to give him his answer. And so, standing up and looking upon him the next time that he said 'what will yee give me and I will deliver him unto you?' the old man answered, 'Marry thou shalt have a good fat bishoprick, and then I am sure thou wilt betray him indeed.' Nowe yee may find out by this, who hath betraied the Kirke of Scotland.

"My brethren, the comparison betweene Christ and our Kirke holds well together, and their troubles have beene in some things alike, for Christ is the head, the Kirke is the body. Ye ken our Savior, when he entred first into the ministrie, he was carried by Satan (God save us) into the wildernes, where he was tempted forty long daies of a mickle Devill, in which time he endured many temptations. But as soone as he began to worke his miracles, then he was carried into Jerusalem with great triumph, where there was nothing but '*Hosanna,*' in their mouthes, 'blessed is he that commeth in the name of the Lord!'" The next newes ye heare of him, they came with halberts and feathered staves, and troups of souldiers, from the high Priest to apprehend him.

"So the Kirke of Scotland for almost 40. yeares by-past hath sate desolate in the wildernes, by you contemned and rejected of all, and endured manie temptations, and nowe in the end having overcome them, shee is riding to Jerusalem in triumph, for now there is nothing in all mens mouthes but '*Hosanna,*' crying, 'blessed is he that comes in the name of the Lord!'

"But in the last place, ye remember when Christ was betraied, how they came to betray him. Therefore, take heed when they come with swords and staves and bands of men from the high Priests against you, that you doe not, with Peter, denie your Master and your religion, and like the rest of the apostles, shewe a faire pair of heeles and forsake him.

"Now, poore fooles, yee have all seen your Church wounded, where shee lyes a wofull spectacle. But what shall wee doe for to heale her? Marry, pray unto the Lord, who hath promised to heale his wounded Sion. And we must put to our helping hands also, for such as put their hands to the plough (as ye have done) and turne back againe, are not fit for the kingdome of heaven."

After his sermon was ended, his prayer said and a psalme sung, he stood up to give the blessing, but first said thus, "I know it is not the custome in this place to say any thing after sermon, yet because I had much to say, and one thing drave another out of my head, therefore I must crave leave to ad a word or two by way of exhortation.

"First, I will speake to such noble men as have not subscribed the Covenant, to know their reason. Yee will say, yee are *Noli me tangere*. Howsoever, I will give you a touch, and it may be ye will answer, yee must goe in a parliamentary way, the meanest first and the best last. Yee would be angry, if yee were told the poore must enter heaven before you. You have a fashion here in the southerne parts of Scotland, that when yee come to the foord of a river, the poore post man must first venture over upon his little nag, to see whether it be deepe or no, and then the Laird comes mounted on his gay steed and he passes over. This is no good fashion where ever you had it. Wee that are highlanders have a better then that our selves. Wee usuallie goe on foote, and when wee come to a foord, wee are loth to lose a man. Therefore, wee joine arme in arme, and hand in hand, and all goe in together, so that the strong suports the weake, and drowne one drowne all. So, put your hand to the Covenant and either live or die with the rest.

"In the second place, yee that are of the Colledge of Justice, yee excuse your subscribing because yee are imployed by his Majestie and so cannot stand with your honors to doe it. Heers a brave reason but a bad example, for so may the very meanest man in the kingdome, that gathers up but 20s per annum, for the King, have such a hole to goe out at. Well, there is but one man betwixt God and you. Get by him and goe to God.

"In the third place, I must speake to you that are of this City Councell, although I see there are fowre of your chiefest chaires emptie. You excuse your selves because you are in office, and when yee are out you will subscribe. Heers a brave reason indeed. Nowe, yee ought to be ringleaders to the rest in this citie, as in all other affaires. Who dares subscribe in the city, till yee have done it? And if God get his worke done ere that time, where be your thanks? Let our chiefe register looke over his bookes and see if ever the towne of Edenburgh suffered for joyning with the Kirke of Scotland.

"Lastly, I must speake a word to you that are strangers." Then, turning himselfe to the Provost, Baylives, and Doctors of Aberden, who sate in a gallerie by themselves, hee said, "It may be, that yee doe not subscribe the Covenant, because when ye came hither on your civill affaires, you promised not to subscribe it. Remember your owne proverb in buying and selling, 'an Aberden man may recant his first bargaine if he please.' Therefore, let me advise you to play Aberden mens parts and take your word againe and goe home and drinke a cup of bon-accord, and joine with the Kirke of Scotland, and subscribe the Covenant."

THOMAS URQUHART

SIR THOMAS URQUHART of Cromartie was born in 1611, son of the elder Sir Thomas Urquhart of Cromartie and Christian, daughter of the fourth Lord Elphinstone. At the age of 11 he enrolled at King's College, Aberdeen but left with no degree. Of his youth we know little except that he spent some time travelling in France, Spain and Italy, appearing thrice in the lists to defend the honour of Scotland. When the Civil War showed signs of breaking out however, and his father chose the unpopular step of refusing to sign the Covenant, Urquhart returned to Scotland and took part in the "Trot of Turiff" on the victorious Royalist side. The position of the Urquharts grew increasingly awkward, in the years immediately following, not only due to the strength of the Presbyterian forces, but also because the father was now deeply in debt. On his death in 1642, Thomas, who had been knighted the year before, left the estate in the hands of trustees and left for the continent. By 1645 he was back on these estates, where matters were worsening. By 1647 Sir Robert Farquhar had gained possession of Cromartie. He sold the rights to Sir John Urquhart, who in turn purchased a commission from Charles I, making him hereditary sheriff of Cromartie. As he let his claims lie dormant for a while, however, Thomas Urquhart still retained the appearance of power. He was involved in the unfortunate rising of the Northern Cavaliers under Thomas Mackenzie, but was mercifully treated by the General Assembly Commission. In June 1650, Charles II landed and was crowned at Scone on January 1st 1651. Urquhart joined the ill fated army, which marched south in that year. He was captured at Worcester in September and imprisoned in the Tower, though he records the generosity of his treatment there. His manuscripts had been lost after the battle, but in a period of less stringent captivity at Windsor Castle he made up for their loss, composing most of his major works. The later period of his life presents no continual record, though the *Continuation of the Pedigree of the Urquharts* indicates a further period of imprisonment. He died suddenly in Holland in 1660. Tradition has it that the cause was a hearty burst of laughter at the news of Charles II's accession. If this is not the truth, it ought to be!

I have included passages from *The Trissotetras*, ἐκεκυβαλαυρομ (or *The Jewel*) and from his translation of Rabelais. His other works are *Epigrams, Divine and Moral* (1645), παντοχρονοχανον (or *A peculiar Promptuary of Time*) (1652) and *Logopandecteision* (or *An Introduction to the Universal Languages*) (1653). The last of these also contains interesting passages, dealing with Urquhart's own character and his future hopes for the estates of Cromarty.

Urquhart has usually appealed to critics, though in the rôle of lovable eccentric, rather than major literary figure. Unstinted praise is usually reserved for the *Rabelais*. Professor Roe notes how translator and original shared "the keenest zest for words, which they handled with exuberant fancy. Both cultivated a taste for a copious, robust, and original vocabulary. To each of them, imagination furnished a rare selection of racy words in extraordinary abundance." Sir Theodore Martin on a more general theme praises "the buoyancy and unembarrassed sweep" of his prose, but one still feels that Urquhart's overall contribution has been sadly underestimated by scholars to date.

My text is based in each case, on that of the first printed edition, *Trissotetras* (1645); *Jewel* (1652) and *Rabelais* (1653).

THE TRISSOTETRAS

14: In all plain rectangled triangles, the ambients are equall in power to the subtendant; for, by demitting from the right angle a perpendicular, there will arise two correctangles, from whose equiangularity with the great rectangle will proceed such a proportion amongst the homologall sides of all the three, that if you can set them right in the rule, beginning your analogy at the main subtendent (seeing the including sides of the totall rectangle prove subtendents in the partiall correctangles, and the bases of those rectanglets, the segments of the great subtendent) it will fall out, that as the main subtendent is to his base, on either side (for either of the legs of a rectangled triangle, in reference to one another is both base and perpendicular) so the same bases, which are subtendents in the lesser rectangles, are to their bases, the segment of the prime subtendent. Then, by the golden rule, we find, that the multiplying of the middle termes (which is nothing else but the squaring of the comprehending sides of the prime rectangular) affords two products, equall to the oblongs made of the great subtendent, and his respective segments, the aggregat whereof, by equation, is the same with the square of the chief subtendent, or hypotenusa, which was to be demonstrated.

THE JEWEL

(The "Admirable Crichton" amuses the Court at Mantua.)

Those fifteen several personages he did represent with such excellency of garb, and exquisiteness of language, that condignely to perpend the subtlety of the invention, the method of the disposition, the neatness of the elocution, the gracefulness of the action, and wonderful variety in the so dextrous performance of all, you would have taken it for a comedy of five acts, consisting of three scenes, each composed by the best poet in the world, and acted by fifteen of the best players that ever lived, as was most evidently made apparent to all the spectators in the fifth and last hour of his action (which, according to our western account, was about six a clock at night, and by the calculation of that country, half an hour past three and twenty, at that time of the yeer) for, purposing to leave of with the setting of the sun, with an endeavour nevertheless to make his conclusion the master-piece of the work, he, to that effect, summoning all his spirits together, which never failed to be ready at the cal of so worthy a commander, did by their assistance, so conglomerate, shuffle, mix and interlace the gestures, inclinations, actions, and very tones of the speech of those fifteen several sorts of men, whose carriages he did personate, into an inestimable ollapodrida of immaterial morsels of divers kinds, sutable to the very ambrosian relish of the Heliconian nymphs, that, in the *peripetia* of this drammatical exercitation, by the inchanted transportation of the eyes and eares of its spectabundal auditorie, one would have sworne that they all had looked with multiplying glasses, and that (like that angel in the scripture whose voice was said to be like the voice of a multitude) they heard in him alone the promiscuous speech of fifteen several actors, by the various ravishments of the excellencies whereof, in the frolickness of a jocound straine beyond expectation, the logofascinated spirits of the beholding hearers and auricularie spectators, were so on a sudden seazed upon in their risible faculties of the soul, and all their vital motions so universally affected in this extremitie of agitation, that, to avoid the inevitable charmes of his intoxicating ejaculations, and the accumulative influences of so powerfull a transportation, one of my Lady Dutchess chief maids of honour, by the vehemencie of the shock of those incomprehensible raptures, burst forth into a laughter to the rupture of a veine in her body, and another young lady, by the irresistible violence of the pleasure unawares infused, where the tender receptibilitie of her too, too tickled fancie was least able to hold out, so unprovidedly was surprised, that, with no less impetuositie of ridibundal passion then (as hath been told) occasioned a fracture in the other young ladies modestie, she, not able longer to support the well beloved burthen of so excessive delight, and intransing joys of such mercurial exhilarations, through the ineffable extasie of an overmastered apprehension, fell back in a swoun, without the appearance of any other life into her, then what, by the most refined wits of theological speculators, is conceived to be exerced by the purest parts of the separated entelechies of blessed saints in their sublimest conversations with the celestial hierarchies. This accident procured the incoming of an apothecarie with restoratives, as the other did that of a surgeon with consolidative medicaments.

The Admirable Crichtoun now perceiving that it was drawing somewhat late, and that our occidental rays of Phoebus were upon their turning oriental to the other hemisphere of the terrestrial globe, being withall jealous, that the uninterrupted operation of the exuberant diversitie of his jovialissime entertainment, by a continuate winding up of the humours there present, to a higher, yet higher, and still higher pitch, above the supremest Lydian note of the harmonie of voluptuousness, should, in such a case, through the too intensive stretching of the already-super-elated strings of their imagination, with a transcendencie over-reaching Ela, and beyond the well-concerted gam of rational equanimitie, involve the remainder of that illustrious companie into the sweet labyrinth and mellifluent aufractuosities of a lacinious delectation, productive of the same inconveniences which befel the two afore-named ladies, whose delicacie of constitution, though sooner overcome, did not argue, but that the same extranean causes, from him proceeding, of their pathetick alteration, might by a longer insisting in an efficacious agencie and unremitted working of all the consecutively-imprinted degrees, that the capacity of the patient is able to containe, prevaile at last, and have the same predominancie over the dispositions of the strongest complexioned males of that splendid society, did, in his own ordinary wearing-apparel, with the countenance of a prince, and garb befitting the person of a so well bred gentleman and cavalier κατ'ἐξοχήν, full of majesty, and repleat with all excogitable civilitie (to the amazement of all that beheld his heroick gesture) present himself to epilogate this his almost extemporanean comedie, though of five hours continuance without intermission, and that with a peroration, so neatly uttered, so distinctly pronounced, and in such elegancie of selected tearmes, expressed by a diction so periodically contexed with isocoly of members, that the matter thereof tending in all humility to beseech the highnesses of the Duke, Prince, and Dutchess, together with the remanent lords, ladies, knights, gentlemen, and others of both sexes of that honorable convention, to vouchsafe him the favour to excuse his that afternoons escaped extravagancies, and to lay the blame of the indigested irregularity of his wits excursions, and the

abortive issues of his disordered brain, upon the customarily-dis-
pensed-with priviledges in those Cisalpinal regions, to authorize
such like impertinences at carnavalian festivals; and that, although
(according to the most commonly received opinion in that country,
after the nature of Load-him (a game at cards, where he that wins
loseth) he who, at that season of the year, playeth the fool most
egregiously, is reputed the wisest man, he, nevertheless, not being
ambitious of the fame of enjoying good qualities, by vertue of the
antiphrasis of the fruition of bad ones, did meerly undergo that
emancipatorie task of a so profuse liberty, and to no other end
embraced the practising of such roaming and exhorbitant diver-
sions, but to give an evident, or rather infallible demonstration of
his eternally-bound duty to the house of Mantua, and an inviolable
testimony of his never to be altered designe, in prosecuting all the
occasions possible to be laid hold on, that can in any manner of
way prove conducible to the advancement of, and contributing
to the readiest means for improving, those advantages that may
best promove the faculties of making all his choice endeavours and
utmost abilities at all times, effectual to the long wished for further-
ance of his most cordial and endeared service to the serenissime
highnesses of my Lord Duke, Prince and Dutchess, and of conse-
crating with all addicted obsequiousness, and submissive devotion,
his everlasting obedience to the illustrious shrine of their joynt
commands. Then, incontinently addressing himself to the lords,
ladies, and others of that rotonda (which, for his daigning to be
its inmate, though but for that day, might be accounted in nothing
inferiour to the great Colisee of Rome, or Amphitheater at Neems)
with a stately carriage, and port suitable to so prime a gallant, he
did cast a look on all the corners thereof, so bewitchingly amiable
and magnetically efficacious, as if in his eys had bin a muster of ten
thousand Cupids eagerly striving who should most deeply pierce
the hearts of the spectators with their golden darts.

And truly so it fell out (that there not being so much as one
arrow shot in vain) all of them did love him, though not after
the same manner, nor for the same end. For, as the manna of the
Arabian desarts is said to have had in the mouths of the Egyptian
Israelites, the very same tast of the meat they loved best, so the

princes that were there did mainly cherish him for his magnanimity
and knowledge; his courtliness and sweet behaviour being that for
which chiefly the noblemen did most respect him; for his preg-
nancie of wit, and chivalrie in vindicating the honour of ladies, he
was honoured by the knights; and the esquires and other gentlemen courted him for his affability and good fellowship; the rich
did favour him for his judgement and ingeniosity, and for his
liberality and munificence, he was blessed by the poor; the old men
affected him for his constancie and wisdome, and the young for
his mirth and gallantry; the scholars were enamoured of him for
his learning and eloquence, and the souldiers for his integrity and
valour; the merchants, for his upright dealing and honesty, praised
and extolled him; and the artificers for his goodness and benignity;
the chastest lady of that place would have hugged and imbraced
him for his discretion and ingenuity; whilst for his beauty and
comelieness of person he was (at least in the fervency of their
desires) the paramour of the less continent; he was dearly beloved
of the fair women, because he was handsom, and of the fairest
more dearly, becaus he was handsomer. In a word, the affections
of the beholders (like so many several diameters, drawn from the
circumference of their various intents) did all concenter in the point
of his perfection.

After a so considerable insinuation, and gaining of so much
ground upon the hearts of the auditory (though in shorter space
then the time of a flash of lightning) he went on (as before) in
the same thred of the conclusive part of his discourse, with a
resolution not to cut it, till the over-abounding passions of the
company, their exorbitant motions, and discomposed gestures,
through excess of joy and mirth, should be all of them quieted,
calmed, and pacified, and every man, woman, and maid there
(according to their humour) reseated in the same integrity they
were at first; which, when by the articulatest elocution of the most
significant words, expressive of the choisest things that fancie
could suggest, and (conforme to the matters variety) elevating or
depressing, flat or sharply accinating it, with that proportion of
tone that was most consonant with the purpose he had attained
unto, and by his verbal harmony and melodious utterance, setled

all their distempered pleasures, and brought their disorderly raised
spirits into their former capsuls, he with a tongue tip't with silver,
after the various diapasons of all his other expressions, and making of a leg, for the spruceness of its courtsie, of greater decore-
ment to him then cloth of gold and purple, farewel'd the companie
with a complement of one period so exquisitely delivered, and
so well attended by the gracefulness of his hand and foot, with
the quaint miniardise of the rest of his body, in the performance
of such ceremonies as are usual at a court-like departing, that from
the theater he had gone into a lobbie, from thence along three
spacious chambers, whence descending a back staire, he past
through a low gallerie, which led him to that outter gate, where a
coach with six horses did attend him, before that magnificent convention of both sexes (to whom that room, wherein they all were,
seemed in his absence to be as a body without a soul) had the
full leisure to recollect their spirits (which, by the neatness of his
so curious a close, were quoquoversedly scattered with admiration)
to advise on the best expediency how to dispose of themselvs for
the future of that licentious night.

During which time of their being thus in a maze, a proper
young lady (if ever there was any in the world) whose dispersed
spirits, by her wonderful delight in his accomplishments, were by
the power of Cupid, with the assistance of his mother, instantly
gathered and replaced, did upon his retiring (without taking notice
of the intent of any other) rise up out of her boxe, issue forth at a
posterne-door into some secret transes, from whence going down a
few steps, that brought her to a parlour, she went through a large
hall; by the wicket of one end whereof, as she entered on the
street, she encountered with Crichtoun, who was but even then
come to the aforesaid coach, which was hers, unto which, sans
ceremony (waving the frivolous windings of dilatory circumstances)
they both stepped up together, without any other in their company, save a waiting gentlewoman, that sate in the furthest side
of the coach, a page that lifted up the boot thereof, and walked by
it, and one lacky that ran before with a kindled torch in his hand,
all domestick servants of hers, as were the coach-man and postillion;
who, driving apace (and having but half a mile to go) did, with

all the expedition required, set down my lady with her beloved
mate at the great gate of her own palace; through the wicket
whereof (because she would not stay till the whole were made wide
open) they entred both; and injunction being given, that forth-
with after the setting up of the coach and horses, the gate should
be made fast, and none, more then was already, permitted to come
within her court that night, they joyntly went along a private
passage, which led them to a lanterne scalier, whose each step
was twelve foot long; thence mounting up a paire of staires, they
past through and traversed above nine several rooms on a floor,
before they reached her bed-chamber; which, in the interim of the
progress of their transitory walk, was with such mutual cordialness
so unanimously aimed at, that never did the passengers of a ship
in a tedious voyage long for a favorable winde with greater uni-
formity of desire, then the blessed hearts of that amorous and
amiable couple were, without the meanest variety of a wish, in
every jot united. Nevertheless, at last they entred in it, or rather
in an alcoranal paradise, where nothing tending to the pleasure of
all the senses was wanting. The weather being a little chil and
coldish, they on a blew velvet couch sate by one another towards
a char-coale fire burning in a silver brasero, whilst in the next room
adjacent thereto, a pretty little round table of cedar-wood was a
covering for the supping of them two together. The cates prepared
for them, and a week before that time bespoke, were of the choisest
dainties and most delicious junkets, that all the territories of Italy
were able to afford, and that deservedly, for all the Romane Empire
could not produce a completer paire to taste them. In beauty she
was supream, in pedigree equal with the best, in spirit not inferiour
to any, and, in matter of affection, a great admirer of Crichtoun,
which was none of her least perfections....

Crichtoun ... by that the sun had deprest our western horizon by
one half of the quadrant of his orb, did, after supper, with his
sweet lady (whom he had by the hand) returne againe to the bed-
chamber, wherein formerly they were; and there, without losing
of time (which by unnecessary puntilios of strained civility, and
affected formalities of officious respect, is very frequently, but too
much lavished away, and heedlessly regarded, by the young

Adonises and faint-hearted initiants in the exercises of the Cytherean Academy) they barred all the ceremonies of pindarising their discourse, and sprucifying it in *à la mode* salutations, their mutual carriage shewing it self (as it were) in a meane betwixt the conjugal of man and wife, and fraternal conversation of brother and sister, in the reciprocacy of their love, transcending both, in the purity of their thoughts equal to this, and in fruition of pleasure, nothing inferior to the other; for when, after the waiting damsel had, by putting her beautiful mistris into her nocturnal dress, quite impoverished the ornaments of her that dayes wear, in robbing them of the inestimably rich treasure which they inclosed, and then performed the same office to the Lord of her Ladies affections, by laying aside the impestring bulk of his journal abiliaments, and fitting him, in the singlest manner possible, with the most genuine habit *à la Cypriana* that Cupid could devise; she, as it became an obsequious servant, and maid observant of her mistrisses directions, bidding them good night with the inarticulate voyce of an humble curtesie, locked the doors of the room behind her, and shut them both in to the reverence of one another, him to her discretion, her to his mercy, and both to the passion of each other; who then, finding themselves not only together, but alone with other, were in an instant transported both of them with an equal kinde of rapture; for as he looked on her, and saw the splendor of the beams of her bright eyes, and with what refulgency her alabaster-like skin did shine through the thin cawle of her Idalian garments, her appearance was like the antartick oriency of a western aurore, or acronick rising of the most radiant constellation of the firmament; and whilst she viewed him, and perceived the portliness of his garb, comeliness of his face, sweetness of his countenance, and majesty in his very chevelure, with the goodliness of his frame, proportion of his limbs, and symmetry in all the parts and joints of his body, which through the cobweb slenderness of his Cyllenian vestments, were represented almost in their *puris naturalibus*, his resemblance was like that of Aeneas to Dido, when she said, that he was in face and shoulders like a god; or rather to her, he seemed as to the female deities did Ganimed, when, after being carried up to heaven, he was brought into the presence of

Jupiter. Thus for a while their eloquence was mute, and all they spoke was but with the eye and hand, yet so persuasively, by vertue of the intermutual unlimitedness of their visotactil sensation, that each part and portion of the persons of either was obvious to the sight and touch of the persons of both; the visuriency of either, by ushering the tacturiency of both, made the attrectation of both consequent to the inspection of either. Here was it that passion was active, and action passive, they both being overcome by other, and each the conquerour. To speak of her hirquitalliency at the elevation of the pole of his microcosme, or of his luxurious-ness to erect a gnomon on her horizontal dyal, will perhaps be held by some to be expressions full of obscoeness, and offensive to the purity of chaste ears; yet seeing she was to be his wife, and that she could not be such without consummation of marriage, which signifieth the same thing in effect, it may be thought, as *definitiones logicae verificantur in rebus*, if the exerced act be lawful, that the diction which suppones it, can be of no great trans-gression, unless you would call it a solaecisme, or that vice in grammar which imports the copulating of the masculine with the feminine gender.

RABELAIS

BOOK I : CHAPTER 37

How Gargantua in combing his head, made the great cannon-ball fall out of his haire.

Being come out of the river of Vede, they came very shortly after to Grangousiers Castle, who waited for them with great longing. At their coming they were entertained with many congies, and cherished with embraces. Never was seen a more joyful company, for *supplementum supplementi chronicorum* saith, that Gargamelle died there with joy. For my part, truly I cannot tell, neither do I care very much for her, nor for any body else. The truth was, that Gargantua, in shifting his clothes, and combing his head with a combe (which was nine hundred foot long of the Jewish canne-measure, and whereof the teeth were great tusks of elephants, whole and entire) he made fall at every rake above seven balls of bullets, at a dozen the ball, that stuck in his haire, at the razing of the castle of the wood of Vede, which his father Grangousier seeing, thought they had been lice, and said unto him, "What, my dear sonne, hast thou brought us thus farre some short-winged hawkes of the Colledge of Montague? I did not mean that thou shouldest reside there." Then answered Ponocrates, "My soveraign Lord, think not that I have placed him in that lousie Colledge, which they call Montague. I had rather have put him amongst the grave-diggers of Sanct Innocent, so enormous is the cruelty and villany that I have known there, for the galley-slaves are far better used amongst the Moors and Tartars, the murtherers in the criminal dungeons, yea the very dogs in your house, then are the poor wretched students in the aforesaid colledge; and if I were King of Paris, the devil take me if I would not set it on fire, and burne both principal and regents, for suffering this inhumanity to be exer-cised before their eyes." Then taking up one of these bullets, he said "These are cannon-shot, which your sonne Gargantua hath lately received by the treachery of your enemies, as he was passing before the wood of Vede.

"But they have been so rewarded, that they are all destroyed in the ruine of the castle, as were the Philistines by the policy of Samson, and those whom the tower of Silohim slew, as it is written in the thirteenth of Luke. My opinion is, that we pursue them whilest the luck is on our side, for occasion hath all her haire on her forehead. When she is past, you may not recal her. She hath no tuft, whereby you can lay hold on her, for she is bald in the hind-part of her head, and never returneth again." "Truly," said Grangousier, "it shall not be at this time, for I will make you a feast this night, and bid you welcome."

This said, they made ready supper, and of extraordinary, besides his daily fare, were rosted sixteen oxen, three heifers, two and thirty calves, threescore and three fat kids, fourscore and fifteen wethers, three hundred barrow-pigs or sheats sowced in sweet

wine or must, elevenscore partridges, seven hundred snites and
woodcocks, foure hundred Loudun and Cornwal-capons, six
thousand pullets, and as many pigeons, six hundred crammed hens,
fourteen hundred leverets or young hares and rabbets, three
hundred and three buzzards, and one thousand and seven hundred
cockrels. For venison, they could not so suddenly come by it, only
eleven wilde bores, which the Abbot of Turpenay sent, and eighteen
fallow deer, which the Lord of Gramount bestowed, together with
seven score phesants, which were sent by the Lord of Essars; and
some dozens of queests, cowshots, ringdoves and woodculvers;
riverfowle, teales and awteales, bittorns, courtes, plovers, francolins,
briganders, tyrasons, young lapwings, tame ducks, shovelers, wood-
landers, herons, moore-hens, criels, storks, canepetiers, oranges
flamans, which are phaenicopters, or crimson-winged sea-fowles,
terrigoles, turkies, arbens, coots, solingeese, curlews, termagents
and water-wagtails, with a great deal of cream, curds and fresh
cheese, and store of soupe, pottages, and brewis with variety. Without doubt there was meat enough, and it was handsomly drest by
snapsauce, hotchpot and brayverjuice. Grangousiers cooks, Jenkin
Trudg-apace and Clean-glasse were very careful to fill them drink.

BOOK 2: CHAPTER 2

Of the nativity of the most dread and redoubted Pantagruel

Gargantua, at the age of foure hundred, fourescore, fourty and
foure years begat his sonne Pantagruel, upon his wife named
Badebec, daughter to the king of the Amaurots in Utopia, who
died in childe-birth, for he was so wonderfully great and lumpish,
that he could not possibly come forth into the light of the world
without thus suffocating his mother. But that we may fully understand the cause and reason of the name of Pantagruel, which at
his baptism was given him, you are to remark, that in that yeare
there was so great drought over all the countrey of Affrick, that
there past thirty and six moneths, three weeks, foure dayes, thirteen
houres, and a little more without raine, but with a heat so vehe-

ment, that the whole earth was parched and withered by it. Neither
was it more scorched and dried up with heat in the dayes of
Eliah, then it was at that time, for there was not a tree to be seen,
that had either leafe or bloom upon it. The grasse was without
verdure or greennesse, the rivers were drained, the fountaines dried
up, the poore fishes abandoned and forsaken by their proper
element, wandring and crying upon the ground most horribly.
The birds did fall down from the aire for want of moisture and
dew, wherewith to refresh them. The wolves, foxes, harts, wild-
boares, fallow-deer, hares, coneys, weesils, brocks, badgers, and
other such beasts were found dead in the fields with their mouthes
open. In respect of men, there was the pity! You should have seen
them lay out their tongues like hares, that have been run six
houres. Many did throw themselves into the wells. Others entred
within a cowes belly to be in the shade; those Homer calls Alibants.
All the countrey was idle, and could do no vertue. It was a most
lamentable case to have seen the labour of mortals in defending
themselves from the vehemencie of this horrifick drought, for
they had work enough to do to save the holy water in the churches
from being wasted; but there was such order taken by the counsel
of my Lords the Cardinals, and of our holy Father, that none did
dare to take above one lick. Yet, when any one came into the
church, you should have seen above twenty poor thirsty fellows
hang upon him that was the distributer of the water, and that
with a wide open throat, gaping for some little drop (like the rich
glutton in Luke) that might fall by, lest any thing should be lost.
O, how happy was he in that yeare, who had a coole cellar under
ground, well plenished with fresh wine!

The philosopher reports in moving the question, wherefore it
is that the sea-water is salt, that at the time when Phoebus gave
the government of his resplendent chariot to his sonne Phaeton,
the said Phaeton, unskilful in the art, and not knowing how to
keep the ecliptick line betwixt the two tropicks of the latitude of
the sunnes course, strayed out of his way, and came so near the
earth, that he dried up all the countreys that were under it, burning a great part of the heavens, which the philosophers call *via
lactea*, and the Huffsnuffs, St. James his way, although the most

coped, lofty and high-crested poets affirme that to be the place where Juno's milk fell, when she gave suck to Hercules.

The earth at that time was so excessively heated, that it fell into an enormous sweat, yea such a one as made it sweat out the sea, which is therefore salt, because all sweat is salt, and this you cannot but confesse to be true, if you will taste of your own, or of those that have the pox, when they are put into a sweating. It is all one to me. Just such another case fell out this same yeare, for on a certain Friday, when the whole people were bent upon their devotions, and had made goodly processions, with store of letanies, and faire preachings, and beseechings of God Almighty, to look down with his eye of mercy upon their miserable and disconsolate condition, there was even then visibly seen issue out of the ground great drops of water, such as fall from a puff-bagg'd man in a top sweat, and the poore hoydons began to rejoyce, as if it had been a thing very profitable unto them, for some said that there was not one drop of moisture in the aire, whence they might have any rain, and that the earth did supply the default of that. Other learned men said, that it was a showre of the antipodes, as Seneca saith in his fourth book *Quaestionum naturalium*, speaking of the source and spring of Nilus. But they were deceived, for the procession being ended, when every one went about to gather of this dew, and to drink of it with full bowles, they found that it was nothing but pickle, and the very brine of salt, more brackish in taste then the saltest water of the sea. And because in that very day Pantagruel was borne, his father gave him that name, for 'panta' in Greek is as much to say as 'all,' and 'gruel' in the Hagarene language doth signifie 'thirsty,' inferring hereby, that at his birth the whole world was a-dry and thirstie, as likewise foreseeing that he would be some day Suprem Lord and Sovereign of the thirstie Ethrappels, which was shewn to him at that very same hour by a more evident signe; for when his mother Badebec was in the bringing of him forth, and that the midwives did wait to receive him, there came first out of her belly threescore and eight tregeneers (that is, salt-sellers,) every one of them leading in a halter a mule heavy loaden with salt; after whom issued forth nine dromedaries, with great loads of gammons of bacon, and dried neats tongues on their backs. Then followed seven camels, loaded with links and chitterlins, hogs puddings and salciges. After them came out five great waines, full of leeks, garlick, onions and chibols, drawn with five and thirty strong cart horses, which was six for every one, besides the thiller. At the sight hereof the said midwives were much amazed, yet some of them said, "Lo, here is good provision, and indeed we need it, for we drink but lazily, as if our tongues walked on crutches, and not lustily like Lansman dutches. Truly, this is a good signe, there is nothing here but what is fit for us. These are the spurres of wine, that set it a going." As they were tatling thus together after their own manner of chat, behold, out comes Pantagruel, all hairie like a beare. Whereupon one of them, inspired with a prophetical spirit, said, "This will be a terrible fellow. He is borne with all his haire. He is undoubtedly to do wonderful things, and, if he live, he shall have age."

GEORGE MACKENZIE

SIR GEORGE MACKENZIE was born in Dundee in 1636, son of the 2nd Earl of Seaforth. His University career took him in turn to St. Andrews and Aberdeen, culminating in that centre of legal studies, Bourges. There he read Civil Law for three years. Fully qualified, he returned to Scotland, and became an Advocate in 1659, being re-admitted after the Restoration. His first major case came in 1661, when along with John Cunningham and others, he defended the Marquis of Argyll, accused of treason in having supported Cromwell. MacKenzie's clever defence rested on "whether passive compliance in public rebellions be punishable as treason". Unfortunately late evidence in the form of letters proved Argyll's support to have been decidedly active and the case was lost. MacKenzie's own performance however, was praised and in the same year he was promoted to Justice Depute. Following his first marriage to Elizabeth Dickson in 1662, success graced his career at the bar, and he sought to extend his influence into parliament. This he entered in 1669, cleverly opposing Lauderdale over the proposed Union of Parliaments, while pretending to support it. Elizabeth Dickson must have died shortly before this, and in 1670 MacKenzie married for the second time, on this occasion to Margaret Haliburton. The culmination of his legal career however, had to wait till 1677, when the Lord Advocate Nisbet was deposed for taking bribes, and MacKenzie rather than his arch-enemy Sir George Lockhart succeeded to the post. He also became a member of the Privy Council and began energetically to make reforms in the procedure for criminal courts. During this period of great power he was to lay for himself that reputation of "Bluidy Mac-Kenzie", eternalised by Scott's Davie Deans and Wandering Willie's

Tale. It is true that he did mercilessly prosecute many Covenanters, although his sincerely held Episcopalian and Royalist principles must go some way to alleviating his guilt. On the matter of tortures, which he did employ, it should be remembered that torture was still a recognised mode of procedure in criminal courts at this time. Nonetheless, there is clear evidence of pre-judging, and of competent lawyers for the defence suddenly being drafted on to the prosecution, as in the case of Johnson of Warriston's son, Baillie of Jerviswood. Yet MacKenzie does give the impression of being a sincere believer in a set of perhaps questionable principles (which included a belief in despotism) rather than the unprincipled rogue of popular tradition. He lost his power and position shortly after the accession of James VII, only briefly to regain them when his successor John Dalrymple proved inadequate. He refused to feign support for James's Catholicism, however, and only an uneasy truce reigned. At the time of the revolution, his Royalist principles triumphed and he was one of a minority who voted against the victorious motion of April, 1689, that James had forfeited his right to the crown. In the midst of these troubles he had still found time to inaugurate the Advocates Library. In exile it was to academic pursuits that he again returned, being welcomed by the students at Oxford. His last days were spent in Westminster. He died in May 1697 and is buried in Greyfriars' Churchyard, Edinburgh.

His major works are the Romance, *Aretina* (1660) from which I have chosen the dramatic account of Sophander's hanging and two highly rhetorical passages, suggestive of Sir Thomas Browne's influence. There followed in 1663, the *Religio Stoici*, indubitably his finest work of literature, and helpful for the historical student, when trying to understand MacKenzie's somewhat complex attitude to religion. From this I have isolated Chapter 7 "Of the Strictness of Churches". His later works are numerous and include *A Moral Essay Preferring Solitude* and *The Moral History of Frugality* (1691), but as a writer he never again matches his early promise. This opinion is borne out by Andrew Lang, who comments "It was only during his youth, when, busy as he was in his profession, he could still find or make time in abundance, that he strove to attain style in literature, and to master the arts of expression". Apart from this, critics are surprisingly silent. The first writer of a successful Scottish Prose Romance, and founder of the country's major library is passed over in silence by Wittig and warrants but a footnote in Craig.

My text is based on the first editions of *Aretina* and the *Religio Stoici*.

ARETINA

(This extract is taken from the end of Book 2. Sophander, then chief minister in Egypt, has secretly allied himself against that country with Prastus, King of Persia and the Egyptian military commander Misarites. Their plans are foiled by the heroes, Megistus and Philarites. Sophander tries to slander Megistus before the King of Egypt, but Monanthropus reveals him to be the real traitor. Further evidence to this effect is forthcoming, and Sophander is sentenced to death.)

Megistus, hearing that the king resolved to cause hang Sophander, thought, that albeit he could not beg his life, as being a traitor, yet that he would endeavour to mitigate the manner of his death, as being his old friend and patron. Whereupon both Philarites and he entreated his majesty, that he would cause cut off his head, and not hang him, as being once honoured by himself with the title of Chief Minister of State; and that it was customary amongst all nations, to punish in the least eminent way those who had been most eminent in dignity, both because the smallest punishment is greater to them, than the greatest would be to others, as also, because punishments being ordinarily inflicted, not for what was past, because that could not be re-called, but for prevention of the like by that rigour for the future; and so seing fewer great ones would probably incurre these guilts, the law needed not punish them so severely, as it did the meaner sort, who would more frequently fall in the crimes forbidden. "That maxime holds only true," answered the king, "in those crimes which degrade not a man of his honours, as in combats and private injuries, which crimes are consistent with true honour. But in treason and treachery, the committer declares himself unworthy of his honours, and consequently should not enjoy those priviledges due to them. Yet, to satisfy your desires, I am content his head be struck off, and his body buried."

At the day appointed for his execution, all the city, yea, and the nation flocked to the market-place; some to satisfie their inhumane revenge (which that circumstance of time made most unjust) others, to remark the period of humane glory; and a third sort, to glut their boundlesse curiosity. After some time so spent, Sophander appeared upon the scaffold, in his gown and night-cap, whose age and gravity drew tears from his most inveterate enemies. After he had setled himself a little, he gave the spectators this farewell.

"Gentlemen, I am by providence presented here as an emblem of unconstant grandour. I wish my case may be remarked by all, but imitated by none. I am set up as a beacon upon the rockie shoar of court-favour, that ye should not approach the place where I have splitted. I mean not that ye should all retire your selves from court, for that were impossible, seing the nation must be governed by some; and unlawfull, seing nature hath bestowed publick spirits upon some, that they might imploy them for the profit of all; but I mean, that none should thrust themselves into the crowd of minions, wherein many have perished in entring, and all have perished almost before they could retire: and that all should be so wise, as to be the last who will go to sea in such storms, and the first who will retire from them. I know many are taken with our greatnesse, but they consider not our hazard; many envie our access to our Prince, but they advert not the misinformations given in to him against us; some eye greedily our riches, but remembers not our vast expences and numerous attendants; and, on the other hand, they see the poverty of a private life, but are strangers to its contentment, and contemns its lownesse without weighing its security. Thus greatnesse, like a whore, presents her self unto us fairded, whereas chast vertue appears only in her homely habite, and, believe me, albeit ye may for a season recreate your self more ticklingly with the first, yet ye will live more contentedly with the second. O, who were lodged but one night in the breast of a grandee, to see what confusion of thoughts were there, would thereafter buy himself off from the ensnaring pleasures of that anxious life! May ye not consider that the gods who have created all things for the use of man, have made things which are most usefull and good to be most common? And so, seing they have ordained many to be governed, and but few to govern, we must conclude those who are governed to be happiest; for, if they had thought crowns and scepters as requisit for mans happiness, as were private estates and cottages, they could have made as many of the one as of the other, and created as many kingdoms as there were men to be kings in them. Yea, I believe that kings and courts were ordained, not to make happy those who lived in them, but to maintain the happinesse of those who lived remote from them. Your sleep is not interrupted, whilst we are disquieted; neither is your danger worth the noticeing, whilst ours is often inevitable. Consider the number of our competitors, the multiplicity of our businesses, our own fears, and the Princes jealousies; and you will soon conclude, that we are like poor peasants who make and sell good wine to others, but drink little or none of it our selves. Since there are so many reasons to dissuade us from being ambitious, we must conclude ambition to be a cunning sophister, which can solve all those unanswerable arguments. I remember that the Christians observe, that seing it tempted the angels, before they were corrupted with any other sin, it is no wonder it should tempt us who are but men, and already tainted with sin; and that since it was the first sin, it must necessarily be the sin we have greatest inclinations for, seing we imbrace first ordinarily that we affect most. Ambition, then, is the devils first-born, and so no wonder it claim precedency before all other vices; and as ordinarily proud men of all men have alwayes the greatest train, so pride it self of all vices hath still the maniest attendants; for it must be waited upon by covetousness, to fill its prodigal coffers; with revenge, to repair its imaginary affronts; with murder, to remove all those who stand in its way; and in fine, it is the great bellyed vice, which spanneth all the rest. Gentlemen, if I were speaking this to you, incircled with my former honours, ye might imagine I enveighed against greatness, as wishing all others to flee it, that I might share alone in it; or, if I were to live banished, ye might say that I disparaged it, because I could not retain it; but being to dye, ye may be confident that all I say are the dictates of meer ingenuity. I am now upon the brink of my grave, and can leave you nothing in legacy but my tears and precepts; which, if ye follow, may repair the great losse this nation hath suffered by me. Farewell."

Thereafter he called for Megistus, and craved him pardon for misinforming his majesty against him, and gave him privately some papers, wherein were some remarks, usefull for those who were to govern Egypt; and prophesied to him his future advancement (which was thereafter no small encouragement to Megistus) for, said he, the soul being certainly of a divine extraction, would fore-know many strange events, if it were not ignoranced by the unproportionatness of the bodily organs to such contemplations, and when it is emancipitated from the power of the body, as in feavers, death-beds, swoonings, extasies, and womens histerick passions, we see it acteth and foreseeth things extraordinary. Thereafter he recommended his friends and nephews to Megistus, and Megistus to the people, and loyalty to all of them; and so had his head struck off by the executioner, and received by Megistus.

The next morning there was this epitaph posted upon his tomb.

Here restless he doth rest, who never could
Get earth enough, till casten in this mould.

Megistus sadned exceedingly, partly by the uncertain condition of mankind, partly puzled with the thoughts of Sophanders prediction, retired to his chamber, where his landlord, a witty fellow, came presently to solace him, and related to him this story, which had occurred that same day in the city.

A young country gentleman, accustomed at home to whistle following the plough, to domineere amongst a great many countrey clowns, and to feed a kennel of dogs, was by his friends brought into the city to court a young citizen, whose beauty lay in her

coffers, and whose perfections were counted by thousands. Yet
this jet was able enough to draw straw to it, and her blacknesse did
cast a curious lustre when enambled upon gold. His friends cared
not whether she had a golden mind, seing she was a golden mine;
neither looked they to her age, seing it was a golden age. To
speak truth, such a statue fitted well such a worshipper. Being
come to the city, he was all gilded with gold, and indeed such an
harsh pill had need to be so; and ye would have sworn that his
cloathes being upon him, were another Jasons fleece, and himself
the sheep. Thus accoutred, he marched up and down the city,
dreaming that all persons were busied in viewing him, and point-
ing out his finger, asking who was that, or the other; which, a
young gallant perceiving, watched till he, holding out his finger
to a coach, to ask what a cart was that so covered, which his
servant not hearing at first, as being as busie as his master, he
asked the second time, with his finger outstretched, what was
that; to which the other gallant, making a low congie, answered,
that it was his honours finger. He admired likewise for what use
served those chests that men carried about the streets (meaning
the sedans) to which a merry bystander answered, that it was to
carry gentlemens hounds and dogs, lest else they should stray, or
be robbed by the courtiers; whereupon the youth addressed himself to the bearers, and commanded them to take in his dogs (for
the other had persuaded him, that if he spoke calmly to them that
they would think him blunt and silly) at which the bearers, thinking he spoke so, only to affront them, and knowing by his garb
that he was but a fresh-water citizen, reviled him most pitifully,
saying that the shepherds in the country were much to blame, who
suffered their sheep so to stray, and that they behoved to fleece
him; whereupon they pulled away his cloak, and had not restored
it, if his servant, who went up and down crying that his Honour
was massacred, had not amazed many people, who caused restore
him his cloak, each one swearing that what he had spoken, was
spoken out of simplicity. Home he went with his cloak lined with
this affront, and the next morning was admitted to see his mistris,
who, albeit she was not fair, yet could go fair to cheat him, and
was able to play her cards so, as that she was able to counter and

beast such a gentleman; and if they had begun the game, doubtless she had by turning up always the ace, made my gentleman
throw down his cards.

The gentlewoman being informed of his pure wit, resolved to
let him see some of hers; whereupon she commanded her maid to
put on her cloathes, and to sit in her chair, and receive the visit
for her; and withall, after the young gallant should begin to extol
her beauty above all others, that she should then ask what he
judged of her maid. All things being thus ordered, she sent to
entreat his friends, that none of them should come to her chamber
with him the first day, because she would be too bashfull if any
else were there to remark her; to which they easily condescended.

Enter Gentleman.

The gallant the next day enters, and putting his arm about
her neck, kisses his mistris loudly, fearing that else that they had
imagined that he had not kissed her at all, and thereafter tumbling
back confusedly, made another low reverence, where he lost mis-
fortunately the paper upon which his complements were written
(which he very often repeated at home to his uncle). He entreated
her to sit down in the highest chair, thinking that to be some
preferment; whereto the gentlewoman wittily answered, "Sir, the
woman should be lowest." After this debate was ended, he insisted
thus.

"Mistris, when I came first to Alexandria, I thought this city the
prettiest thing in the world, but now when I see you, I esteem
nothing of it, for I think that all our country maids, may be hand-
maids to you, whose beauty is as far preferable to theirs, as this
city is to ours." Here he stopt, hearing a horse pass by upon the
street, and called for his servants to look if that was his young
horse or not, and thereafter insisted thus, "Madam, I believe that
my father's house hath all accomplishments requisit for sweetning
the harshness of a solitary life. Only it wants such an accomplished
lady as you are, to be mistris of all." (And there he recounted to
her what choice fields for hunting, and what excellent pasturages
for herding, were there). "But Sir," replyed she, "seing we see
country gentlemen leave all these rural pleasures, pretending to
come to the city for converse, and those who are in the city leave

their well deckt chambers and sumptuous parlors, and go abroad
to recreate themselves with their friends, we may infer, that society
is preferable to all these; for, when ye come to the city, ye acknowledge it is to better your spirits; and when we go to the country,
our end is only to refresh our bodies, so that the country may be
thought as justly to cede to the city, as the soul is preferable to
the body." "O Madam, but ye could make any place happy, and
happy were the son of that father who might be husband to such
a compleat lady as ye are!" "What think you of my maid, if compared with me," said she. "I think her a beautifull young gentlewoman," quoth our gallant, "but no beauty, when compared with
you." Whereupon the mistris, who had played the maid hitherto,
did now sit down in her own chair, and commanding her waiting-
maid to stand by her, she thundred thus the poor simple gentleman.

"Sir, I admire the lesse what hath past, that I expected to hear
what I now hear; but I admire that men should lavish out so
profusely praises of what they know not. For, Sir, if we were so
simple as to believe, that your heart conceived what your tongue
brings forth, ye might rather wish us in Bedlam than in your beds;
and if we are so wise as to discern your dissimulation, ye may
conclude, that we think you as unfit to be our husbands, because
of this last, as ye might judge us unworthy to be your wives because
of the first. Wherefore, Sir, consider for the future, that albeit
women are so discreet as to connive at your dissimulation, yet they
are not so ignorant, as not to know it. Ye wrong our sex hugely,
by thinking us so simple, and your own, by making us conclude
that ye are all dissemblers. And of all vices, dissimulation is one
of the worst, because it not only is evil in it self (as being a
cheat) but likewise is an abuse of what is good, even of respect and
friendship, making them bawds to your vicious cheats. Sir, those
strings are not well tuned, which are tuned too high; and those
praises are but flatteries, which are palpable lyes. Yet, Sir, I
pardon you more than others; for, as those who shoot seldom,
must be pardoned when they shoot over, so those who complement
but unfrequently, must be pardoned, albeit they do it imprudently."

The gentleman struck dead by these thunder-bolts of wit, remained speechless, as if his soul had fled away for shame. He essayed often to speak, but his words no sooner peeped out, but smelling this reply, they retired back to their old quarter in great disorder, leaving their master helpless without them, who had been formerly but little holpen by them. "Since his own soul hath left him," said Megistus, "it is reason we leave him also." And so he went to bed.

*

(This extract is taken from the beginning of Book 4. The lovers —Philarites and Aretina; Megistus and Agapeta—are re-united. They celebrate the occasion in a lighthearted rhetorical interchange in a garden of great beauty.)

Agapeta desired them to end these complements, and that each of them would remark something in that garden, where every thing was remarkable. "And that I may begin, look how the flourish peeps out of its green palace, to behold this sweet moneth, and to smell that excellent perfume, wherewith the sun hath powdered the heads of the undergrowing hills." Aretina remarked how time had borrowed youth from an old apple-tree, to lend it to a young cherry-tree which grew not far from it, whose coat was so long worn, that it was now all in rags. "See ye not", continued she, "how it hath stood so long that it is now weary, and would willingly lie down, if the carefull gardener had not provided a staff for its age to lean upon? And yet in spight of age, ye see how its fruits do flourish, ripening alwayes as the tree grows old, and bringing seeds in their bosome wherewith to plenish the earth after they are gone, and the tree fallen." "Observe, fair ladies," said Megistus, "how these red roses blush, and these tulips grow pale, through anger to see their beauty so outstript by yours, and how these cherries, albeit they be but hard hearted creatures, yet understand their duty so well as bow downwards to do you obeisance, and would willingly throw themselvs at your feet, if their stalks did not hinder them; and how yonder pond hath drawn your picture, and placed it in its bosome, presenting it to you when ye approach,

to indicate the high value it sets upon your beauty, and concealing it when ye are gone, fearing lest any should rob it." Philarites
recommended to them, to advert, how the gods had cleared the
sky purposely that morning, that they might have the fuller view
of them; and how the grass propined their shoes with their pearly
drops, which seemed to kiss their feet in token of subjection. This
gave them occasion to laugh at one anothers pretty conceits, wherein their wanton inventions seemed to sport themselves.

*

*(This extract is taken from Book 3, that portion of the Romance,
which presents in allegorical form an account of the death of
Charles I and the events leading up to the Restoration. In this
episode, Theopemptus (Charles II) has returned to rule the
country.)*

In this senate Theopemptus is called home; not limited by conditions, as some desired (for how could subjects give law to a
king, and possibly these conditions would have been by the next
ensuing senate, declared treason, and the treaters declared traitors)
but absolutely; each endeavouring who should strengthen his pre-
rogative most.

At his Proclamation the people kindled innumerable bonfires,
as if by them they intended to purge the air of these nations,
which had been polluted with blasphemy against the gods, and
rebellion against the king formerly; or else, as if they intended to
bury in these graves and burn to ashes those cares, wherewith
they had been formerly afflicted. Their flames mounted so high,
that one might have thought that they intended to carry news of
those solemnities to heaven, and the smoke covered the towns
pend-ways, lest heaven should have discerned the extravagancies
whereof the inhabitants were guilty; for gravity was banished as an
enemy to their duty, and madnesse was judged true loyalty; the
trumpets were ecchoed by the vociferations of the people, and
those vociferations seemed to obey the summons of the trumpets;
the bells likewise kept a part with the singing multitude, so that

both bells and people did both sing and dance all at once; and
the air no sooner received these news, but it dispersed them to
all the corners of the city, and ears of the citizens, it being no
crime to be in this a talebearer; and the bullets did flee out of
the cannons, as if they intended to meet him half way. Wine was
sent in abundance to the earth, that it might drink his majesties
health also, and the glasses capreoled in the air, for joy to hear
his name. Some danced through the fire, knowing that the wine
had so much modified them, that they needed not fear burning;
and others had bonfires kindled in their faces by the wine which
they had drunk.

RELIGIO STOICI, THE VIRTUOSO OR STOICK

OF THE STRICTNESS OF CHURCHES

Most of all churches do, like coy maids, lace their bodies so strait,
that they bring on them a consumption, and will have the gates
of heaven to have been only made for themselves. And as this
nigardliness hath possest churches, so from that root hath stem'd
the churlishness of some private Christians, who will allow God
but a most inconsiderate number of these whom He hath admitted
to make up His visible church. Thus, some pastors will only admit
two or three to be guests at the Lord's table, allowing no wedding
garment, but what is of their own spinning; and others, with their
uncharitable hands, blur the names of all their acquaintances out
of the books of life, as if they were keepers of His registers and
rolls, and will only have seats kept in the church triumphant, for
three or four sisters, who are so frugal of their devotions, as to
spare them at home, to the end they may be liberal in publick.
But both these should consider, that the New Jerusalem is said to
have moe gates then one; that John, in his *Revelation*, tells us,
that numberless numbers were seen following the Lamb; and that
it is not probable, that the wise framer of the world made such a
spacious dwelling as heaven, to be inhabited by so inconsiderable

a number, whereas hell (in the geography of believed tradition) is only the small kernel of this small shell the Earth. I know, that many are called and few chosen, and that the way is strait, and few enter in at it. But we should consider, that these chosen are said to be few, in respect only of these many who are called; which is most certain, for ten parts of eleven are pagans or Mahumetans (and all are called). Of that eleventh part, many are malitious hereticks, and amongst the residue many are flagitious and publick sinners, so that albeit the greatest part of the regular members of the visible church were sav'd, yet the number would be small in comparison of these others. The body of the visible church must (like all other bodies) be compounded of contrary elements. And albeit I am not of opinion, that this body should be suffer'd to swell with humours, yet I would not wish, that it should be macerated with purgations. It's nails (though but excrementitious parts) should not be so nearly pair'd, as that the body may bleed, yet they should be so pared, as that Christians may not scratch one another. They should feed not upon blood, but milk, and they are unmannerly guests, who will not suffer others to sit at their masters table with them.

It pleases my humour to contemplat, how that albeit all religions war against one another, yet are all of them governed by the same principles, and even by these principles, in effect, which they seem to abominat. Thus, albeit the cessation of miracles be cryed down by many, yet do the most bigot relate, what miracles have been wrought by the founders of their hierarchies, and what prophesies they have oraculously pronounced. And seing all confess, that God in our dayes breaks the prosperous upon the same wheel, on whose top they did but lately triumph, making fortune adopt the opprest in their vice, why should we talk so much of the ceasing of miracles? For, doubtless, these effects are in policy as contrair to nature, as are the swimming of iron, or sweetning of rivers; or rather more, seing in the first, mans will is forc'd (without which, such revolutions could not be effectuated) whereas in the last, dull and sensual qualities are only wrested, which as they are not so excellent, so, doubtless, are not able to make such resistance, as the soul of man. Yea, I should rather think, that the world being become old, must, doubtless, be more dim-sighted (as all old things are) then formerly; and therefore God doth now present greater objects of admiration to our eyes, then He did formerly. For man is become so atheisticall, that if God did not presse His meditations with such infallible testimonies of the being of an irresistable power, He would, doubtless, shake off all resolutions of submitting. Thus, we see that in all the tract of John's *Revelations*, miracles grow still more frequent the nearer the world draweth to it's grave; and, like all other bodies, the weaker it becomes, the more subject it is to all alterations, and the less is nature able to resist. And it would appear, that if miracles were requisit at first, for the establishment of religion, even when no older religion was to cede to it, and to make an exit at it's entry, much more should miracles be necessar, for fixing any religion against the received constitutions of a previously settled church. But to prosecute my first design, it is remarkable, that albeit infallibility be not by all conceded to any militant church, yet it is assumed by all. Neither is there any church under the sun, which would not fix the name of heretick, and account him (almost) reprobat, who would refuse to acknowledge the least rational of their principles; and thus these church-men pull up the ladders from the reach of others, after they have by them scal'd the walls of preferment themselves. That church-men should immerse themselves in things civil, is thought excentrick to their sphere, even *in ordine ad spiritualia*: and yet, even the Capuchins, who are the greatest pretenders to abstract Christianity and mortification, do, of all others, dipth most in things civil. The Phanaticks enveigh against presbyterian gowns. The Presbyterian tears the episcopal lawn sleeves, and thinks them the whore of Babel's shirt. The Episcopist flouts at the popish robes, as the livery of the beast. The Antinomian emancipats his disciples from all obedience to the law. The Protestant enjoyns good works, and such are commanded, but place no merit in them. The Roman-Catholick thinks he merits in his obedience. The Phanatick believs the Lords Supper but a ceremony, though taken with very little outward respect. The Presbyterian allowes it, but will not kneel. The Episcopist kneels, but will not adore it. The Catholick mixeth adoration with his kneeling. And thus, most of all religions are made up of the same elements, albeit their asymbolick qualities predomine in some more then in others. And if that maxime hold, that *majus et minus non variant speciem*, we may pronounce all of them to be one religion.

The church, like the River Nilus, can hardly condescend where it's head lyes; and as all condescend that the church is a multitude of Christians, so joyn all their opinions, and you shall find that they will have it to have, like the multitude, many heads. But in this (as in all articles, not absolutely necessar for being saved) I make the laws of my countrey to be my creed. And that a clear decision herein is not absolutely necessar for salvation, is clear from this, that many poor clowns shall be saved, whose conscience is not able to teach their judgments how to decide this controversie, wherein so many heads have been confounded, so many have been lost, and so many have been shrewdly knockt against one another; from which flinty collisions much fire, but little light, hath ever burst forth.

God, by His omniscience, foreseeing, that it was too dazeling a sight for the pur-blind eyes of man's soul, to behold Him invironed with the rayes of divine majesty, did bestow upon us three mirrours, wherein we might contemplat Him (as we use to look upon the sun in a tub of water, not daring eye his native splendor). The one was the mirrour of the law; the second is the works of the creation, and the third is the soul of man, which He Himself hath told us, is framed after His own glorious image.

As for the first mirrour, the law; God knowing that instinct, or as we terme it, a natural conscience, were compleat digests of all that man was to observe, He did make that mirrour very little, a volumne of only two pages, but that mirrour is, of late, so mullered about, by marginal notes and commentars, that the mirrour it self is almost over-spread by them; and it is very observable, that in the holy registers, the law is still abridged, but we never see it enlarg'd. For, albeit the fundamental laws of both tables were packed up in narrow bounds, yet our Saviour sums them in these two, 'Fear the Lord thy God with all thy heart, and love thy neighbour as thy self.' And the apostle Paul, in his divine epistles, professes, that he desires to know only Christ, and Him crucified;

so that I am confident, that if our Saviour were to preach in
person once more to the world, He would enveigh against our
casuists, as much as He did against the Jewish Talmudists; for
the one, as well as the other, are equally guilty of burdening the
shoulders of weak Christians, with the unnecessary trash of
humane inventions. For I remember to have seen a late Casuist
dispute contentiously amongst his other cases, whither tobacco,
taken in the morning, did break a commanded fast or not. To
which, after a feaverish conflict, his wisdom, forsooth, returns
this oraculous answer, that if tobacco be taken at the nose, it
breaks not the fast, but if it be taken at the mouth, then it breaks
the fast. Which, because I made a collasterion betwixt the Casuists
and the Talmudists, I shall only mention out of the Talmude
(which was the Jews comment upon the law) a case exactly parallel
to this; wherein is decided, that if a man carry a burden on the
sabbath day upon both his shoulders, then he is guilty of breach of
sabbath, but that he is not guilty, if he carry it upon one shoulder.
As to my own private judgment (which I submitt to my spiritual
tutors) I think, that seeing the conscience of man is the same faculty
with the judgment, when conversant about spiritual employments
(as the word σμνειδησις, which imports a knowledge reflexive
upon a man's own self, doth abundantly evidence) that therefore,
as there are judgments of different tempers, so there are likewise
consciences of different frames, and which vary as much amongst
themselves, as natural constitutions do. And therefore, as the same
dose would prove noxious to one constitution, wherein another
would find his health, so in one and the same act, that resolution
may be saving to one conscience, which may condemn another.
For, seing God hath kindled a torch in each mans breast, by whose
flame he may see what path he should beat (in which sense it is
said, Prov. 20.27, that the understanding of man is the candle of
the Lord, and can that light mislead) and seing man must be
answerable according to what it prescrives to him, doubtless it is
fitter that he should hearken to the reiterated dictates of his conscience, than to the resolution of any School-Casuist, and that for
the same reason, that it is more rational to obey the law it self,
than the wisest lawier, who may either be deceived himself, or

have a design to deceive others. For if God hath endued man with every thing necessary for working out the work of his own salvation with fear and trembling, He hath doubtless bestowed upon him an internal touch-stone, by whose test he may discern betwixt good and evil; seing to command man to walk uprightly, and not to bestow on him eyes to see the road, were to command a blind man to walk, and to punish him if he went astray. And as the composure of man's body would be imperfect and manck, if he wanted a palate to discern betwixt the tast of what is wholsome or what is putrid, so if the soul of man were not able to know its own duty, and by the palate of a natural conscience, to difference betwixt lawfull and unlawfull, certainly the soul might be thought to be but ill appointed. Thus, beasts are by an intrinsick principle taught their duty, and do accordingly shun or follow what is convenient for them, without consulting any thing from without. And shall man be less perspicacious, or more defective then these? As also seing man is oftimes, by thousands of occasions, removed far from the assistance of chair or pulpit-informers; and in that his retiredness hath most of these cases to be resolved; it were absurd to think, that he then wants sufficiency of help for their resolution. And it is most observable in scripture, that men are oft check'd for quenching the spirit, but never for not consulting Casuists. I know it may be thought, that when the soul of man rages at sometime in a feaver of lust, revenge or some such sin, that then the conscience may rave; yet I dare say, that albeit the soul, out of an inordinat desire to enjoy its own pleasures, may set its invention a work, to palliat the sinfulness of what it desires; yet by some secret knell, the conscience sounds still its reproof. And I dare say, that never man erred without a check from his conscience; nor that ever any sinned, after an approbation obtained from his conscience of what he was about. And when we assent to these doctors, is it not because our consciences, or our judgments (which are the same) assent to what they inform? Which evidences, that our consciences are more to be believed then they, by that rule, *propter quod unumquodq, est tale* etc. But to convince us of the folly of our addresses to these doctors, it may, and often doth fall out, that that may be a sin in me, which a Casuist pronounces to be none; as, if my breast did suggest to me, that it were a sin to buy church-lands, if there-after I did buy them, it were doubtless a sin, albeit my doctors, following the canons of their particular church, assured me, that the sale of church-lands were no sin in it self. I am confident then, that this Casuist-divinity hath taken its rise from the desire church-men had to know the mysterie of each man's breast, and to the end, nothing of import might be undertaken without consulting their cell; per-suading men, that *in ordine ad spiritualia*, their consciences, and consequently their salvation, may be interested in every civil affair. And to confirm this, it is most observable, that this trade is most used by Jesuits and innovators, who desire to know all intrigues and subvert all states, whereas the primitive church knew no such divinity, neither hath its doctors left any such volumns.

It may be urged, that seing the conscience is but a reflex act of the judgment, that as the judgment is an unsure guid, the con-science cannot pretend to be infallible; and that the one as well as the other, is tutor'd by the fallacious principles of sense and custom. And I my self have seen my lands-lady in France, as much troubled in conscience for giving us flesh to eat in Lent, as if she had cast out the flesh of a Christian to be devoured by dogs; and so atheisme may attribute to custom, these inclinations where-by we are acted on to believe a deity; and may tell us, that the Mahumetans find themselves as much prickt in conscience, for transgressing their prophets canons, as we for offending against the moral law. And thus the adoring of a deity might have at first been brooded in the council-chamber of a statesmans head, and yet might have been at that time, by the vulgar, and thereafter by the wisest pates, worshipped with profound respects. Yet if we pry narrowly into this conceit, we shall find in it something of instinct, previous to all forgeries possible. For, what was it (I pray you) which encouraged, or suggested to these politicians, that such a thing as the deity might be dissembled to their people? For their imposing that cheat, presupposed some pre-existing notion of it. Or, how entred that fancie first in their wild heads? Or how could so many contemporary and yet far distant legislators fall upon the same thoughts, especialy it being so remote from sense;

and for framing of which idea, their experience could never furnish a pattern? Conscience then must be something else then the fumes of melancholy, or capricio's of fancie, for else roaring gallants, who are little troubled, or can easily conquer all other fancies, would not be so haunted by these pricking pangs, which, if they were not infallibly divine, behooved to be meerly ridiculous, and to want all support from reason or experience.

There is another fyle of cases of conscience, which is a cadet of that same family; and these are such cases as were the brood of these late times, which, like insects and unclean creatures, may be said *generari ex putri materia*; an instance whereof was that famous sister, who ask'd if she was oblidg'd to execute her catt for killing a mouse upon the sabbath. This was a theology, taught by old dotting wives, and studied by state-expectants, who, to gain applause, and in hope to mount preferment's sadle, made use of this gilded stirrop. I shall not inveigh against this foppery, seing it hath not possest mens conceit so long, as to have prescrived the tittle of divinity; but, like a meteor, which because it is fixt to no orbe, and is but a mass of inflamed vapours, doth therefore disappear immediatly, how soon its substance flashes out; and its ashes are now entomb'd in the same clay with its brother twain, that pious Non-sense, wherein God Almighty was treated with in familiar and not in superiour.

SAMUEL RUTHERFORD

SAMUEL RUTHERFORD was born about 1600 at Nisbet, a village in Renfrewshire. After attending the Grammar School in Jedburgh, he went to Edinburgh University, graduating M.A. in 1621. Two years later he became Regent of Humanity there, but in 1625, gave up the post due to some indiscretion reputedly connected with his marriage to Eupham Hamilton. He then studied theology under the calvinist, Andrew Ramsay, becoming minister of Anwoth in Kirkcudbrightshire in 1627. There, after a long illness, his first wife died. Despite this, Rutherford came to enjoy his ministry there, making many friends, notable among whom was Marion McNaught, wife of Kirkcudbright's provost, William Fullerton. But the struggle over episcopacy, found Rutherford strongly opposed to any increase in government by bishops. Due to this and a recent book of his criticising Arminianism, he was tried by a Church court in 1636 and sentenced to be confined within the town of Aberdeen. This imprisonment lasted eighteen months and during it Rutherford composed 220 of his 365 letters. On his return the Covenanting party viewed him as too talented a preacher to remain buried in Anwoth. Reluctantly he took up the post of Professor in Divinity at New College, St. Andrews and later was one of the five ministers, chosen to attend the Westminster Assembly. After his return from this Assembly he married his second wife, Jean McMath, a match which produced seven children, only one of whom outlived their father. Rutherford's later years were not without trials. He was opposed to the more moderate Resolutioners on the problem of Charles II and the Covenant, a stand, which estranged him from many of his closest friends. Then, on the Restoration of Charles, his political work, *Lex Rex*, with its comment that the power to elect a King lay with the people alone, became regarded as heretical, and was publicly burned at the Cross of Edinburgh. In March 1661, Rutherford died, experiencing, it is reported, great joy at the thought of at last "crossing the threshold" to his Maker.

I have chosen from his Letters one to Marion McNaught, showing Rutherford's misery at his imprisonment, along with his deep friendship for the Provost's wife. Against this may be set the tones of forceful exhortation addressed to the backsliding Laird of Cally and the more generally philosophical themes reserved for Alexander of Knockgray. The letters were and have remained his most popular literary contribution, for the *Lex Rex*, after its moment of notoriety has sunk back into oblivion. Of the contributions made by Rutherford to ecclesiastical controversy, mention should be made of, *A Peaceable and Temperate Plea for Pauls Presbytery* (1642); *The Due Right of Presbyteries* (1644); *The Divine Right of Church Government and Excommunication* (1646); *Survey of the Spiritual Antichrist* (1648).

The charms of Rutherford's letters are many, and the basis of this charm is in many cases non-literary. Robert Gilmour, in *Samuel Rutherford, a Study*, joins together some of the questions asked by earlier and later commentators, "What is it that draws the reader so irresistibly to these old epistles? Is it their style, which, often hasty and ragged, is also sometimes almost classical in its beauty? Or their subject matter, for they certainly deal with the realities and not with the superficialities of the spiritual life? Or is it their intensity of feeling, their soul-subduing earnestness?" He concludes by arguing for a transcendant synthesizing force, based on the writer's mystical desire to see "one Face, which is yet unseen".

My text is based on that of the first edition of Rutherford's letters, the *Joshua Redivivus* of 1664.

JOSHUA REDIVIVUS or MR. RUTHERFORD'S LETTERS

TO MARION MCNAUGHT

Dearly beloved in our Lord Jesus Christ.

Grace, mercy and peace be to you. Few know the heart of a stranger and prisoner. I am in the hands of mine enemies. I would honest and lawfull means were essayed for bringing me home to my charge, now when Mr. A.R. and Mr. H.R. are restored. It concerneth you of Galloway most, to use supplications and addresses for this purpose, and try if by fair means I can be brought back again. As for liberty, without I be restored to my flock, it is little to me, for my silence is my greatest prison. However it be, I wait for the Lord; I hope not to rot in my sufferings. Lord give me submission to wait on; my heart is sad that my dayes flee away and I doe no service to my Lord in his house, now when his harvest and the souls of perishing people require it; but his ways are not like my wayes, neither can I finde him out. O that he would shine upon my darkness and bring forth my morning light from under the thick cloud, that men have spread over me! O that the Almighty would lay my cause in a ballance and weigh me, if my soul was not taken up, when others were sleeping, how to have Christ betrothed with a Bride in that part of the land! But that day that my mouth was most unjustly and cruelly closed, the bloom fell off my branches, and my joy did cast the flower. Howbeit I have been casting my self under Christ's feet, and wrestling to beleeve under a hidden and covered Lord; yet my fainting cometh before I eat, and my faith hath bowed with the sore cast, and under this almost insupportable weight. O that it break not! I dare not say, that the Lord hath put out my candle, and hath casten water upon my poor coal, and broken the stakes of my tabernacle, but I have tasted bitterness and eaten gall and wormwood, since that day, my Master laid bonds upon me to speak no more. I speak not this, because the Lord is uncouth to me, but because beholders, that stand on dry land, see not my sea-storm. The witnesses of my cross are but strangers to my sad dayes and nights. O that Christ would let me alone and speak love to me and come home to me and bring summer with him! O that I might preach his beauty and glory as once I did, before my clay-tent be removed to darkness, and that I might lift Christ off the ground and my branches might be watered with the dew of God, and my joy in his work might grow green again and bud and send out a flower! But I am but a short sighted creature and my candle casteth not light afar off. He knoweth all that is done to me, how that when I had but one joy and no more, and one green flower, that I esteemed to be my garland, he came in one hour and dried up my flower at the root, and took away mine onely eye, and mine onely one crown and garland. What can I say? Surely my guiltiness hath been remembered before him, and he was seeking to take down my sails and to land the flower of my delights and to let it lie on the coast like an old broken ship, that is no more for the sea. But I praise him for this wailed stroke; I welcome this furnace. God's wisdom made choice of it for me, and it must be best because it was his choice. O that I may wait for him till the morning of this benighted Kirk break out! This poor afflicted Kirk had a fair morning, but her night came upon her before her noonday, and she was like a traveller, forced to take house in the morning of his journey: and now her adversaries are the chief men in the land, her wayes mourn, her gates languish, her children sigh for bread, and there is none to be instant with the Lord, that he would come again to his house, and dry the face of his weeping spouse, and comfort Zion's mourners, who are waiting for him. I know, he shall make corn to grow upon the top of his withered mount Zion again. Remember my bonds and forget me not. Oh that my Lord would bring me again amongst you, with abundance of the Gospel of Christ! But O that I may set down my desires, where my Lord biddeth me! Remember my love in the Lord to your husband (God make him faithfull to Christ) and my blessing to your three children. Faint not in prayer for this Kirk. Desire my people not to receive a stranger and intruder upon my ministery. Let me stand in that right and station, that my Lord Jesus gave me. Grace, grace be with you.

Yours in his sweet Lord,

Aberd. 1637.   and Master, S.R.

TO THE LAIRD OF CALLY

Much honoured Sir.

Grace, mercy and peace be to you. I long to hear how your soul prospereth. I have that confidence, that your soul mindeth Christ and salvation. I beseech you in the Lord, give more pains and diligence to fetch heaven, then the countrey-sort of lazie professors, who think their own faith and their own godliness, because it is their own, best; and content themselves with a coldrife custom and course, with a resolution to summer and winter in that sort of profession, that the multitude and the times favour most, and are still shaping and clipping and carving their faith, according as it may best stand with their summer-sun and a whole skin; and so breath out both hot and cold in God's matters, according to the course of the times. This is their compass they sail toward heaven by, in stead of a better. Worthy and dear Sir, separate your self from such, and bend your self to the utmost of your strength and breath, in running fast for salvation; and in taking Christ's Kingdom, use violence. It cost Christ and all his followers sharp showers and hot sweats, ere they won to the top of the mountain. But still our soft nature would have heaven coming to our bed-side, when we are sleeping, and lying down with us, that we might goe to heaven in warm clothes, but all that came there found wet feet by the way, and sharp storms, that did take the hide off their face, and found to's and fro's and up's and down's, and many enemies by the way. It is impossible, a man can take his lusts to heaven with him. Such wares as these will not be welcome there. O how loath are we to forgoe our packalds and burdens, that hinder us to run our race with patience! It is no small work to displease and anger nature, that we may please God. O if it be hard to win one foot or half an inch, out of our own will, out of our own wit, out of our own ease and worldly lusts, and so to deny our self, and to say, "It is not I but Christ, not I but grace, not I but God's glory, not I but God's love constraining me, not I but the Lord's word, not I but Christ's commanding power as King in me!" O what pains, and what a death is it to nature, to turn 'me, my self, my lust, my ease, my credit,' over in, 'my Lord, my Saviour, my King and my God, my Lord's will, my Lord's grace!' But alas, that idol, that whorish creature, 'my self,' is the master-idol we all bow to. What made Evah miscarry and what hurried her headlong upon the forbidden fruit, but that wretched thing, 'her self'? What drew that brother-murtherer to kill Abel? That wilde 'himself.' What drove the old world on to corrupt their wayes? Who but 'themselves,' and their own pleasure? What was the cause of Solomon's falling into idolatry, and multiplying of strange wives? What but 'himself,' whom he would rather pleasure then God? What was the hook that took David, and snared him first in adultery, but his self-lust; and then in murther, but his self-credit and self-honour? What led Peter on to deny his Lord? Was it not a piece of himself, and self-love to a whole skin? What made Judas sell his Master for 30 pieces of money, but a piece of self-love, idolizing of avaritious self? What made Demas to goe off the way of the Gospel, to embrace this present world? Even self love and love of gain for himself. Every man blameth the devil for his sins, but the great devil, the house-devil of every man, the house-devil that eateth and lieth in every man's bosom, is that idol that killeth all, 'himself.' O blessed are they, who can deny themselves, and put Christ in the room of themselves! O would to the Lord, I had not a 'my self,' but Christ; nor a 'my lust,' but Christ; nor a 'my ease,' but Christ; nor a 'my honour,' but Christ! O sweet word, Gal. 2:20, "I live no more, but Christ liveth in me!" O if every one would put away himself, his own self, his own ease, his own pleasure, his own credit and his own twenty things, his own hundred things, that he setteth up as idols above Christ! Dear Sir, I know ye will be looking back to your old self, and to your self-lust and self-idol, that ye set up in the lusts of youth, above Christ. Worthy Sir, pardon this my freedom of love. God

is my witness, that it is out of an earnest desire after your soul's
eternal welfare, that I use this freedom of speech. Your sun I know
is lower, and your evening-skie and sun-setting nearer, then when
I saw you last. Strive to end your task before night, and to make
Christ your-self, and to acquaint your love and your heart with
the Lord. Stand now by Christ and his truth, when so many fail
foully and are false to him. I hope ye love him and his truth. Let
me have power with you to confirm you in him. I think more of
my Lord's sweet cross then of a crown of gold, and a free Kingdom lying to it. Sir, I remember you in my prayers to the Lord,
according to my promise. Help me with your prayers, that our
Lord would be pleased to bring me amongst you again, with the
Gospel of Christ. Grace, grace be with you.

Yours in his sweetest Lord
and Master, S.R.

Aberd. 1637

TO ALEXANDER GORDON OF KNOCKGRAY

Dear Brother,

Grace, mercy and peace be to you. There is no question but
our mother-church hath a father and that she shall not die without an heir, that her enemies shall not make mount Zion their
heritage. We see, whethersoever Zion's enemies goe, suppose they
dig many miles under the ground, yet our Lord findeth them out,
and he hath vengeances laid up in store for them, and the poor
and needy shall not alwayes be forgotten. Our hope was droup-
ing and withering, and man was saying, "what can God make
out of the old dry bones of this buried Kirk?" The Prelats and
their followers were a grave above us. It is like our Lord is to
open our graves and purposeth to cause his two slain witnesses
rise the third day. O how long wait I to hear our weeping Lord
Jesus sing again and triumph and rejoyce and divide the spoil!
I finde it hard work to beleeve, when the course of providence
goeth cross-wayes to our faith, and when misted souls in a dark
night cannot know east by west, and our sea compass seemeth

to fail us. Every man is a beleever in day light. A fair day seemeth to be made all of faith and hope. What a trial of gold is it, to smoke it a little above the fire? But to keep gold perfect yellow-coloured amidst the flames, and to be turned from vessel to vessels, and yet to cause our furnace sound and speak and cry the praises of the Lord, is another matter. I know, my Lord made me not for fire, howbeit he hath fitted me in some measure for the fire. I bless his high name, that I wax not pale, neither have I lost the colour of gold, and that his fire hath made me somewhat thin, and that my Lord may pour me in any vessel he pleaseth. For a small wager, I may justly quite my part of this world's laughter, and give up with time, and cast out with the pleasures of this world. I know a man, who wondered to see any in this life laugh and sport. Surely our Lord seeketh this of us, as to any rejoycing in present perishing things. I see above all things, and that we may sit down and fold legs and arms, and stretch our selves upon Christ, and laugh at the feathers, that children are chasing here. For I think the men of this world like children in a dangerous storm in the sea, that play and make sport with the white foam of the waves thereof, coming in to sink and drown them. So are men making fool's sports with the white pleasures of a stormy world, that will sink them. But alas, what have we to doe with their sports that they make! If Solomon said of laughter that it was madness, what may we say of this world's laughing and sporting themselves with gold and silver and honours and court and broad large conquests, but that they are poor souls, in the height and rage of a fever gone mad? Then a straw, a fig for all created sports and rejoycing out of Christ. Nay, I think, that this world at it's prime and perfection, when it is come to the top of it's excellency, and to the bloom, might be bought with an half-penny, and that it would scarce weigh the worth of a drink of water. There is nothing better then to esteem it our crucified idol, that is dead and slain, as Paul did; Gal. 6, 14. Then let pleasures be crucified, and riches be crucified, and court and honour be crucified, and since the Apostle saith, the world is crucified to him, we may put this world to the hanged man's doom and to the gallowes; and who will give much for a hanged man? And as little should we give for a hanged and crucified world. Yet what a sweet smell hath this dead carrion, to many fools in the world? And how many wooers and suiters findeth this hanged carrion? Fools are pulling it off the gallowes and contending for it. O when shall we learn to be mortified men, and to have our fill of these things, that have but their short summer-quarter of this life! If we saw our father's house, and that great and fair citie, the new Jerusalem, which is up above sun and moon, we would cry to be over the water, and to be carried in Christ's arms out of this borrowed prison. Grace, grace be with you.

Yours in his sweet Lord

Aberd. 1637   Jesus. S.R.

TRACTS ON THE SUPERNATURAL

LITTLE is known of George Sinclair until he became Professor of Philosophy at Glasgow University in 1654, although on the title page of his *Ars Nova*, he does describe himself as "Scoto Lothiani". He held his professorship till 1666, when he resigned after refusing to comply with the increased Episcopal Government in Scotland. For a long time however, he had been interested in physics and especially in problems involving water. On leaving the academic profession, he became a practical engineer and was employed by Sir James Hope and others in this capacity. In 1670 he was employed by the magistrates of Edinburgh to superintend the introduction of water from Comiston into the city, while it is also known, that he was one of the first men to use a barometer in measuring heights and depths. His major technical works are the *Ars Nova* (1669), *The Principles of Astronomy and Navigation* (1688) and the *Hydrostaticks* (1672). The last of these was powerfully attacked by James Gregory, Professor of Mathematics at St. Andrews, using the pseudonym of "Patrick Mather, archbedal to the University". Despite a number of obvious errors, Sinclair's work did make a significant contribution to the problems of coal-beds and their drainage. Certainly, Sinclair's interests had now become more fixedly scientific than they had earlier been. After the Revolution, then, it came as little surprise, when he was appointed to the Chair of Mathematics in Glasgow University, a post which had been allowed to lapse for lack of money. Sinclair died in 1696.

None of Sinclair's technical treatises could possibly find a place in this volume. In the *Hydrostaticks*, however, there is one passage dealing with the practices of the witches of Glenluce, and reflecting yet another aspect of the professor's manysided personality. His interest in the supernatural led him to collect into one volume, various accounts of otherworldly experiences, ranging from the supposed prophecy to James IV before Flodden to the witchcraft trials of his own day. Although the work, *Satans Invisible World Discovered*, is little known to-day, it enjoyed an immense popularity in the late seventeenth and early eighteenth centuries. As Sinclair often cites his authorities directly, his own clear style is not always in evidence. The selected account of the Flodden prophecy and the strange tale of the Colonel and his deceased friend, the Major, however, do not fall into this category. Here, Sinclair is throughout the reporter, effectively creating the necessary atmosphere of mystery and masterfully holding his reader's attention (and credulity) till the end. My text is based on the first edition of 1685.

The other author considered in this section is Robert Kirk, youngest son of James Kirk, the minister at Aberfoyle. Born in Aberfoyle about 1641, he attended Edinburgh University and graduated M.A. in 1661. His lecture notes at this time prove him to have been deeply interested in Neoplatonism. Already too, magic seems to have intrigued him for they are covered with cabalistic signs. By 1664 he had become minister at Balquhidder, then accepted his father's old charge in 1685. There he continued till his death in 1692. Married twice, his chief claim to fame lies in having been the first person to complete a translation of all the Psalms into Gaelic. Working night and day, he managed to finish his *Psalma Dhaibhidh an Meacrachd*, in 1689, just before the Synod of Argyle's rival version was ready for the press. His interest in Celtic studies also is reflected in *The Secret Common-Wealth*, from which the present selection is drawn. More philosophical in his approach, than Sinclair, the two provide an interesting contrast in style and approach to closely related themes. My text is based on La. III. 551 (Edinburgh University Library). The best edition is that by Mario Rossi in *Il Cappellano delle Fate* (Naples, 1964). Rossi also provides a detailed biography and an extensive introduction.

SATANS INVISIBLE WORLD DISCOVERED

by George Sinclair

RELATION VII

An Apparition to King James the fourth, and his Courtiers, in the Kirk of Lithgow.

While the King stayed at Lithgow, attending the gathering of his armie, which was defeat at Flowdon, being full of cares and perplexity, he went into the Church of Saint Michael, to hear evening-song, as then it was called. While he was at his devotion, an ancient man came in, his amber coloured hair hanging down upon his shoulders, his forehead high, and inclining to baldness, his garments of azure colour, somewhat long, girded about with a towel or table-napkin, of a comely and very reverend aspect. Having enquired for the King, he intruded himself into the prease, passing through, till he came to him. With a clownish simplicity, leaning over the Canons-seat, where the King sate, "Sir," said he, "I am sent hither to entreat you, to delay your expedition for this time, and to proceed no further in your intended journey; for if you do, you shal not prosper in your interprise, nor any of your followers. I am further charged to warn you, not to use the aquaintance, company or counsel of women, as you tender your honour, life and estate." After this warning, he withdrew himself back again into the prease.

When Service was ended, the King enquired earnestly for him, but he could be no where found, neither could any of the bystanders (of whom diverse did narrowly observe him, resolving afterwards to have discoursed with him) feel or perceive how, when or where he passed from them, having in a manner vanished in their hands.

RELATION VIII

*Anent the Major who returned from Death, to tell the Captain,
whether there was a God or not.*

Concerning the apparition of the ghost of Major George Syden-
ham (late of Dulverton in the county of Somerset) to Captain
William Dyke (late of Skilgate in this county also, and now likewise deceased) be pleased to take the relation of it, from a worthy
and learned gentleman, Doctor Thomas Dyke, a near kinsmans of
the Captains, thus. Shortly after the Majors death, the Doctor was
desired to come to the house to take care of a child, that was sick
there, and in his way thither he called on the Captain, who was
very willing to wait on him to the place; because he must, as he
said, have gone thither that night, though he had not met with
so encouraging an opportunity. After their arrival there at the
house, and the civility of the people shewn them in that entertainment, they were seasonably conducted to their lodging, which they
desired might be together in the same bed; where after they had
lyen a while, the Captain knockt, and bids the servant bring him
two of the largest and bigest candles lighted, which he could get.
Whereupon the Doctor enquires what he meant by this. The Captain answers, "You know cusin, what disputs my Major and I
have had touching the Beeing of God, and the Immortality of the
Soul, in which points, we could never yet be resolved, though we
so much sought for and desired it. And therefore it was at length
fully agreed between us, that he of us who dyed first, should
the third night after his funeral, between the hours of twelve and
one, come to the little house which is here in the garden, and
there give a full account to the surviver, touching these matters,
who should be sure to be present there at the set time, and so
receive a full satisfaction. And this," says the Captain, "is the very
night, and I am come on purpose to fulfill my promise."

The Doctor dissuaded him, minding him of the danger of following strange counsels, for which he could have no warrant, and
that the Devil might by some cunning device make such an advan-

tage of this rash attempt, as might work his utter ruine. The Captain replies, that he had solemnly engaged, and that nothing should discourage him. And adds, that if the Doctor would wake a while with him, he would thank him; if not, he might compose himself to rest. But for his own part he was resolved to watch, that he might be sure to be present at the hour appointed. To that purpose, he sets his watch by him, and as soon as he perceived by it, that it was half an hour past 11, he rises, and taking a candle in each hand goes out by a back door, of which he had before gotten the key, and walks into the garden-house, where he continued two hours and a half, and at his return declared, that he neither saw nor heard any thing more than what was usual. "But I know," said he, "that my Major would surely have come, had he been able."

About six weeks after, the Captain rides to Eaton to place his son a scholar there, when the Doctor went thither with him. They lodged there at an Inn, the sign whereof was the Christopher, and tarried two or three nights, not lying together now as before at Dulverton, but in two several chambers. The morning before they went thence, the Captain stayed in his chamber longer than he was wont to do, before he called upon the Doctor. At length he comes into the Doctors chamber, but in a visage and form much differing from himself, with his hair and eyes staring, and his whole body shaking and trembling. Whereat the Doctor wondering, presently demanded, "What is the matter, cousin Captain?" The Captain replies, "I have seen my Major." At which, the Doctor seeming to smile, the Captain confirms it, saying, "If ever I saw him in my life, I saw him but now." And then he related to the Doctor what had passed thus.

"This morning after it was light, some one comes to my bed-side, and suddenly drawing back the curtains, calls 'Captain, Captain,' (which was the term of familiarity that the Major used to call the Captain by) to whom I replied, 'What, my Major?'. To which he returns, 'I could not come at the time appointed, but I am now come to tell you, that there is God and a very just and terrible one, and if you do not turn over a new leaf (the very expression, as by the Doctor punctually remembred) you shall find it so.' " The Captain proceeded. "On the table by, there lay a sword, which the Major had formerly given me. Now after the apparition had walked a turn or two about the chamber, he took up the sword, drew it, and finding it not so clean and bright as it ought, 'Captain, Captain,' says he, 'this sword did not use to be kept after this manner, when it was mine.' After which words, he presently disappeared."

The Captain was not only throughly persuaded of what he had thus seen and heard, but was from that time observed to be very much affected with it. And the humour, which before in him was brisk and jovial, was then strangely altered. Insomuch as very little meat would pass down with him at dinner, though at the taking leave of their friends, there was a very handsome treat provided. Yea, it was observed, that what the Captain had thus seen and heard, had a more lasting influence on him, and it was judged by those who were well acquainted with his conversation, that the remembrance of the passage stuck closs to him, and that those words of his dead friend were frequently sounding fresh in his ears, during the remainder of his life, which was about two years.

THE SECRET COMMON-WEALTH

by Robert Kirk

CHAPTER I: OF THE SUBTERRANEAN INHABITANTS

These sith's or fairies, they call sluaghmaith or the good people: (it would seem, to prevent the dint of their ill attempts, for the Irish use to bless all they fear harme of) and are said to be of a midle nature betwixt man and angell (as were daemons thought to be of old); of intelligent studious spirits and light changable bodies (lik those called astrall) somewhat of the nature of a condens'd cloud, and best seen in twilight. These bodies be so plyable thorough the subtilty of the spirits, that agitate them, that they can make them appeare or disappear at pleasure. Some have bodies or vehicles so spungious, thin and defecate, that they are fed by only sucking into some fine spirituous liquor that pierce like pure air and oyl. Others feed more gross on the foyson or substance of cornes and liquors, or on corne itselfe, that grows on the surface of the earth; which these fairies steall away, partly invisible, partly preying on the grain as do crows and mice. Wherfore in this sam age they are somtimes heard to bake bread, strike hammers, and to do such like services within the litle hillocks, where they most haunt. Som whereof of old befor the gospel dispell'd paganism, and in som barbarous places at yett, enter houses after all are at rest and set the kitchins in order, cleansing all the vessells. Such drudgs goe under the name of Brownies. When we have plentie, they have scarcity at their homes, and on the contrarie, (for they are not impowered to catch as much prey everie where as they please). Their robberies notwithstanding, oftimes occasione great ricks of corn not to bleed so well (as they call it) or prove so copious by verie far as was expected by the owner.

Their bodies of congealed air are som times carried aloft, other whiles grovell in different shapes, and enter in anie cranie or cleft of the earth (where air enters) to their ordinary dwellings; the earth being full of cavities and cells, and their being no place or creature but is supposed to have other animals (greater or lesser) living in or upon it, as inhabitants; and no such thing as a pure wilderness in the whol universe.

Wee then (the more terrestriall kind) having now so numerous-lie planted all countreyes, do labour for that abstruse people, as well as for our selves. Albeit when severall countreys were unin-habited by us, these had their easy tillage, above ground as we now, the print of whose furrowes do yet remaine to be seen on the shoulders of very high hills, which was don when the Cham-pain ground was wood and forrest.

They remove to other lodgings at the begining of each quarter of the year, so traversing till doomsday, being impatient of stay-ing in on place, and finding som ease by sojourning and change-ing habitations. Their chamaeleon-like bodies swim in the air, neer the earth with bagg and bagadge. And at such revolution of time, seers or men of the second sight (females being but seldom so qualified) have verie terrifying encounters with them, even on high-wayes, who therefor usually shune to travell abroad at these four seasones of the year, and thereby have made it a custom to this day among the Scotish-Irish, to keep church duly everie first Sunday of the quarter, to sene or hallow themselves, their corns and cattell, from the shots and stealth of these wandering tribes. And many of these superstitious people will not bee seen in church again till the nixt quarter begin, as if no dutie were to be learned or don by them, but all the use of worship and sermons were to save them from those arrowes that fly in the dark.

They are distributed in tribes and orders; and have children, nurses, marriages, deaths and burials, in appearance even as wee, (unless they so do for a mock-show, or to prognosticate som such things to be among us).

They are clearly seen by these men of the second sight to eat at funerals, banqueetts. Hence many of the Scotish-Irish will not tast meat at those meetings, least they have communion with, or be poysoned by them. So are they seen to carry the bier or coffin with the corps, among the midle-earth men to the grave. Some men of that exalted sight (whither by art or nature) have told me, they have seen at those meetings a double man, or the shape of the same man in two places; that is, a superterranean and a sub-terranean inhabitant perfectly resembling one another in all points, whom he notwithstanding could easily distinguish one from another by some secret tockens and operations, and so goe to speake to the man his neighbour and familiar, passing by the apparition or resemblance of him. They avouch that every element and different state of being have animals resembling those of an-other element, as there be fishes sometimes caught at sea, resembling monks of late order, in all their hoods and dresses, so as the Roman invention of good and bad daemons, and guardian angells particularly assigned, is call'd by them an ignorant mistake sprung only from this originall. They call this reflex-man a coimjmeadh or co-walker, every way like the man, as a twin-brother and companion, haunting him as his shadow and is oft seen and known among men (resembling the originall) both befor and after the originall is dead; and was els often seen of old to enter a house, by which the people knew that the person of that liknes was to visit them within a few dayes. This copy, eccho or living picture goes at last to his own herd. It accompanied that person so long and frequently, for ends best known to itselfe, whit(h)er to guard him from the secret assaults of som of its own folks, or only as a sportful ape to counterfeit all his actions. However, the stories of old witches prove beyond contradiction, that all sorts of spirits, which assume light aery bodies, or crazed bodies coacted by forrein spirits, seem to have som pleasure (at least to assuage som pain or melancholy) by frisking and capering like satyrs, or whistling and shreeching (like unluckly birds) in their unhallowed synagogues and sabbaths. If invited and earnestly required, these companions make them selves known and familiar to men, otherwises, being in a different state and element, they neither can nor will easily converse with them. They avouch that a heluo or great eater hath a voracious elve to be his attender called geirt coimitheth, a joynt-eater or just-halver, feeding on the pith and quintessence of what the man eats, and that therefore he continues lean like a hawke or heron, notwithstanding his devouring appetite. Yet it would seem they convey that substance elswhere, for these subterraneans eat but litle in their dwellings, their food being exactly clean and served up by pleasant children, like inchanted puppets. What food they extract from us is convey'd to their homes by secret pathes, as some skilfull women doe the pith of milk from their neighbours cows, into their own cheishold, thorow a hair-tedder, at a great distance by art magic, or by drawing a spickot fastned in a post, which will bring milk as far off as a bull will be heard to roar. The cheise made of the remaining milk of a cow, thus strain'd, will swim in water like cork. The method they take to recover their milk is a bitter chyding of the suspected inchanters, charging them by a counter-charme to give them back their own, in God or their masters name. But a litle of the mothers dung stroakt on the calves mouth befor it suck any does prevent this theft.

Their apparell and speech is like that of the people and countrey under which they live. So are they seen to wear plaids and varie-

gated garments in the high-lands of Scotland and suanochs here-
tofore in Ireland. They speak but litle, and that by way of whistling, clear, not rough. The verie devils conjured in any countrey,
doe answer in the language of the place. Yet sometimes these subterraneans speak more distinctly then at other times. Their women
are said to spin verie fine, to dye, to tissue and embroyder, but
whither it be as manual operatione of substantiall refin'd stuffs with
apt and solid instruments, or only curious cob-webs, impalpable
rainbows, and a phantastic imitatione of the actiones of more terrestriall mortals, since it transcended all the senses of the seer to
discern whither, I leave to conjectur as I found it.

ANONYMOUS

THE SCOTCH PRESBYTERIAN ELOQUENCE

In 1690 the Presbyterian system of Church government was restored in Scotland. It is seldom realised that this involved depriving more than half of the ministers of their charges, a much larger number than that involved, when James VI revived episcopacy. (See Donaldson *Charles II and James VII*, pp 365-6). Much bitterness ensued and the next decade was characterised by an abnormally large number of pamphlets, the vast majority of which considered the relative merits of episcopacy and presbytery. At the higher level of argument one has the learned work of John Sage, *The Principles of the Cyprianic Age, with regard to Episcopal Power and Jurisdiction, 1695* countered by Gilbert Rule's *The Cyprianick Bishop examined*. Our selection is taken from a more vicious and more popular tract, *The Scotch Presbyterian Eloquence*, the first edition of which appeared in 1692. Opening with a mock dedication to the Earl of Crawford, who at that time presided over Parliament, the pamphlet mercilessly parodies and satirises the leading Presbyterian ministers and beliefs. Its popularity in its own day can be judged by the number of heated replies and counter replies it produced, as well as by the many subsequent editions of and additions to the tract itself.

The most detailed discussion of the pamphlet, its contents, editions and authorship is that by the Rev. Thomas Maxwell in *Records of the Scottish Church History Society* Vol VIII. He is right to be guarded on the matter of authorship as neither of the most popular attributions (to Robert Calder, minister at Nenthorn or to Gilbert Crockett and John Monroe) can be regarded as more than hypotheses. The author of a later tract, *An Apology for the Clergy of Scotland* notes with some satisfaction, that the outraged

Presbyterian pamphleteers have been unable to pierce behind the pseudonym of 'Jacob Curate', used by the creator of the *Eloquence*. That anonymity remains till this day, but it is almost certain that the writer in question was a Scottish minister with strong episcopalian leanings.

Although the pamphlet has little formal organisation, it is divided ostensibly into four separate sections:— I, The true character of the Presbyterian Pastors and People in Scotland; II, Containing some expressions out of their printed books; III, Containing Notes of the Presbyterian Sermons taken in writing from their mouth; IV, Containing some few Expressions of the Presbyterian prayers. My selections are taken from the first and third sections. References will be found to a number of prominent Presbyterians, including:

David Williamson: Deprived of his charge at St. Cuthberts, Edinburgh in 1661, but returned 29 years later, thus fulfilling his prophecy that he would "return and die minister of this kirk".

John Ker: Minister at Lyne in Teviotdale; famed for his generosity to the poor and for his ferocious sermons.

William Guthry: Once tutor to James Lord Mauchline, and later preacher at Fenwick, denounced by Bishop Burnet as "a ringleader and a keeper-up of schism".

John Livingstone: Chaplain to the Countess of Wigton; refused ordination so long as the Five Articles of Perth stood; ministered for a time in Ireland; after a chequered career, came to Ancrum in 1648; a leading protester, he disowned the General Assembly's power and formed the first schism in the reformed church.

John Semple: A precentor in County Down, he became a preacher when the regular minister was late one Sunday and Semple decided to expound on the psalm, which had just been sung; became Minister at Carsphairn; joined Protesters, 1651; imprisoned and sequestrated 1660; granted pardon, 1667.

Robert Blair: A regent at Glasgow University, he was licensed to preach in 1616; like Livingstone he went to Ireland for a time and was involved in the Presbyterian negotiations with Charles in 1645; was forced to resign his charge at the Restoration and was confined in turn at Musselburgh, Kirkcaldy and Meikle Couston.

My text is based on the first edition of 1692 (New College Library, Edinburgh). It is catalogued B. c. 10.8. Although close to the second edition of 1693, it is not "the same pamphlet word for word" as Maxwell claims.

FROM SECTION I.

The True Character of The Presbyterian Pastors and People in Scotland.

In the first place, then, I am to give you the true character of presbyterian pastors and people. I shall begin with the people, for they are truly the guides, and their pastors must follow them, whom they pretend to conduct. For the preachers of the new Gospel, knowing that their trade hath no old nor sure foundation, they are forced to flee to this new and unaccountable notion, that the calling and constituting of ministers is the power of the mob. Now the world knows by too long and sad experience, that their mobile is not led by reason nor religion, but by fancy and imagination, so that we may be sure when the election of ministers is put in their hands, they will chuse none but such as will readily sooth and indulge them in their most extravagant and mad humors. What ministers can be expected from the choice of a people void of common sense, and guided by irregular passions, who torture the scripture, making it speak the language of their deluded imaginations. They will tell you, that ye ought to fight the battels of the Lord, because the scripture says in the Epistle to the Hebrews, "Without shedding of blood there is no remission." They are generally covetous and deceitful, and the preaching they are bred with, hath no tendency to work them into the contrary virtues. They call peace, love, charity and justice, not gospel, but dry morality only. I had once very great difficulty to convince one of them, that it was a sin for him to cheat and impose upon his neighbour in matters of trade, by concealing the faults of his goods from the buyer. He ask'd my reason. I told him, because he would not wish one to deal so with himself. "That is," said he again, "but

morality, for if I shall believe in Christ, I shall be saved." I ask'd
him, "Was not this Christ's saying, 'Whatsoever ye would that
others should do unto you, that do you unto others'?" "Yes",
he said, that was good, but that Christ, because of the hardness
of the Jews hearts spake very much morality with his gospel. The
poor man spoke as he was taught and bred in the conventicles,
for it will be very long e're they hear a sermon upon just dealing, or restitution of ill-gotten goods. And who knows not, that
despising of dominions, speaking evil of dignities, and rising in
arms against the Lord's anointed, is with them but fighting the
battels of the Lord. One George Flint, in the parish of Smalholm,
in the shire of Teviotdale, was look'd upon as a very great saint
among them, and yet out of zeal against the government, he kept
a dog whom he named Charles, after the King; and a cat which
he named Katherine, after the Queen; and another dog whom he
named Gideon, after the minister of the parish. They are a people
that will not swear in common discourse for a world, yet they
never scruple before a Judge, any perjury that may seem to
advance the cause, nor stand in their ordinary dealings to cheat for
a penny. Nay, murther it self becomes a virtue when the work of
the Covenant seems to require it; and the new Gospel which they
profess, is so far from condemning lying, cheating, murther and
rebellion, when committed to fulfil the ends of the Solemn League,
that many of these, whom they reckon martyrs, have at their execution gloried in these crimes, as the sure evidences of their salvation.

Morality being thus discountenanced by the generality of that
party, the poor people are thereby lock'd up in a cell of ignorance.
This did clearly appear, when the laws, in the former government,
discharg'd conventicles, the people being brought thereby home
to the churches. When the ministers began to catechise them
in the principles of the christian religion, they found them
grossly ignorant, for when they were desired to repeat the Creed,
Lord's-Prayer and Ten Commandments, they told they were above
these childish ordinances, for if they believed in Christ, they were
certainly well. And yet these ignorants would adventure to pray
ex tempore, and in their families to lecture on the most mysterious

chapters of Ezekiel, Daniel or the Revelation. A grave and good minister told me, that upon a certain occasion he desired a very zealous she-saint to repeat the Creed; and that she return'd this answer, "I know not what ye mean by the Creed." "Did not your father," says the minister, "promise to bring you up in that faith?" "Indeed did he not," said she, "for, I thank my Saviour, that superstition was not in my father's time." "What then was in your father's time?" said the minister. "It was," said she, "the holy Covenant, which you have put away." "Whether was it the Covenant of works, or grace?" said the minister. "Covenant of works!" said she, "That is handy labour. It was the Covenant of grace, which was made with Adam, and which all of you have put away." At night she went home, and a number of the sighing fraternity flock'd after, pretending to hear her pray. Their family exercise being ended, she told them the conference that pass'd betwixt the curate and her; and they all concluded she had the better, and that she was certainly more than match for the ablest curate in that country.

Generally their conventicles produced very many bastards, and the excuses they made for that, was "Where sin abounds, the grace of God super-abounds. There is no condemnation to them that are in Christ." Sometimes this, "The Lambs of Christ may sport together. To the pure all things are pure." Nay, generally they are of opinion, that a man is never a true saint, till he have a sound fall, such as that of David's with Bathsheba. The following narration of a well known truth shall serve for instance.

A party of King Charles II. his guards being sent to apprehend Mr. David Williamson (one of the most eminent of their ministers now in Edenburgh) for the frequent rebellion and treason he preached then at field meetings; and the party having surrounded the house where he was, a zealous lady, mistress of the house, being very solicitous to conceal him, rose in all haste from her bed, where she left her daughter of about eighteen years of age; and having dressed up the holy man's head with some of her own night cloaths, she wittily advis'd him to take her place in the warm bed with her girl; to which he modestly and readly consented; and knowing well how to employ his time, especially upon such an extraordinary call, to propagate the image of the party, while the mother, to divert the troopers enquiry, was treating them with strong drink in the parlour, he, to express his gratitude, applies himself with extraordinary kindness to the daughter; who finding him like to prove a very useful man in his generation, told her mother she would have him for her husband; to which the mother, though otherwise unwilling, yet, for concealing the scandal, out of love to the cause consented, when the mystery of the iniquity was wholly disclosed to her. This whole story is as well known in Scotland, as that the Covenant was begun, and carried on by rebellion and oppression.

Nor was the actor, who is at this day one of the chief props of the cause, more admired for his extraordinary diligence and courage in this matter, than for his excellent invention in finding a passage of St. Paul's, to prove that the scandal of this was very consistent with the state of a person truly regenerate. "Verily, I do not," said he, "deny, but that, with St. Paul, I have a law in my members, warring against the law of my mind, and bringing me into captivity into the law of sin, which is in my members." Now, according to the gloss which that whole party puts upon this scripture, saying that St. Paul here speaks of himself, and does not personate an unregenerate man, this defence of Williamson's must be allowed to be good; as also, that the height of carnality is consistent, with the greatest grace. Even so the hereticks in St. Peter's days, wrested some things hard to be understood in St. Paul's Epistles, to their own destruction.

There was among them a married woman, near Edenburgh, who had paid several fines for not going to church, yet scrupled not to commit adultery with one of the Earl of Marr's regiment, and the fellow himself that was guilty, told, out of detestation to their damnable hypocrisie, that the vile woman had the confidence, in time of her abomination, to say to him, "O you that are in Marr's regiment, but you be pretty able men, but yet ye are great Covenant breakers! Alas, few or none of you are godly."

There are very many instances of this nature, but I shall only add one more, which was told me by a gentleman of good reputation and credit, who himself confessed to me, with regret, that in the heat of his youth he had been guilty of the sin of fornication with a gentlewoman of that holy sect. He says, that being with her in a garret, and she hearing some body coming up stairs, she said to him, "Ah, here's my aunt. I must devise a trick to divert her." Upon which, she fell a whining and howling aloud, as these people use to do at their most private devotions. "Oh, to believe, to believe! Oh, to have experience!" said she. And by that means she diverted her aunts further approaching, who instantly retired, commending her niece's zeal and devotion. The gentleman conceals the woman's name, out of regard to her honour and his own; begs pardon for the sin, and tells it only to discover the abominable nature of their hypocrisie.

FROM SECTION III

Containing Notes of the Presbyterian Sermons taken in Writing from their Mouths.

At first I begin with one I heard from Zetland, who preaching on David and Goliah, he told the hearers, "Sir, this David was but a little manekine like my beddle Davie Gaddies there, but Goliah was a meckle strong fellow, like the Laird of Quandal there. This David gets a scrippie and baggie, that is, a sling and a stone in it. He flings a stone into Goliah's face. Down falls Goliah and David above him. After that, David was made a King; he that was keeping sheep before, in truth he came very well too, Sirs. Well said, Davie, see what comes of it, Sirs; after that he commits adultery with Uriah." "Nay," said the beddal Davie Gaddies, "it was but with Uriah's wife, Sir." "In faith, thou art right. It was Uriah's wife, indeed man," said Mr. John.

One Ker, at his entring into a church at Teviotdale, told the people the relation that was to be between him and them in these following words: "Sirs, I am coming home to be your shepherd, and you must be my sheep, and the Bible will be my tar-bottle, for I will mark you with it." And, laying his hand on the Clark or Precentor's head, he saith, "Andrew, you shall be my dog." "The sorrow a bit of your dog will I be," said Andrew. "O Andrew, I speak mystically," said the preacher. "Yea, but you speak mischievously," said Andrew.

Mr. William Guthry, preaching on Peter's confidence, said, "Peter, Sirs, was as stalliard a fellow as ever had cold iron at his arse, and yet a hussie with a rock feared him."

Another preaching against drunkenness, told the hearers, there were four sorts of drunkenness. "1. To be drunk like a sow, tumbling in the mire, like many of this parish. 2. There is to be drunk like a dog. The dog fills the stomach of him, and spues all out again, and thou John Jamison was this way drunk the other day. 3. There is to be drunk like a goose. Of all drunkenness, Sirs, beware of the drunkenness of the goose, for it never rests, but constantly dips the gobb of it in the water. You are all drunk this way, Sirs, I need name none of you. 4. There is to be drunk like a sheep. The silly sheep seldom or never drinks, but sometimes wets the mouth of it in the water, and rises up as well as ever, and I my self use to be drunk this way, Sirs. But now, I see," said he, "two gentlemen in the kirk, and gentlemen, you are both strangers to me, but I must vindicate my self at your hands. I have here the cursedest parish that ever God put breath in. For all my preaching against drunkenness, they will go into a change-house after sermon, and the first thing they'll get, is a meckle cup full of hot ale, and they will say, 'I wish we had the minister in the midst of it.' Now, gentlemen, judge ye how I am rewarded for my good preaching." After sermon the Clerk gives him up the name of a fornicatrix, whose name was Ann Cantly. "Here is," saith he, "one upon the stool of repentance. They call her Cantly. She saith her self she is an honest woman, but I trow scantly."

Mr. John Levingstone in Ancrum, once giving the sacrament of the Lord's Supper, said to his hearers. "Now, Sirs, you may take Christ piping hot," and finding a woman longsome in taking the bread out of his hand, he says, "Woman, if you take not Christ, take the meikle devil then".

One John Simple, a very zealous preacher among them, used to personate and act sermons in the old monkish stile spoken of Sect 1. 16. At a certain time he preached upon that debate,

'Whether a man be justified by faith or by works,' and acted it after this manner. "Sirs, this is a very great debate. But who is that looking in at the door, with his red cap? Follow your look, Sir. It is very ill manners to be looking in. But what's your name? 'Robert Bellarmine.' 'Bellarmine,' saith he, 'whether is a man justified by faith, or by works?' 'He is justified by works.' 'Stand thou there man. But what is he, that honest-like-man, standing in the floor with the long beard and Geneva cowl, a very honest-like man? Draw near! What's your name, Sir?' 'My name is John Calvin.' 'Calvin, honest Calvin, whether is a man justified by faith or by works?' 'He is justified by faith.' 'Very well John, thy leg to my leg and we shall hough down Bellarmine even now.'"

Another time, preaching on the Day of Judgment, he told them, "Sirs, this will be a terrible day. We'll all be there, and in the throng I John Simple will be, and all of you will stand at my back. Christ will look to me, and he will say, 'Who is that standing there?' I'll say again, 'Yea, even as ye ken'd not, Lord.' He'll say, 'I know thou's honest John Simple. Draw near, John. Now John, what good service have you done to me on earth?' 'I have brought hither a company of Blew Bonnets for you, Lord.' 'Blew Bonnets, John, what is become of the brave hats, the silks, and the satins, John?' I'll tell, 'I know no, Lord. They went a gate of their own.' 'Well, honest John, thou and thy Blew Bonnets are welcome to me. Come to my right hand, and let the devil take the hats, the silks, and the sattins.'"

This John was ordinarily called Fitch-cape and Claw-poll, because in the time of preaching or praying, he used to claw his head, and rub his callet. At a certain time he was called to preach in a neighbouring church, and his preface was in these words:

"Sirs, I know what you will be saying among your selves the day. Ye will say, 'Here is Fitch-cape come to preach to us the day.' But as the Lord lives, I had a great deal of do e're I could come to you, for by the way I met the devil. He said to me, 'What now Fitch cape, whither are you going?' 'I am going,' said I, 'to preach to the people of God.' 'People of God!' said the foul thief. 'They are my people!' 'They are not yours, thou foul thief,' said I. 'They are mine, Claw-poll,' said he again to me. So the foul thief and I tugg'd, rugg'd and riv'd at one another, and at last I got you out of his clooks. Now here is the good that Fitch-cape hath done to you. Now that ye may be kept out of his gripes, let us pray."

Another, lecturing on the first of Job, said, "Sirs, I will tell you this story very plainly. The devil comes to God one day. God said, 'What now deel, thou foul thief, whither are you going?' 'I am going up and down now, Lord you have put me away from you now, I must even do for my self now.' 'Well, well, deel,' says God, 'all the world kens that it is your fault. But do you not know that I have an honest servant they call Job? Is not he an honest man, deel?' 'Sorrow to his thank,' says the deel. 'You make his cup stand full even, you make his pot play well, but give him a cuff, I'll hazard he'll be as ill as I am called.' 'Go, deel,' says God, 'I'll yoke his honesty with you. Fell his cows, worry his sheep, do all the mischief ye can, but for the very saul of you, touch not a hair of his tail.' "

Mr. Robert Blair, that famous presbyterian preacher at St. Andrews, was very much thought of for his familiar way of preaching. He preached often against the observation of Christmass, and once in this Scotch jingle, "You will say, Sirs, 'Good old Youleday;' I'll tell you, 'good old Fool-day.' You will say, it is a brave Haly-day; I tell you, it is a brave Belly-day. You will say, these are bonny formalities; but I tell you, they are bonny fartalities."

Another, enveighing against the vanity and gaddiness of women, spake thus, "Behold the vanity of women, look to them. You'll see first a sattin petticoat; lift that, there is a tabby petticoat; lift that, there is a flanning petticoat; lift that, there is a holland smarck; lift that and there you will see what they ought not to be proud of, that's no very cleanly spectacle. Eve," said he, "was never so vain. She sought no covering but fig-leaves."

Mr. Simple (whom I named before) told, that Samson was the greatest fool that ever was born, for he revealed his secrets to a daft hussie. "Samson! You may well call him fool Thomson, for of all the John Thomson's men that ever was, he was the foolest."

I have a sermon, written from the preachers mouth by one of their own zealots, whereof this is one passage, "Jacob began to wrestle with God, an able hand forsooth. I Sirs, but he had a good second, that was faith. Faith and God gave two or three tousles together. At last God dings down faith on its bottom. Faith gets up to his heels, and says, 'Well, God, is this your promise to me? I trow I have a ticket in my pocket here.' Faith brings out the ticket and stops it in God's hand, and said, 'Now God! is not this your own write? Deny your own hand-write if you dare! Are these the promises you gave me? Look how you guide me when I come to you.' God reads the ticket, and said, 'Well, well, faith, I remember I gave you such a promise. Good sooth faith, if you had been another, thou should get all the bones in thy skin broken.' "

DIARISTS

JAMES MELVILLE was born in 1556, the son of Richard Melville, the minister of Marytoun. He gained his early schooling at Montrose before attending St. Andrews University from 1569-73. He was profoundly influenced by his uncle, Andrew Melville and when the latter became Principal of Glasgow University, James followed him, holding the position of Regent from 1575-80. In 1580 he became Professor of Hebrew and Oriental Languages at St. Andrews. His staunch upholding of Presbyterian principles brought him into conflict with the influential Archbishop Adamson, and in 1584, Melville fled to Berwick, fearing reprisals. After a period in Newcastle and London, he was called to the parish of Anstruther-Wester in November 1585. Three other parishes were then joined to this charge and in 1589, Melville became Moderator of the General Assembly. In this post he continued to oppose fearlessly both Archbishop Adamson and all attempts to establish conformity of worship with England. At this time the Earl of Bothwell was trying to gain the support of the Presbyterian ministers, and Melville's name became linked with his, and thus with various anti-royalist plots. James VI retained his faith in Melville throughout this period, but after the Union of Crowns, grew tired of his rigorous opposition to all the proposed increases in episcopal government for Scotland. Thus, when his more illustrious uncle was summoned to London in 1606 and imprisoned, James too was questioned. His punishment was not so severe, but he was ordered to remain within a ten-mile radius of Newcastle and forbidden to cross back into Scotland. On his wife's death he did return once, briefly, but when final negotiations for his release were completed, he died on the journey north, at Berwick on Tweed. This was in 1613.

Melville did compose some poems, including two sonnets, at a time when that genre was enjoying great popularity in Scotland. Of his prose works, *A Spirituall Propine of a Pastour to his People* (1598) is almost entirely neglected. On the other hand, his *Autobiography and Diary*, along with its continuation *Ane True Narrative of the Declyning Aige of the Kirk of Scotland* (1596-1610), has long remained popular, mainly among historians. This tradition was begun as early as Calderwood, who in his *History*, uses Melville as his chief authority, citing long passages from the *Diary*. For the student of Scottish Prose, however, Melville is a fine exponent of the less stylised, personal prose written at the turn of the century. His unpretentious yet controlled descriptive technique is exemplified in the passage dealing with his escape to Berwick, which also provides some memorable moments of wry humour. Like Knox, however, he is especially adept at recapturing the fieriness of dialogue, as he does in the account of James VI's argument with his uncle and himself over the value of David Black's ministry. Finally, there are a few passages of rich, natural description, such as that dealing with the appearance of a meteor in 1604.

Most critics have been impressed more by the *Diary* as a revelation of its author's personality, than as a work exhibiting any literary skill. Thus, J. G. Fyfe notes, "*The Autobiography and Diary* is indeed, full of interest to the student of history and to the general reader, though the author's 'piety' is inclined to be tiresome. This open show of religious conviction was, however, merely the custom of the time, and in James Melville it was absolutely sincere, and free from all traces of sanctimoniousness." Diaries do share many of the charms of the first person novel, but these can only be inadequately reflected in an anthology, which must limit itself to isolating interesting incidents and showing the author's range. Even so, a fair glimpse of the "confidential", "inimitable" Melville may be obtained.

My text for the first two extracts is based on Advocates MS 34.4.15 (National Library of Scotland); the third is based on

Laing MS Dc.4.10 (Edinburgh University Library).

Alexander Brodie was born on 25th July 1617. He spent the years from 1628-32 in England, but then returned to study at King's College Aberdeen. He did not graduate, and in 1635 married Elizabeth, daughter of Sir Robert Innes of Innes. She died when he was 23, leaving one son and one daughter. The next period in his life was marked by a growing involvement in the political and religious issues of the time. He sided firmly with the Presbyterian faction and in December 1640 was one of the party, who demolished two oil paintings and much of the carved work in Elgin Cathedral. By 1643 he was representing the County of Elgin in Parliament, and on Charles I's death was one of those sent to The Hague to test Charles II's attitude to the National Covenant and the Solemn League and Covenant. Appointed a Lord of Session in 1649, he was also one of those who greeted Charles II on his arrival in Scotland during 1650. Despite being summoned to London by Cromwell, he refused to hold office during the Commonwealth, only giving way after Cromwell's death in 1658. Ironically, on the restoration of Charles II, he was then demoted, and later fined for compliance with the Puritan government. From 1672, illness afflicted him, till, eight years later, he died. His son, James (b.1637) took over his estates. Married to Mary Ker, younger daughter of William 3rd Earl of Lothian, he continued the staunch Presbyterian traditions and was frequently fined for attending conventicles. He died in March, 1708.

Alexander Brodie's habit of keeping a diary seems to have stemmed from the notes he took of various sermons over the period from 1642-54. This later broadened into a fuller account of the domestic, political and religious problems with which he was beset during the later years of his life. Of the two passages given, the first is predominantly political and the second concerns an incident at once domestic and religious in its overtones. To these has been added the moving passage contributed by James (as good a stylist, though a less persevering diarist) on the death of his father. The text is based on MSS of the various volumes of the Diary, all of which still remain in the hands of the Brodie of Brodie.

THE DIARY OF JAMES MELVILLE

About the beginning of May, I was compellit throw necessitie, bathe of the furnesing of the foundat persones in the Collage, and my awin famelie, to tak jorney athort Angus and Merns, whar the Collage leiving lyes, and gather in the rent dew to the Collage. In this mean tyme, the bischope is retourned from his embassage. A parliament is keipit at Edinbruche, in the quhilk lawes is sett down for restraining of the frie pretching of the Word, and owerthraw of the haill establissed discipline of the Kirk; and that of speciall purpose to be snares to tak the fathfull ministers in. For, do what they could, they sould nocht eschape ather treassone against Chryst or the King. For preaching frilie the treuthe, they sould fall under the danger of these lawes; and keiping sylence, or pretching to the pleasour of men, they suld betrey the cause of Chryst. These lawes ar promulgat at the mercat-cross of Edinbruche, and vowes maid be Captean James, the Chancellar, and cheif hand of that cause, that gif Mr James Lawsones head war als grait as a haystak, he sould cause it lope from his hause! The quhilk, when Mr James perceavit, be advys of his brethring of the Presbyterie, and of the best of his flok, and godlie barones and gentlemen about, with his brother and coleag, Mr Walter Balcanquall, withdrew him self secreitlie from Edinbruche, and past in Eingland. Bot befor they past, Mr Robert Pont, accompanied with Mr Walter Balcanquall and certean of the breithring, cam to the mercat-cros at the verie publication of the actes of parliament, and tuk publict documents, that they protested against the said actes (sa far as twitched the Kirk, in the nam of the Kirk of Scotland, etc.

Returning from Angus, all thir newes is tauld me, and that the bruit was, that I was away with the rest. Whowbeit indeid, as yit it cam na wayes in my mynd to leave the Collage, bot was resolvit to be fund ther when ever it pleasit God to visit me. Sa, the Sabbathe efter my ham-coming, I went to the Kirk; and efter noone my uncle Roger, knawing fordar nor I did, comes ower from Dondie, and finding a frind of his in St Androis, tauld him that the bischope was coming hame with a commission to tak me, and thairfoir besought him nocht to leave me till I aggreit to go ower to Dondie with him. Sa he delt with Mr Robert Bruce and uthers my frinds, and importuned me sa, that it behoved me to go with him, as I did that night, to Dondie. The newes that comes to me the morn was, that the bischopes men, with the magistrats, haid bein cersing the Collage and my hous for me, and haid sought out all my lettrones and wryttes; and that my dittay was allready inacted, interteining of intelligence with my uncle, the Kings rebell, etc.

Sa, seiking resolution cairfullie of my God what to do, a cusing of my awin name, of his awin frie motion and accord, offerit to me, be the assistance of God, to put me saif in Berwik within twentie-four houres be sie. To this also my uncle Roger, and uther frinds, aggreit. Sa, efter consultation with my God, and finding of his warrand in my hart, I concludit to go, albeit nocht without grait tentationes and mikle heavines, yit on the part rejoysing, that God gaiv the hart to leave native countrey, house, and sweit loving new-maried wyf, and all for the love of him and his Chryst. Thus my cusing, being a mariner, conducit a bott to carie a town of his portage wyn about to Carell, and decking me upe in his sie attyre betymes in the morning, about the simmer solstice, tuk me in down under Dondie as a shipbroken sie-man; and rowing about, behovit to go to the heavin of St Androis, to lose a certean of skleatt steanes; and because it was law water, we behoved to ly a whyll in the road till the water grew, whare, the bott wanting ane owerlaft, the seall was cassen ower hir ta end, and ther I leyed upe, lest I sould be spyed of sum shipes rydding besyde. Bot within schort space, partlie be rokking in the sie, and partlie for want of eare, I grew sa extream seik, that manie a tyme I besaught my cowsing to sett me a-land, schosin rather anie sort of dethe, for a guid cause, nor sa to be tormented in a stinking holl. And yit, whowbeit it was extream peanfull, I gatt ther notable medicin of vomitine, quhilk was a preservative to my helthe all that yeir. Sa, coming hard to the steppes of the Archbischopes peire at St Androis, we loste our skleattes, and tuk in vivers, and rowit out agean immediatlie, and cam that night to Pitmillie-burn-mouthe, wher I gead a-land, and reposit me in my sie abbat. And efter offers of grait kyndnes be the Lard, and furnitour of a rubber of starke Merche eall, betymes in the morning we rowit out about the Nes. The day was hat. Ther was bot twa men in the bott, by twa cusings of myne, with my self. Of these twa, we haid an at our devotion. The uther was the awner of the bott, and verie evill-affected; bot the hat rowing, and the stope with the stark eall hard besyd him, maid him atteanes to keave ower aslipe. And it pleased God to send a prettie pirlye of wound, wherby getting on a seall upon hir, or ever our schippar wakned we was a guid space besouthe the May; wha, seing he could nocht mend him self, was fean to yeild and agrie with his merchant for a hyre to Berwik. Bot being af and on with Dumbar, about ane efter noon comes af the hilles of Lamermure-age a grait mist with a tempestuous schoure and drow, quhilk, or we could gett our sealles taklit, did cast us about, and, or my cusing was awar, caried us bak almaist to the May, with such a how wa and spene drift, that the bott being opin, he lukit for grait danger gif the stormie schoure haid continowed. Bot the young man being verie skilfull and able, starts to his kist, and tuk out a compas, and finding us contrare our course, with mikle ado, wanting helpe, and schipping of mikle water, he cust about and pykit on the wind, halding bathe the helme and scheit, susteining in the mean tyme evill langage of the schippar in stead of helpe, till it pleasit God mercifullie to luik upon us, and within an houre and an half to dryve away the schoure and calme the drow, sa that it fell down dead calme about the sune drawing leache.

To keipe the sie all night in an opin litle bott, it was dangerus, and to go to Dumbar we durst nocht, sa, of necessitie, we tuk us toward St Tab's Heid. Bot we haiving, but twa eares, and the boot slaw and heavie, it was about alleavin houres of the night or we could win ther. Whowbeit, na man was ydle. Yea, I rowit my self, till the hyd cam af my fingars, mair acquented with the pen nor working on an are. Coming under the crag, we rowit in within a prettie lytle holl betwix the mean and the head, whare easelie going a-land, we refreschit us with cauld water and wyne; and returning to our boot, sleipit the dead of the night, bot neidit nan to wakin us, for soon, be the day light piped, ther was sic a noyse of foulles on the crag, and about us, because of thair young annes, that we war almaist pressed to launche out. Now we haid Cawding-ham Bay and Hay-mouth to pas by, and that but slawlie, rowing be the land, whar the residence of Alexander Home of Manderston, an of our cheif confederat enemies, and wha haid intercepted a boot of the Earle of Angus coming about from Tamtallon to Berwik nocht lang befor. This put us in grait feir; but our guid God gardit us, making a sweik thik mist till aryse, wherby we might bot skarslie gis at the sight of the land, and thairfra nane could sie us. Sa we cam on hulie without fear till we wan within the bounds of Berwik, whar we was in graitest danger of all, umbesett in the mist be twa or thrie of the cobles of Berwik, quhilk war sa swift in rowing, that they ged round about us. Bot we being fyve within burd, and haiving twa pistolets, with thrie swords, and they na armour, they war fean to let us be, namlie, when they understud that we was making for Berwik.

Thus gratiuslie protected by my guid God, I cam to Berwik, whar I fand Mr. James Lawsone and Mr Walter Balcanquall, my uncle, Mr Andro, with Patrik Forbes, appeirand of Cors, and sum uther gentlemen, but twa dayes befor entred in their jorney southe ower. And Mr James, with his colleg, war evin upon thair voyage to follow, as they did within thrie or four dayes, acquenting me with thair frinds, and leaving me in thair rowm to pretche in the Kirk, as I was desyrit.

*

The yeir following, Mr David Blaks ministerie in St Androis, quhilk haid wrought notable guid effects, bathe in the town for the weill of all the peiples saulles, and ther republict, and guid ordour of provisioun for the pure, as also to landwart for purpose of biging of kirks, and in the Presbyterie moving non residents to tak tham to thair kirks and charges, began now, be the devill invying it, to be branglit. The instruments war the Manse-moungar, (sa Mr David named him) Wilyeam Balfour, and his favourars, wha, fearing Mr Davids prevaling against him, and evicting of his hous in the Abbay to be a manse to the minister, causit, be divers courtiours and uthers, the Kings eares to be filled with calumnious informationes of the said Mr David his doctrine and ministerie: as lykwayes be his occasioun, of Mr Andro, my uncle, Rector of the Universitie, being the principall mean of the said Mr Davids bringing and placing thair, and meantiner and assistar of him in his ministerie.

Sa, in the monethe of August 1595, the said Mr David and my uncle ar chargit to compeir befor the King and Counsall at Falkland, to answer for certean speitches uttered be tham in thair doctrin against his majestie's progenitours, of the quhilk I knew na thing bot be advertisment fra my uncle from St Androis to keipe the dyet. Coming to Falkland, the King inquyres of me, what I thought of Mr David Blak. I answerit, I thought him a guid and godlie man, and a mightie preatchour, and a man whase ministerie haid bein verie forcible and fruitfull in St Androis.—"O," sayes the King, "yie ar the first man, and onlie, that ever I hard speak guid of him amangs ministerie, gentilmen, or burgesses!"—"Surlie, then," says I, "I am verie sorie, Sir, that your Majestie hes nocht spoken with the best sort of them all."—"I ken," sayes the King in coler, "the best, and hes spoken with tham; bot all your seditius deallings ar cloked, and hes bein with that name of the best men." —"Then, surlie," says I, "Sir, your Majestie sall do weill to gif Mr David a syse of anie in all tha thrie ranks, excepting nan bot sic as hes knawin particulars, and gif they fyle him, I sall speak na mair in this maner to your Majestie, till your Majestie find what he is in effect." The King slipping away fra me, goes to a speciall courtier, and sayes to him, "Fathe, Mr James Melvill and I ar at our graitest, for I perceave he is all for Mr David Blak, and that sort!" The King, lest he sould irritat the Kirk be calling befor his Counsall anie minister for thair doctrine, quhilk haid nocht succeidit weill of befor, called onlie a number of the breithring of the ministerie (namelie, sic whilk war offendit with Mr Davids scharpe and plean form of doctrine, sparing nather King nor minister) to try the mater, and judge thairupon.

Mr David compeiring, declynit the King's judicator, in doctrine; and as for the breithring, he refusit tham nocht, being anie sort of assemblie of the Kirk, rightlie callit for that effect, or utherwayes

in privat to confer with thame, and satisfie tham in anie dout con-
ceavit of his doctrine. The King summarlie and confusedlie passit
ower all, and put nan of these things to interloquutor, bot called
for the witnesses. And Mr David, called to sie what he haid to say
against tham, answerit, gif that was a judicator, he sould haiv an
answer concerning the unlawfulnes and incompetencie alleagit; as
lykwayes, put ceas it war, as it is nocht, he sould haiv an accusar
fortifeit with twa witnesses, according to the rewll of the apostle,
etc. That in lyk maner is past, and a nomber of witnesses is
examined, Burley, the delatter and accusar, being alwayes present;
whilk, when my uncle, Mr Andro Melvill, perceaving, chapping
at the chalmer dure, whar we war, comes in, and efter humble
reverence done to the King, he braks out with grait libertie of
speitche, letting the King planlie to knaw, that quhilk dyvers tymes
befor with small lyking, he haid tooned in his ear, that thair was
twa Kings in Scotland, twa kingdomes, and twa jurisdictiones.
Thir was Chryst Jesus, &c.; and gif the King of Scotland, civill
King James the Saxt, haid anie judicator or cause thair, presentlie,
it sould nocht be to judge the fathfull messanger of Jesus Chryst,
the King, etc., bot (turning him to the Lard of Burley, standing
there) this trator, wha hes quitted divers poincts of hie treasone
against his majestie's civill lawes, to his grait dishonour and offence
of his guid subjects, namlie, taking of his peacable subjects on the
night out thair houses, ravishing of weimen, and receatting within
his hous of the King's rebels and forfauld enemies! etc.

With this, Burley falles down on his knies to the King, and
craves justice. "Justice!" sayes Mr Andro, "wald to God yow haid
it! Yow wald nocht be heir to bring a judgment from Chryst upon
the King, and thus falslie and unjustlie to vex and accuse the
fathfull servants of God!" The King began, with firme counten-
ances and speitches, to command silence and dashe him; bot he,
insurging with graiter bauldnes and force of langage, buir out
the mater sa, that the King was fean to tak it upe betwix tham
with gentill termes and mirrie talk, saying, they war bathe litle
men, and thair hart was at thair mouthe etc. Sa that meitting was
demissit the forenoone.

*

No further that yeir, bot a strang meteor, quhilk wes hard and sein in the seventh day of December. About ane houre befoir the sone rose, the moone schyneing cleir two dayis befoir the chainge, in ane calme and pleasant morneing, thair wes at ane instant sein gryt inflamatiounes of fyre-flauchtis in the eisterne hemisphere, and suddentlie thaireftir wes hard a gryt crack, as of a gryt cannoun, and sensibilie markit a gryt glob or bullat, fyrrie-cullorit, with a mychtie quhissilling noyse, flieing from the north-eist to the south-west, quhilk left behind a blew traine and draught in the air, most lyk ane serpent in mony faulds and linkit wimples; the heid quhairof breathing out flames and smooke, as it wald directlie invaid the moone, and swallowit hir up; but immediatlie the sone ryseing, faire and pleasant, abolischit all.

The crack wes hard of all, alsweill within as without the house, and sic as wer without, in the tyme, or hastilie ran out to sie, did verie sensibilly sie and mark the rest above rehearsit. Heir wes a subject for poyetis and prophettis to play upoun, as wes also the strange comett so much discoursit upoun and written on, togidder with the starr that appeirit and cleirly schynit abone Edinbruche, hard on by the sonne, at 10, 11, 12 and ane of the clock, in the middel day, prognosticatting, undoutidlie, strang alteratiounes and changes in the world, namely under our climat.

THE BRODIES' DIARY

ALEXANDER BRODIE

I perceavd this parliament is lyk to have much fire and contentions, heat and passion in it. This I desir to mention befor God, and to pray that he would extinguish it, and quench the sinful passions of men, and if not, turn their sin and wrath unto his prais. Ther are men seiking, I hear, to mak friends with the chaunges, even corrupt men, that for ther ends wil serv al tyms, parties, factions and designs, thogh never so unjust and wild, or never so contrari one to another. Ther ar mani base and wild men, unrighteous,

bribing, fals and profan. Let God glorifi himself in discovering
and bringing doun, if I may ask this without carnal passion and
sinister ends, and mak wickednes manifest and ashamd, that we
may see good in the land yet. I aprehend, that albeit the violent
may outshut himself, yet the craftie and doubl minded may escap,
and God cannot reach them. Lord! correct thes thoghts, and help
me to submission, and patienc, and sobernes, to wait for Thee,
and to remitt the ordouring of thes things to Thy infinit wisdom
and soveraintie. Thou wilt be knowen to be God; and they shal
know it.

*

Efter dinnar, good Mr. Th. Hogg cam to me anent Alr. Chisolm,
but did fal to expostulat with me for the favours which I bear to
wicked men. I desird not to speak, but to hear. And yet he prest
on me, and I said, I durst not tak on me to judg the estat of others,
and I thoght it might consist with a seid of grac to fall in wicked
acts frequentli, of drunkennes, lying, or the lyk. He, and on in
the estat of grac may be frequentli, mor then onc or twic, overtaken with thes sinful acts. He said, that to be frequent in wicked
acts of the lyk kind, he could not but judg them in the way to
hell. I said, ther actions I disalowd, so did they, perchanc, themselves, and wer burthend with it. But for ther failing, so I durst not
cal them, or rekon them amongst the wicked. Grac may be smotherd
with much and frequent corruptions and weakneses. The holi man
exprest so much indignation at my expression and opinion, and
that he abhord it, and that I stumbld him greatlie. My woful heart
kindld, and I said I did noe less dislyk his severiti in censuring
the condition and estat of others, and that he took the keys, and
judgd rashlie and rigidlie; and that I could not imbrac the opinion
becaus Mr. Tho. Hogg said it, and if he stumbld at me, he might
forbear me. He was sorri that my children should hear such doctrin. Lord! piti both my hastines, rashnes, and ignoranc, and the
want of charitie to that holi man, quhom I had in great esteem;
and quherin I may be in an errour, the Lord discover it to me, and
convince, and let me not goe on in it, for Thy nams sak. In speak-

ing he shew a letter of Tho. Watsons; on which I took occasion
to explain my poor opinion, and said, that man had a hopd good
in him: He lovd thes that feard God. 2. He had Gods worship
in his hous. 3. He did shew charitie to honest folks in distress,
and had other moral good qualities, yet he had a habit of drinking. I durst not seclud him from charitie, nor judg his estat towards
God, nor reckon him as a wicked man, to quhom I should shew noe
favour, and with quhom I should hav noe familiariti ...

I adducd for my opinion of men that may fall in and continue
in evel courses and frailties, and yet may have Gods seid under al
that, Salomon, Jacob, Judah, som of the patriarchs.

I did afterward cal Mr. Tho. asid, and lovingli askd, why he
kindld soe vehementli against me. I hopd we minded the sam
thing, and had the sam object of our love and hatred, albeit his
was mor intens for good and against evel then min. But I desird
unfeindli to hat evel and lov good. Ani sin continud in, and
fallen in, without repentance, condemns, but how oft a child of
God may fall, and ris, and repent, it is hard to define.

JAMES BRODIE

17 April, 1680.—This night, betwixt 12 at night and two of the
morning, being sabbath morning, dyed my precious, worthie and
dear father, of a fitt of the gravel. I had come hom only the night
before betwixt 12 and on of the morning. I was not apprehending
that this strok was so near. It found me secur and stupid, and
asleip; which has been the plaug and dyseas I have been held by
long before. This has a loud cry, if I could hear it. I can hardly
aprehend the consequenc of it to the land, and church, and
famely. The Lord give instruction, and open the ear, and awaken
out of securitie!

We wer further threatened with a dismal sad symptom in his
being removd. He was like to have passed away without a word
to anie of us, in a swound. It pleased the Lord in his mercie and
goodnes to give som blink of reviving, so that, with the intermission of sleip and slumbring now and then, we had sweit, savorie,

seasonable words, thrie or four hours before his death. His advise
to myselfe at the last was, "My son, be strong in the Lord, and
the power of his might, my sone, to the Law and to the Testimonie." Mr. Jas. Urquhart prayd, and I hop was heard in it, that
the Lord would not tak him away in such anger against us, and
that the Lord would open his mouth, and that his death might be
edefying. These words wer alwais in his mouth, "My father and
my God, Lord Jesus leave me not! Take me with Thee!" and
being asked a word concerning his hop and expectation of the
Church and interest of Christ, he said, the Lord would redeem
his people. He longd to be ridd of a body of death and sin. He
was afraid whil he lived, and in the tym of his sicknes, to have
bein in great pain and distraction, but it pleasd the Lord to give
him a quiet passage and end, without complaint of pain, or working, or thraching. In his lyf also, he thought it would be desyrabl
to pass out of tyme to eternitie on the morning of a sabbath, and
to begin an eternal sabbath, quhilk he obtained. He was brought
so weak and low by his continued sickness and enervitie of bodie
and mind since the 5 of May last, at which tym he took the
beginning of his sicknes at Ballachastel, quhilk has continued and
encreased upon him ever since. I desire to be instructed and tak
warning, and to be awakened by this strok, and to hear what it
speaks to myself, the poor famely, the land and church. There are
many things in it, if I could winn to read or be instructed by it. As
to myselfe, I have had the benefit of instruction, warning, means
of knowledg, and has not profited in and by the company of such
a one since ever I had it, and now I am deprivd of it. This speaks
anger. I have seen the godly conversation, holy and christian walk
of a father,—his watchfulnes, fruitfulnes,—his secret communion
with God,—yet cannot say that my hart has bein gaind or winn to
the folowing his exampl. I have not made that use of his company
that anie other would have done. The famely has not profited.
O! how unlik and unsutabl to the pains taken on them. He has
keepd up a light amongst us. I and others have bein weakning his
hands, drawing back. He has, in some measure, fard the wors of
such a person, and now, whil I am under thes and many such con-
victions, I cannot recal or get back those occasions quhich I have

lost, mispent, and sind away. And now, if the Lord should say he would not reprove or be at anie mor pains with me, he wer just and holy, and it wer bot the just punishment of my iniquity. Bot let his mercy, and grace, and love in Jesus Christ com over al these provocations.

Now, what can or wil this sad strok do to me? If the Lord strik not in by his spirit with it, I wil sleip on. O, that this night, and dark cold winter would kill and nipp bitter roots quhilk ar within me, of securitie, worldines, passion, pride, carnalitie! O, that the Lord would give a tender, spritual, holy, zealous, form of hart, and to be watchful, that this be a tym of getting acquaintance with Christ; a tym of weaning affections from the world, and things in it. O, that the Lord would com in and fill the room and place in the famely, and in harts, and make up the want of a dear anger. I have seen the godly conversation, holy and christian walk father and instructor.

18.—Die Dom. Mr. A.D. only prayd in the famely, in the morning. It was our complaint that sabbaths wer desolate formerlie, bot alas, al our sun seims now to be gon doun! I read with the famely a pairt of the 3 Lamentations, and prayd, if I may cal it prayer. Mr. A. spok a word in the evening ... Main and his wife wer heir. Ther cam one from Castl Forbes to enquir anent my dear father. I wrot a line to my daughter, and dispatchd the bearer that sam day.

GLOSSARY

JOHN KNOX

bourding jesting
bruyted rumoured
bukkill other by the byrse seize one another by the bristles
chymlay brazier
comptis accounts
cummer hamper
deprehend detect
diosey diocese
a feg for the fead a fig for the feud
fowsea ditch
garte made
glorious vainglorious
glowmyng scowling
Gukstoun Glaikstour Mr. Trifling Folly
hetterent hatred
jackmen attendants
knapped cracked
kystes chests
manrent vassalage
neattis nets
nefelling fisticuffs
seinye synod
sentence judgment
stog sweard thrusting sword
strook struck
walking awake
whingar short sword

THOMAS MAITLAND

in aventure in case
bourd jest
bruit din
circumvein get the better of
cleif adhere
gogie silly (?)
halk hawk
lychtnes wantonness
pance think
spang crack
speid prosper
stokado thrust
stur harsh
umbre shadow
wait know
wittie wise

GEORGE BUCHANAN

contrebank to in line with
doubilnes duplicity
ee eye
endommage injure
engyne mind
fenyeitlie feignedly
murthour murder
revaris robbers
vyerwayis otherwise

JOHN LESLIE

assistance company
ballettis songs
benefest provided with a benefice
conye money
dimished dismissed
fianzeillis marriage
hingers loops for carrying swords
joyses enjoys, possesses
licklie suitable
parochynns parishes
promoves restores
propyned endowed
quhill until
samin same
scarmishis skirmishes
tareit stayed

ROBERT LINDSAY

in ane rayit battell in order of
    battle
battellis battalions
is bidden remains
cast throw
disconfeit defeated
ellis already
glied counterfeit (Lit: cross-eyed)
haiknay horse used for ordinary
    riding
haschatur gambler
junitt met
langest levar survivor
leir teach
makdome form
myans influence
peirandlie apparently
raknit reckoned
rose nobill coin valued at about
    £1.20
sloghorne battle cry
sowtaris cobblers
staillit trained
unconsable deaf to advice
vessie inspect
vott vote

wight fellow
witter token
wyspe wisp
yett gate

WILLIAM FOWLER

adventur accident
bordel brothel
deborded overflowed
displesant unpleasant
drouth thirst
furthye enterprising
hantit frequented
incace in the event that
inlaiketh is lacking
of newe again
rampiers ramparts
requeseit necessary
slokned quenched
swillted poured freely
umbre shade
wood mad

JAMES IV

airt branch of learning
belay secure
blok draft
cautelis cautions
cavalcado raid
eschewit avoided
Flowing alliteration
list wish
makdome beauty
mollicies luxuries
ordinary tavern
pantoun slipper
Ryming in termes identical
    rhymes
seindil seldom
sensyne since then
stewes brothel

WILLIAM DRUMMOND

doome judgment
euripe channel
happelie perchance
phanes temples
proper his own
tapist conceals itself
tideous tedious
toyles webs

JAMES ROW

bogled was terrified (?)
halberts halberds
hopshackled hobbled
lowns rascals
ordinarie judge in ecclesiastical
   matters
poakmantie bag
post man courier riding 'post'
sick such

THOMAS URQUHART

accinating accenting
acronick at nightfall
alcoranal from the *Koran*
antiphrasis figure where words
   are used in a sense opposite to
   their meaning
aufractuosities excursions
barrow castrated
brasero brazier
canepetiers bustards
cates delicacies
chibols type of onion
condignely suitably
congies bows
diapasons harmonies
entelechies actualities
francolins pheasants
gnomon rod
hirquitalliency delighted shouts
isocoly equal length

journal daily
lacinious prolix
Lansman dutches German rustics
logofascinated fascinated by words
miniardise caressing treatment
ollapodrida incongruous mixture
phaenicopters (fr.) phoenicopteres
queests wood pigeons
quoquoversedly in all directions
scalier staircase
sheats pigs under one year old
spectabundal eager to see
terrigoles (fr.) terrigoles
tyrasons woodcocks
vertue industry

GEORGE MACKENZIE

collasterion analogy
enambled enamelled
manck deficient
mullered ground
pend-ways arched-ways

SAMUEL RUTHERFORD

coldrife chilly

TRACTS ON THE SUPERNATURAL

defecate refined
dint assault
hairtedder rope made from hair
heluo one who destroys himself
   by drinking and overeating
humour disposition
narrowly closely
prease crowd
sene sanctify
sith's people resting in peace
spickot spiggot
suanochs cloaks

tarried stayed
tissue weave

ANONYMOUS

beddle church-officer
callet cap
clooks claws, clutches (glossed in text)
hough down trip (glossed in text)
John Thomson's men henpecked men
meckle cup large dish (glossed in text)
mobile rabble
riv'd tore
rock distaff (glossed in text)
rugg'd tugged
silly deserving of sympathy
smarck underskirt
stalliard stalwart
stops thrusts

DIARISTS

abbat dress
are oar
aslipe asleep
athort across
biging building
branglit thrown into confusion
cassen thrown
cersing searching
chapping knocking
cobles rowing-boats
delatter denouncer
dittay indictment

drow squall
eall ale
eare air
eares oars
enervitie weakness
fean contented
fyle convict
fyre-flauchtis flashes of lightning
hause neck
how wa hollow wave
hulie slowly
interloquutor judgment
invying railing against
judicator position as judge
keave ower topple over
keipe the dyet appear at court on the day appointed
leache into a low position
lettrones desks
to lose a certean of skleatt steanes deliver a cargo of slates
mean mainland
outshut overshoot
owerlaft upper deck
pirlye slight motion
portage cargo
put ceas suppose
pykit on the wind tacked next the wind
quitted rid himself of
spene drift swelling current
stope flagon
sweik such (?)
swound faint
syse judgment
thraching thrashing
umbesett surrounded
vivers provisions
wound wind
wryttes documents

ACKNOWLEDGMENTS

I wish to express my gratitude to the National Library of Scotland, the British Museum and the Bodleian Library for allowing me to consult the manuscripts in their care, and to the Brodie of Brodie for making the Brodie Diaries available to me. The committee of the Scottish Text Society kindly permitted me the use of their editions, for comparison with the original manuscripts. For a number of helpful suggestions on choice and approach, I am indebted to Mr. Jack Aitken, to Professor John MacQueen and to Mr. Alexander Scott. Any problems of a historical or biographical nature were patiently considered by members of the Scottish History Department of Edinburgh University, and particularly by Mr. Edward Cowan. Other aid was willingly proffered by Professor William Beattie, Mr. Ian Campbell, and Mr. J. G. Howie. Finally I am grateful to my wife for checking the proofs and to Miss A. Wheelaghan for typing the selections and Introduction.